principles of
MODERN
ARCHITECTURE

christian norberg-schulz

principles of
MODERN
ARCHITECTURE

ANDREAS PAPADAKIS PUBLISHER

Acknowledgments

My text is dedicated to the memory of my teacher Sigfried Giedion. His famous book *Space, Time and Architecture* (Cambridge, Mass., 1941) also aimed at explaining what modern architecture is all about, and it still remains the most inspiring and essential text on the two first phases of the "new tradition." I also want to remember the others who taught me modern architecture: Walter Gropius, Mies van der Rohe, Pier Luigi Nervi and Arne Korsmo. Thanks are furthermore due to the many colleagues with whom I have had the occasion to discuss the problems, above all Jørn Utzon, Paolo Portoghesi, Charles Jencks, Donlyn Lyndon, Giancarlo de Carlo, Colin St. John Wilson, Vincent Scully, Robert Stern, and, last but not least, Eduard Neuenschwander, who at an early moment made an essential contribution to my love for modern architecture. Special thanks to my son, Christian E. Norberg-Schulz, for the design of the book, and to my Publisher Andreas Papadakis for his support of the project.

Design and layout: Christian Emanuel Norberg-Schulz
Front cover: Jørn Utzon: Sydney Opera House, detail
Frontispiece: Theo van Doesburg: Spatial Composition, 1920

First published in the United Kingdom in 2000 by
Andreas Papadakis Publisher
An imprint of NEW ARCHITECTURE GROUP LTD.
107, Park Street, London W1Y 3FB, United Kingdom

ISBN 1-901092-24-0 PB
ISBN 1-901092-27-5 HB

Printed and bound in Singapore

CONTENTS

Preface

This is not a history of modern architecture. The aim of the book is theoretical, and represents an attempt at explaining what modern architecture is all about. Rather pretentious, it might seem, but so many misunderstandings are today circulating that a clarification becomes an urgent need. For reasons of justice it is necessary to remember what the modern movement really wanted, and to demonstrate what it in fact accomplished. Today, some writers on the subject maintain that the modern movement is a "mystification;" in reality, they say, modern architects did not possess any common "ideology," and a modern architecture therefore does not exist. As an active participant in the movement after the second world war and a delegate to the CIAM, I must oppose such distortions of our recent history. The modern movement certainly had a basis and a direction, and only when that is understood can we arrive at a fair evaluation of its results, comprising the recent post-modern endeavours. Thus we gain a point of departure for the further pursuit of a democratic architecture for our time

The approach adopted is a concrete, phenomenological one. Nothing is achieved by writing "around" architecture, giving pride of place to social or political problems. Architecture has to be understood in terms of architecture. This does not mean, however, that I consider architecture an "autonomous" discipline. As an *art,* architecture belongs to life. Its purpose is to provide *places* where life can "take place." A place is not a set of resources or a neutral container; it is a concrete environment possessing order and character. It is therefore meaningless to talk about life on the one hand and place on the other. "Design for life" was in fact a slogan used to indicate the general aim of the modern movement. In order to explain what that really means, the present book takes man's being-in-the-world as its point of departure.

The exposition starts with a brief discussion of the new world, and man's need for orientation and identification therein. In general, architecture satisfies this need by means of spatial organization and formal articulation. The modern answer to this problem is explained in two chapters on the "free plan" and the "open form." The fundamental importance of these concepts was recognized long ago, but so far they have never been properly discussed. Three chapters on the "house," the "institution" and the "city" show how the free plan and the open form were given concrete implementation. Thus, the basic aims and results of modern architecture have been stated. In three further chapters, however, it is indicated how the movement – after its "heroic" phase – aimed at expanding its scope to comprise the problem of *meaning* in architecture. Thus the notions of "regionalism," "monumentality" and "place" are discussed.

The exposition is not chronological but organized according to the problems taken up by the modern movement, and follows the line of development which Giedion called the "new tradition." A certain chronology is, however, implicit, and is indicated by the headings "pre-modern," "modern," and "post-modern."

Obviously, the book presupposes a certain knowledge of the history of architecture, and in particular of the history of modern architecture. I may in this connection recommend my own book *Meaning in Western Architecture* (London 1975), and as a concise and useful supplement Kenneth Frampton's *Modern Architecture, a Critical History* (London 1980). Frampton has also presented the history of modern architecture in two profusely illustrated special issues of *GA Documents* (Tokyo 1982-83). In order to understand our situation, it is also important to consider the writings of leading architects of the present, such as Robert Venturi, Charles Moore, Paolo Portoghesi, Aldo Rossi, Oswald Matthias Ungers and, in particular, the critic Charles Jencks.

The present book is a thoroughly revised edition of *Roots of Modern Architecture*, published in Tokyo in 1988 (manuscript 1983). The illustrations of the new edition are almost entirely my own and follow the text more closely. The purpose of the reissue is not only to bring the book up to date, but to make it accessible to students.

Fifteen years have passed and architecture has gone through a series of difficult phases. Whereas about 1980 post-modernism was a promising and vital current, it soon faded away, or dissolved into superficial playfulness. (Not to mention the sterile eclecticism of the "Urban Renaissance" movement.) The different varieties of *deconstruction* that followed similarly led to a dead end, partly because of the lack of basic knowledge of man's being-in-the-world.

At the turn of the century, therefore, we are left empty-handed. Or rather, we have to reconsider the only valid current of the twentieth century: *modernism.*

This aim asks for understanding in the sense of relinquishing the present subjectivism, and renewing the socially founded belief that marked the early stages of the modern movement. The title of the present book has therefore replaced "Roots" with "Principles." About 1980 post-modernism looked for roots. Today we need *principles*, that is, a return to the original source of architectural expression.

Christian Norberg-Schulz

1 *the* New World

Modern architecture came into existence to help man feel at home in a new world. To feel at home means something more than shelter, clothing and food; primarily it means to *identify* with a physical and social environment. It implies a sense of belonging and participation, that is, the possession of a known and understood world. Man has to feel that he stands under and among, known and meaningful things. We are all aware that such an identification has become problematic in the modern world. The closed and secure environments of the past have disintegrated, and new social and physical structures demand new forms of understanding.[1]

Modern architecture is one of these forms. Its general aim is to provide man with a new "dwelling." The new dwelling should satisfy the need for identification and thus be an expression of a renewed "friendship" between man and his environment. "The problem of the house is the problem of the epoch," Le Corbusier wrote in 1923. "The equilibrium of society depends upon it. Architecture has for its first duty, in this period of renewal, that of bringing about a revision of values, a revision of the constituent elements of the house."[2] The first great international manifestation of the new architecture, the Weissenhofsiedlung in Stuttgart in 1927, was in fact organised as an exhibition called *The Dwelling* (*Die Wohnung*). Taking the dwelling as its point of departure, the modern movement turned the traditional hierarchy of building tasks upside-down. The leading tasks of the past, the church and the palace, were dethroned, and from now on public institutions were considered *extensions* of the house. A new democratic attitude thereby came to the fore, in accordance with the structure of the new world.

Over and over again the pioneers of modern architecture refer to the *newness* of the modern world, and insist that it cannot be served by the forms of the past. Le Corbusier's battle-cry is well known: A great epoch has begun. There exists a new spirit . . . Architecture is stifled by custom. The styles are a lie . . . Our own epoch is determining, day by day, its own style."[3] And Mies van der Rohe echoed: "Not yesterday, not tomorrow only today can be given form."[4] The belief here expressed was shared regardless of political convictions, although it often went together with a radical attitude. In an article called "The New World," the Marxist Hannes Meyer wrote: "Each age demands its new form. It is our mission to give the new world a new shape with the means of today. But our knowledge of the past is a burden that weighs upon us..."[5] As a consequence, architecture had to start anew, "as if nothing had ever been done before," an aim which was advanced already about the turn of the century. In 1914 the Futurist Antonio Sant'Elia stated: "Architecture breaks with tradition: of necessity it begins again from the beginning. ... The formidable antithesis between the modern world and the old is determined by everything that was not there before. ... We must invent and build *ex novo* the modern city . . ."[6] All the statements quoted here were prefigured in Schinkel's more modest question of 1826: "Should we not try to find our own style?"

Modern architecture in fact appeared as something radically new. Its forms seemed to have been invented from scratch, as embodiments of a new vision of the world. Hector Horeau's project for the 1867 World's Fair in Paris already illustrates that. Here the massive and enclosed forms of past buildings are abolished; space extends infinitely in all directions, as indicated by a limitless horizon, and the building appears as a transparent and open volume which is an integral part of total space. The volume is defined by slender members in cast iron, which offer rhythm and scale, without however depriving space of its basic continuity and openness. Thus the building expresses the new "global" situation which was the point of departure for the exhibition as such,[7] and invites man to participate in a world characterized by a new freedom of movement and choice. To understand the aims and results of modern architecture, we therefore have to consider the

OPPOSITE: Walter Gropius: Total Theatre, 1927.

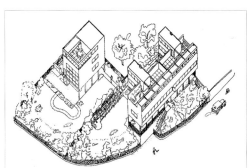

FAR RIGHT TOP: Hector Horeau:
Paris World Fair, 1867, project.
FAR RIGHT BOTTOM: Le Corbusier:
Weissenhofsiedlung, Stuttgart, 1927.
RIGHT: Manchester in the
nineteenth century.

"newness" of the modern world, and ask how architecture serves to make it manifest.

The new conception of space

Sant'Elia offered a key to the discussion of the newness of the modern world, saying that it is characterized by "everything that was not there before." In the article already quoted, Hannes Meyer describes the things that were not there before, such as "racing cars that dash along our streets, and aircraft which slip through the air, widening our range of movement and the distance between us and the earth."

But mobility is only one of the aspects of the new sense of space and time. Meyer also points to the "simultaneity of events" brought about by advertisements and displays (today we would say "the media"), and the interaction caused by "radio, marconigram and proto-telegraphy," which "liberate us from our national seclusion and make us part of a world community." Finally Meyer points out that "our homes are more mobile than ever. Large blocks of flats, sleeping cars, house yachts and transatlantic liners undermine the local concept of "homeland." "We become cosmopolitan," Meyer wrote in 1926, but the coming of what he described had already been felt about the middle of the nineteenth century, and the situation is certainly not different today. The open, global world is there, and it has come to stay. "The new era is a fact: it exists, irrespective of our 'yes' or 'no'," Mies van der Rohe said in 1930.[8]

The new "things" are certainly interesting in themselves, but more important are the general changes in the relationship between man and his environment which they express. Thus we have talked about "openness," "mobility," "interaction" and "simultaneity." All these words refer to spatiotemporal structures, and suggest that the newness of the modern world primarily has to be understood in terms of such. To many this understanding appears impossible. Being a world of "complexity and contradiction," it seems futile to look for

common denominators or structural properties. And yet the pioneers evidently believed that such properties exist, and took the understanding of them as their point of departure. In particular they concentrated their attention on the "new conception of space," assuming that architecture is the art which expresses the "spatiality" of the world.[9]

"Every cultural period has its own conception of space," László Moholy-Nagy wrote in 1928, introducing with these words his "theory of architecture."[10] About the same time Walter Gropius stressed the need for a "new spatial vision," which he considered "far more important than structural economy and functional emphasis."[11] The spatiality of the new world is particularly well indicated by the word "simultaneity." Thanks to media and potential mobility, we are so to speak in several places simultaneously. Physically we are of course in one place at a time, but existentially we experience a "simultaneity of places." This is the basic property of the new spatiality and the content of the "new vision." How, then, does a particular place make this state of affairs manifest? Not necessarily by assimilating a multitude of traits from other places, but rather through a "virtual openness," that is, a form which is ready for interaction rather than closed and self-sufficient. Evidently the new conception of space is related to a "new way of life." It is not something in itself, but tells us how modern man "is" in the world. By setting the new conception into work, architecture allows for modern life. "Modern life" does not here primarily denote a set of particular actions, but rather structural properties as indicated above.

An illuminating illustration is offered by Gropius's project for a "Total Theatre" from 1926. In addition to the traditional stage forms – the proscenium, the apron, and the arena – the Total Theatre also comprised a ring stage, on which the action could take place all around the audience, supported by the projection of films on numerous screens. According to Gropius the aim was to "move the spectator into the centre of the happening."[12] In the classical theatre man faces a limited,

FAR RIGHT: Karlsruhe in the
eighteenth century.
RIGHT: Bedstead at the
Paris World Fair, 1889.

particular image of the world. Although a sense of participation may be present, a certain distance always remains; the two spaces, auditorium and stage, represent different aspects of reality. In the Total Theatre performers and spectators are brought together in the same "total" and limitless space, and a new kind of interaction is thereby achieved. Thus we obtain that sense of participation which is one of the aims of the new open world. In the Total Theatre the spatial vision of Horeau becomes alive as the presentation of a new way of life.

In general, the new conception of space gives primary importance to openness and continuity, in contrast to the isolated, semi-independent "places" which made up the spatial structure of past worlds. This openness is, however, primarily *horizontal*; a global situation implies that the surface of the earth is integrated, whereas the vertical direction correspondingly loses in importance. The relationship to the sky, the "sacred dimension" of past cultures, tends to be forgotten when the earth is opened up as horizontal extension.

Baroque architecture prepared for the conquest of the horizontal. During the seventeenth century the universal, ordered cosmos of the Middle Ages was substituted by a multitude of competing systems, religious, political, or economic. Because of their explicit or implicit competition, "propagation" was essential, and dynamic, centrifugal patterns became usual. "Propagation is only meaningful and effective in relation to a centre, which represents the basic axioms of the system."[13] In this centre a vertical reference is expedient to make it appear as a focal point. Departing from this point, the system could be infinitely extended. The plans for cities such as Versailles and Karlsruhe are typical examples of the open but centralized Baroque conception of space.

The new space conception, which came to the fore during the second half of the nineteenth century took over the notions of extension and mobility, but abolished the symbolic centre. In the modern world human understanding is no longer administered by some centrally placed authority, but is set free and, at least in theory, put within the reach of everybody. The "loss of the centre," however, makes our understanding of the world extremely difficult.[14] How is human orientation and identification possible in a dynamic world of interaction and change? To solve this problem is the task of modern architecture.

When the pioneers of modern architecture rejected the "forms of the past," they did not only intend particular motifs, but also general space conceptions such as the linear perspective of the Renaissance, or the totalitarian patterns of the Baroque. In particular they turned against the "academic" compositions of the official architecture of the nineteenth century, where the meaningful centres and axes of Baroque planning degenerated into a play with formalistic figures. Evidently such artificial and static layouts could not cope with the form of life of an open and dynamic world.[15] Last but not least they rejected the "styles" as systems of building types and symbolic elements. By means of the styles the space conceptions of the past were set into work. As ordering systems, the styles consisted of interrelated parts, which reflected an understanding of the world as a hierarchy where every part was assigned a particular place and value. During the nineteenth century the parts were taken out of their context, and history was reduced to a "department store," where forms could be borrowed when "needed." Giedion has described this eclecticism as a "devaluation of symbols," and has shown how it served to give the new "self-made man" a "humanistic alibi."[16]"No matter how clever he may be, an eclectic is but a feeble man; for he is a man with neither star nor compass . . . An eclectic is a ship which tries to sail before all winds at once," Charles Baudelaire wrote about 1850.[17] No wonder that Le Corbusier, echoing Henry van de Velde, called the styles a "lie."

The rejection of the styles implied that a new language of forms was necessary to set the new conception of space into work. "Contemporary architecture had to take the hard way."

The New World

Etienne-Louis Boullée,
Temple of Reason, c.1793, project.

As with painting and sculpture, it had to begin anew. It had to reconquer the most primitive things, as if nothing had ever been done before. It could not return to Greece, to Rome, or to the Baroque, to be comforted by their experience. In certain crises man must live in seclusion, to become aware of his own inner feelings and thoughts. This was the situation for all the arts around 1910."[18] It would, however, be superficial to interpret the demand for new means of expression as a mere "formalistic" problem. We have already emphasized that the new architecture aimed at helping man to gain an "existential foothold." The devaluation of symbols was in fact part of a general human "alienation" which developed during the nineteenth century. Deprived of meaningful symbols, man could no longer identify with his environment, and lost his sense of belonging. The new space conception represented a promise, but so far it was stifled by a ruling taste which took refuge in sentimental stimuli. To win this state of alienation, a new *art* was needed, an art which could give man emotional access to "everything that was not there before," and make him feel safe with openness and mobility. Modern architecture is part of this new art, and developed in accordance with the evolution of modern art in general, and with modern painting and sculpture in particular.

The needle-eye of modern art

To modern man it might not seem obvious that a new art is needed in a world dominated by science and technology. Do we not believe today that understanding is a matter of reason alone? Do we not believe that all problems may be solved by technical means? The faith in reason stems from the Enlightenment. In general it implies a refusal of any kind of *a priori* dogma, and a belief in the study of the phenomena as such. "We must never say: let us begin by inventing principles according to which we attempt to explain everything," Voltaire wrote, "We should rather say: let us make an exact analysis of things . . ."[19] And John Locke added: "Whence has

the mind all the materials of reason and knowledge? To this I answer in one word, from *experience*."[20] Thus, empiricism was adopted as the guiding method of the new world, and other, intuitive forms of understanding were pushed aside. As a consequence, education became an acquisition of mere factual "knowledge," whereas art was reduced to a pastime or even an "unnecessary luxury."

In his grandiose project for a *Temple of Reason* (c. 1793), Etienne-Louis Boullée gave the new "belief" an architectural interpretation.[21] Here man's world is presented as "nature," in the form of two complementary semispheres, one visualizing the earth as a deep rocky ravine and the other the sky as an embracing, smooth dome. On a plateau inside the ravine a statue of Nature, shown as the chthonic goddess Artemis Ephesia, is placed. Man's power of reason and knowledge is symbolized by an encircling, anthropomorphous colonnade between the two spheres. From his position he may look down to reveal the secrets of the earth and up to contemplate the wonders of the sky. Although Boullée's vision gives support to the belief in natural science, it also indicated its limits: being an "image" Boullée's project reaches beyond the acquisition and ordering of data; it "presents" the new world to us as a meaningful whole, and thereby illustrates the function of art as a complement to reason.

The belief in reason was, however, taken over by modern art, and a "scientific" study of artistic phenomena was attempted, especially at the Bauhaus.[22] However, most of the pioneers realized that man cannot gain an existential foothold through reason alone. Natural science reduces the world to what is "measurable," that is, to abstract quantities, while the "qualities" of the concrete things which constitute our everyday world wither away.[23] In a quantified world, man's feelings are left to chance, and tend to oscillate between sudden outbursts and introvert passivity. "The rift between the newly created reality and emotional feeling started with the industrial revolution: ungoverned machines – outcast feeling, production as

FAR RIGHT: Paul Klee: "Rain."
RIGHT: Constantin Brancusi: "Bird."

an end in itself – escape into romanticism," Giedion wrote. "This dichotomy explains the rise of the official art of the last century, which is still the standard of taste of the general public. The accepted art of the exhibitions, the academies, the press, the art that had real power and that came to govern the emotional world of the general public proved to be merely a drug, a narcotic."[24] "The nineteenth century witnessed a greater expansion of material goods than had ever been known before. Its thinking was concentrated upon obtaining a rational mastery over all the world . . . At the same time the nineteenth century lived in a fog of inarticulate feelings. It floundered between one extreme and another, reaching out blindly in all directions. It sought its release by escape into the past . . ."[25] To heal this "split of thinking and feeling" was a basic aim of the modern movement in art and architecture.

What, then, is the purpose of art in general, and particularly in an epoch of scientific understanding and industrial production? By different means man has to understand and "keep" the transient world of phenomena to which he belongs. Thus he abstracts similarities, classifies and arrives at "natural laws". Or he constructs practical tools which enable him to handle situations according to his purposes. But this is not enough. "Understanding means something more than theory and practice. It also means to keep the vision of how things "are," of their "true nature," which includes their interrelationships. That is, we have to grasp the situation as a qualitative totality, as that meaningful "life-world" which escapes science and technology. Thus we create *works of art*, which as images do not describe the world but make it stand forth as a concrete reality. "Only image formed keeps the vision," Heidegger says, "yet image formed rests in the poem."[26] The work of art therefore keeps and makes visible a world. It does not represent an object, but shows what it is as a "thing," that is, as a "gathering" of a world. A thing is never alone, it is related to other things, and its "thingness" consists in these relationships,

or in Heidegger's words, in the world it gathers.[27] When the artist presents the *thing*, he reveals this world and thereby makes the *thing* become meaningful.

During the first decade of the twentieth century a "visual revolution" took place in the plastic arts. Basically it consisted in a departure from the realistic representation of the objects of everyday life, which had been the norm in past epochs. In cubism this was achieved through the use of a number of simultaneous viewpoints whereby several aspects of the thing were unified into one image. Thus pictorial art left perspective behind and became "abstract" or "non-figurative." The traditional "figure" is disposed of, and a new kind of "open form" comes into existence. This revolution happened about the same time as some architects abolished the historical styles, and the pioneers of modern music moved away from tonality. All these experiments may be understood as parallel attempts at developing a "modern" art which could express the new open world. In general it aimed at a return to the "things themselves," and thus represented a complement to the quantitative abstractions of scientific thinking.[28] "Art does not reproduce what is visible, but makes visible," Paul Klee said, and in his works he confirmed this tenet making us see the essential quality of phenomena.

His drawing *Rain* brings forth the trickling of the downpour, its varying density and force, and its origin in a distant "firmament." Thus, modern art did not deny nature. Rather it wanted to penetrate to the real nature of things through an abstraction of their qualities. Sometimes simple forms reveal this nature, as Constantin Brancusi confirms: "Simplicity is not an aim in art, but one arrives at simplicity when one approaches the real meaning of things."[29] Thus Brancusi's *Bird* conquers verticality "to fill the vault of the sky," as he himself said, because its simple form reveals the essential potentialities of the bird. Even the orthogonal compositions of Piet Mondrian aimed at a "unification of man with the universe," through a visualization of the basic properties of the world.[30] In this way

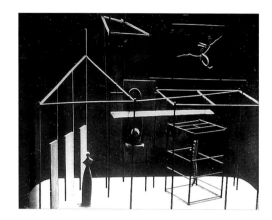

FAR RIGHT: Umberto Boccioni:
"Bottle developing in space."
RIGHT: Alberto Giacometti:
"The Palace at 4 o'clock."

modern art fought against the "devaluation of symbols," but it had to "take the hard way and reconquer the most primitive things, as if nothing had ever been done before."

Umberto Boccioni's *Bottle which develops in space* (1912) illustrates particularly well the new conception of the thing as essence and relationship. Thus, the bottle "develops in space" to tell us that the most basic property of the world of any object is its relation to earth and sky. But Boccioni's bottle also "gathers" the mobility of the fluid contained, the reflexes of light on the surface, and its position in space as a "centre" from which water and wine are offered to the surrounding "users." The bottle rises out of the transitory phenomena to take a stand as a "gathering thing," at the same time as it defines space as a concrete, lived entity rather than a mathematical abstraction. In *The Palace at 4 o'clock in the Morning* by Alberto Giacometti, the new conception of space becomes the main theme. A composition of thin sticks here defines a space which is simultaneously infinite and differentiated. It is kept and directed by a few vertical and horizontal planes placed within the linear skeleton. In this space strange figures appear: a hovering bird, a suspended spinal column (or is it a caterpillar?), a standing woman and a small sphere. All these figures represent different ways of being between earth and sky. Moreover they have the character of "memories" which appear and disappear, thus relating the present to the past, at the same time as they seem to be charged with the future. Uniting elements which do not logically belong together, the work of art becomes "surreal;" it reaches beyond what is immediately given and opens up a world of hidden meanings. The meanings revealed by Giacometti's *Palace* are evidently the mysteries and structures of the new, open world, which is here presented as a kind of imaginative "architecture."

After the intuitive syntheses of the pioneers, however, the dangers inherent in the modern approach to art came to the fore. Under the influence of the current analytic attitude, many artists tended to give ever more importance to the means of expression as such, whereby art was reduced to a new kind of play with effects.[31] This approach was supported by the pseudo-scientific belief that man constructs his image of the world, his understanding, from "below" by adding up sensations. "Of a feeling of warmth, the smell of milk, the touch of hands, the looming of features," Georgy Kepes says, "the child compounds a united picture of the mother. Image making is the integration of sense data into a coherent experience of something . . ."[32] This atomistic approach to the world can only lead to disintegration. The world does not consist of sense data, but is immediately given as a multitude of "things."[33] Art is the only means to grasp the *thingness* or quality of these things, and its success in this pursuit depends on an adequate "vision."

The examples given above illustrate the new way of seeing and understanding which was needed to establish a meaningful relationship between man and his new environment.[34] Its pictorial counterpart consists in open and "surreal" collages which gather the modern world. Sometimes these collages are reduced to the simplest possible essentials, as in Mondrian's compositions with orthogonal grids and primary colours. Sometimes they are saturated with poetic detail, as in Klee's unfathomable fairy tales. Without the new vision the modern world would remain unintelligible. Therefore Giedion had to emphasize that, "Nobody becomes an architect today without having gone through the needle-eye of modern art."

The new architecture

Modern art and modern architecture belong together. Both aim at helping man to find an existential foothold in the new world through the visualization of its qualities. The artistic character of modern architecture was recognized by the pioneers. Already Louis Sullivan said: ". . . a building which is truly a work of art (and I consider none other) is in its nature, essence and physical being an emotional expression."[35] Le Corbusier gave particular emphasis to this view, introducing all

Louis Sullivan:
Wainwright Building, St. Louis, 1890.

the three chapters on "Architecture" in his book *Towards a New Architecture* with the same statement: "You employ stone, wood and concrete, and with these materials you build houses and palaces. This is construction. Ingenuity is at work. But suddenly you touch my heart, you do me good. I am happy and I say: 'This is beautiful.' That is Architecture. Art enters in."[36] And Walter Gropius wrote in *The New Architecture and the Bauhaus*: . . . "Rationalization, which many people imagine to be the cardinal principle of the new architecture, is really only its purifying agency . . . The other, the aesthetic satisfaction of the human soul, is just as important . . ."[37] Even Mies van der Rohe, who is generally considered the most "puritan" of the pioneers, in his preface to the official publication of the Weissenhofsiedlung stated the same belief: "It is necessary today to stress that the new dwelling is an artistic (*baukünstlerisch*) problem, in spite of its technical and economic aspects. It is not a composite problem, and cannot therefore be solved by means of analysis or organization, but only through creative effort."[38] We may also add that Le Corbusier was an important modern painter in his own right, while Gropius engaged artists such as Kandinsky, Klee, Schlemmer, Albers, Feininger and Moholy-Nagy as major teachers at the Bauhaus. Mies van der Rohe, finally, was a collector of Klee's paintings (not of Mondrian's!). Thus, the modern movement in architecture was an artistic movement.

But does this not contradict the common interpretation of modern architecture as "functionalism?" Le Corbusier, Gropius and Mies certainly gave due attention to function, but none of them believed that forms simply "follow" from functions.[39] In the heading already quoted, Le Corbusier went on saying: "By the use of inert materials and "starting from" conditions more or less utilitarian, you have established certain relationships which have aroused my emotions. They are a mathematical creation of your mind. This is architecture." The functions, thus, may be taken as a point of departure, but the relationships which arouse our emotions do not "follow" from them;

rather they are a "creation of the mind." A radical functionalism was not pursued at the Bauhaus either, during the years of Gropius's leadership. This approach was only introduced in 1928 when Hannes Meyer took over. The same year Meyer stated in the bulletin of the school: "All things in this world are the product of the formula (function x economy), all these things are therefore not works of art. All art is composition and therefore useless. All life is function and therefore unartistic."[40] As a consequence Meyer wanted to do away with Gropius's "formal" approach and introduce a "scientifically founded theory of building." Meyer's radical functionalism remained peripheral to the modern movement. It was, however, taken over after the second world war by forces which were interested primarily in economy and efficiency, and led to what has been labelled "vulgar functionalism."[41] Instead of developing the artistic aim of modern architecture, vulgar functionalism reduced building to a mere rational activity guided by logical analysis and "design methods."

Before we consider how modern architecture set its artistic aims into work, we must add a few words about the artistic dimension of architecture in general. As an art, architecture makes a world visible. Evidently this world does not correspond to that of the plastic arts. A work of architecture does not present to us the essences or interrelations of human beings, animals or other things. In general, it does not portray anything. What, then, does architecture do? Rather than representing something else (as is assumed by semiologists), it visualizes a "different way of being between earth and sky." *All* things are, of course, related to earth and sky, and this relationship is part of their world. In buildings this aspect gains primary importance or, in other words, the buildings reveal what we have called the "spatiality" of the world. They do that by *standing* on the ground, *rising* towards the sky, *extending* in the direction of the horizon, and *opening* and *closing* on their surroundings. Thus buildings define a general frame of reference, a place or *milieu*, which makes the other things stand

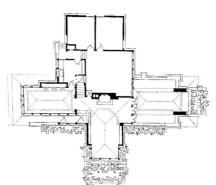

Frank Lloyd Wright: Isabel Roberts House, River Forest, 1907.

out as what they "are."[42] Le Corbusier was aware of that when in the *manifesto* already quoted, he said: ". . . Suppose that walls rise towards heaven in such a way that I am moved. I perceive your intentions. Your mood has been gentle, brutal, charming or noble. The stones you have erected tell me so." This implies that architecture is something more than an art of spatial organization. It is certainly a basic property of any work of architecture to offer a "space" which allows life to "happen." But this space has to be set into work by means of "built forms" to become a "place," that is, a concrete "here" where life can "take place." When something happens we in fact say that it "takes place," implying that it is meaningless to talk about life on the one hand and place on the other. Place is an integral part of human existence, and it is the scope of architecture to offer places suited for human life. To be suited, the place does not only have to admit functions; it also has to visualize a way of being between earth and sky, through the use of modes of standing, rising, extending, opening and closing. These modes are "embodiments" of "characters," that is, of a general sense of being in the world, or "mood," to use the word introduced in the English translation of Le Corbusier's book.[43]

It follows that architecture may be understood in terms of two basic aspects: the organization of space and the built form or, in short, "space" and "form." The first is related to man's orientation in his surroundings (comprising the functional patterns of his actions); the second to his identification with an environmental character (comprising his need for "expression").

Both aspects are general as well as circumstantial. Organization of space is not only a consequence of circumstantial functions, but also of a general conception of space, that is, of an understanding of space as closed or open, centralized or directed, additive or continuous. The general properties are, moreover, based on local as well as "absolute factors," the latter being structures such as the cardinal points and the difference between up and down. The built form

similarly expresses the character of "what a building wants to be," to use the words of Louis Kahn, as well as a set of common characters, as indicated by Le Corbusier with the words "gentle," "brutal," "charming" and "noble."[44] Both aspects are subject to temporal changes, and visualize man's understanding of the world as "lived space" at a particular moment.

In the past the conceptions of space and form were united in *images* which were simultaneously archetypal (general) and local (circumstantial). Such images were the column, the arch, the gable, the tower, the pyramid, and the rotunda. Le Corbusier intuited this when he defined architecture as the "masterly, correct and magnificent play of volumes brought together in light . . . cubes, cones, spheres, cylinders and pyramids are the great primary forms . . ."[45] although he described the primary forms in too abstract, mathematical terms. By means of such images the work of architecture could act as a true *imago mundi*.

As we have already pointed out, modern architecture defined new conceptions of space and form, taking the "simultaneity of events" as its point of departure. These conceptions have their roots in the iron-and-glass structures of the nineteenth century and were developed into a consistent "grammar" of design by Frank Lloyd Wright before 1900. In 1914 Le Corbusier designed a skeletal structure for his *Domino* houses with the aim of "liberating space from the slavery of load-bearing walls" and permitting "innumerable combinations of interior dispositions and facade openings." With his *Five Points for a New Architecture* of 1926, he offered a precise definition of the new ideas. One of the points is called the *plan libre*, or "free plan," a term which has ever since remained of basic importance to the theory of modern architecture.[46] We shall later give an account of its phenomenology; for the present we shall only affirm that the free plan came into existence to satisfy the spatial needs of modern life. Related to the free plan is the point called the "free facade,"

FAR RIGHT: Le Corbusier: Five Points for a New Architecture, 1926.
RIGHT: Le Corbusier: Immeuble Villas, project, 1923.

which is conceived as the result of an interaction between interior and exterior, rather than a formal composition in its own right. The free facade forms part of a new conception of built form. In two of his other points Le Corbusier defines the new relationship of the building to earth and sky. The *pilotis* raise the building over the ground, which is thus preserved in its infinite continuity, whereas the *toit-jardin* "receives" the sunlight and the rain and expresses that life always takes place "under the sky." In general, the built form, as defined by Le Corbusier, may serve a new, active way of life, and visualize the freedom of modern spatiality.[47] The new forms developed by the pioneers could also to some extent substitute the "images" of the past. The *pilotis*, the *fenêtres en longueur* and the flat roof have in fact gained a kind of emblematic importance. The new elements were not, however, united into a "language" of forms like the styles, although a certain uniformity of appearance during the 1920s seemed to indicate the birth of a new "international style."[48]

In his project for the *League of Nations* in Geneva from 1927-28, Le Corbusier set the new conceptions into work on a grand scale, expressing the general as well as the circumstantial aspects of the task. Here space is opened up and the built form liberated, thus integrating the building with its surroundings, at the same time as clearly defined and variously articulated volumes give the parts and the whole identity. Thus the *League of Nations* project illustrates the new conceptions of space and form, as well as the need for realizing these "as something," that is, as *house*, as *factory*, as *school*, as *theatre*. Architecture is in fact not only a question of "how" things are done, but also of "what" is done. The "what," the building task, is a manifestation of a way of life, and the problem of modern architecture was to redefine the tasks in accordance with the spatiality of the new world, to arrive at solutions which were truly contemporary.

We have already pointed out that the dwelling is the basic architectural problem of our epoch, and the "house" has in

fact been the leading building task in modern architecture. After the intuitions of the "proto-modern" masters, Frank Lloyd Wright gave a radically new interpretation to the house. In his book *The Natural House* he summed up his ideas: "I began to see a dwelling primarily not as a cave but as broad shelter in the open, related to vista, vista without and vista within."[49] The concept of the free plan is here implied, and the early houses of Wright also illustrate the emergence of a new built form where the closed masses and formal facades of the past give way to a free juxtaposition of vertical and horizontal planes. The early work of Wright was published in Germany in 1910 and 1911, and caused a revolution in the approach of European architects. In the introduction to one of the German editions, C.R. Ashbee wrote: Wright has understood how to apply the new ideas (i.e. of Louis Sullivan) to the private house, and has created a new type which is completely without any precedent . . ."[50] and in the official publication of the Weissenhofsiedlung he was still remembered: "Frank Lloyd Wright already twenty years ago possessed the necessary quality to lead the way towards a new dwelling."[51] We shall discuss later the problem of the new dwelling in detail; for the present, we would just like to emphasize that the development of the modern house was of decisive importance for the definition of the new conceptions of space and form.

The new way of life, however, also demanded a revision of the public building tasks. During the nineteenth century a multitude of new ones had come up in connection with the restructuring of society. Some of them were interpretations of already known tasks, but many were entirely new, such as those connected with the means of production and distribution: the factory, the railway station, the exhibition hall and the department store. Some of the old tasks also gained new importance, in particular the theatre and the museum, which as "aesthetic temples" replaced the church as the *leading* building tasks. The official architecture of the period

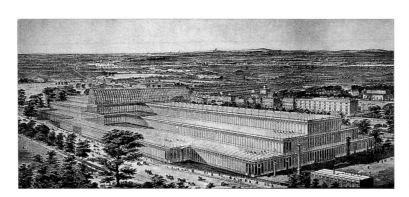

Joseph Paxton:
Crystal Palace, London, 1851.

employed the historical styles to their solution, and were careful to make the chosen style "correspond" to the task in question.[52] Iron-and-glass structures were, however, also used to a certain extent, and a new public architecture slowly emerged to replace the devalued symbols of the styles.

In general the new tasks were solved by means of two basic building types: the large unitary "hall" and the high-rise "skyscraper." Both stem from known models, such as churches, cityhalls and towers, but these models were given an entirely new interpretation. The hall and the skyscraper were in fact understood as manifestations of the new open world. In a contemporary description of the *Crystal Palace* we read that there was "nothing between (the things inside) and the open sky;"[53] and Louis Sullivan, who made a decisive contribution to the development of the skyscraper, defined it as having "an indefinite number of storeys."[54] We may add that the *Crystal Palace* was conceived as a space of indeterminate extension which was given rhythm and scale by means of a repetitive, articulate construction. Being horizontally open, it formed a counterpart to the vertically open skyscraper.

The problem of the city was given particular attention by the pioneers of modern architecture. Being the primary place where human life takes place, the city more than any single building embodies the way of life of an epoch. This is especially the case today, when life is becoming ever more urbanized. The closed and relatively static historical city evidently does not correspond to the structure of the new open world, a fact which caused a gradual decay of the old cities during the nineteenth century. Overcrowding, unhealthy living conditions, and urban sprawl became the order of the day, and a radical renewal seemed to be necessary. The vision thus emerged of a "green" city, which aimed at giving back to man the "essential joys" of *sun*, *space* and *verdure*,[55] at the same time as it made manifest the open world. To concretize this idea, the free plan was transferred from the building to the city, and a new urban pattern of free-standing, slab-like buildings came to replace the streets, squares and blocks of the traditional city. Le Corbusier gave the new vision its "classical" interpretation in numerous projects, starting with his *Contemporary City for Three Million Inhabitants* of 1922, and he also played a decisive role in developing its theory.[56] It is, however, doubtful whether the free plan can be blown up to form a city. It is related to the movements and moods of the individual human being, and thus linked to a smaller environmental scale. A city is, moreover, "a place of assembled institutions," to use the definition of Louis Kahn, and therefore "a place where a small boy, as he walks through it, may see something that will tell him what he wants to do with his whole life." [57] The cities of the past had this quality, whereas the green city hardly allows for such participation. This does not mean, however, that the city should return to a closed and static form. A modern city should be open and dynamic, without however losing its identity as a place. Modern architects have approached this problem, first by pointing out the necessity of giving the city a "heart" or "core,"[58] and later by introducing patterns of dense, but open growth.

As a place of assembled institutions, the city is also a symbolic form which makes the way of life of a people manifest. Because of the relative weak image quality of the public buildings erected between the two world wars, the demand for a "new monumentality" came to the fore. In their *Nine Points on Monumentality* of 1943, the architect José Luis Sert, the painter Fernand Léger and the historian Sigfried Giedion stated: "Monuments are human landmarks which men have created as symbols for their ideals, for their aims, and for their actions. They are intended to outlive the period which originated them, and constitute a heritage for future generations. As such, they form a link between the past and the future." "The people want the buildings that represent their social and community life to give more than functional fulfilment." "Monumental architecture will be something more than strictly functional. It will have regained its lyrical

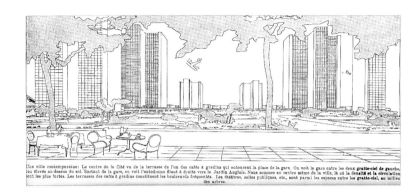

Le Corbusier: "The green city."

value."[59] The demand for a new monumentality does not mean a departure from the basic goal of modern architecture – to visualize the new world – but rather that we ought to draw the full con-sequences of this aim. Evidently a *monumental* building gathers a more comprehensive, interhuman world than a private dwelling, and therefore it may serve as a focus to a whole environment.

The need for a more meaningful architecture also comprises the demand for a "new regionalism." Whereas early modernism primarily paid attention to the general structures of the new world, and therefore tended towards becoming "international," it later became clear that an open world does not mean that the individual places should lose their identity and come to look alike.[60] An open world is a world of interaction and exchange, which implies diversity. In other words, life is necessarily related to a local character, and the visualization of any world has to comprise the expression of this character. The possibility of a locally rooted modern architecture was first shown with conviction by Alvar Aalto in the 1930s. "Finland is with Aalto wherever he goes," Giedion wrote. "It provides him with that inner source of energy which always flows through his work. It is as Spain is to Picasso and Ireland to James Joyce."[61] The importance of this widening of the scope of modern architecture was also understood by Giedion: "There is one thing that the modern architect has learnt: that first and foremost, before making any plans, he must make a careful – one might almost say a reverent – study of the way of life (the climate of living) of the place and the people for whom he is going to build. This new regionalism has as its motivating force a respect for individuality and a desire to satisfy the emotional and material needs of an area.[62]

The "new monumentality" and the "new regionalism" are interrelated demands; both are concerned with meaning, and both presuppose the existence of a "tradition," one stressing the general, and the other the local aspects of the situation.

Giedion in fact summed up his understanding of the principles and development of modern architecture as the "growth of a new tradition."[63]

The new place

To provide man with a new dwelling implies something more than the building of modern houses. Man does not only "dwell" in his own home; he also dwells together with his fellow men in public institutions and urban spaces. A comprehensive identification is hence necessary to experience belonging and participation. The object of this identification is the quality of *place*, which is determined by natural as well as man-made structures.[64] The ultimate aim of architecture is therefore the creation and preservation of places. Let us repeat that a place may be understood as a synthesis of spatial organization and built form (analogously, "dwelling" is a synthesis of orientation and identification). We could also say that architecture is not only the question of "how" and "what," but of "where" as well.

Our final question, therefore, is whether modern architecture has succeeded in creating satisfactory places for the new way of life. A modern place is still a place in the sense of having an identity of its own. At the same time, however, it has to possess a virtual openness which indicates the simultaneous presence of "innumerable places." We have suggested that some of the necessary tools to solve this problem have been developed, that is, the new conceptions of space and form. We have also pointed out that these tools have been taken into use to solve those building tasks which determine the man-made place. Finally we have reiterated the fact that the modern movement already a long time ago recognized the need for a new monumentality and a new regionalism, that is, for new symbolic forms. The prerequisites for the creation of contemporary places are there, and we may also point to many significant contributions to the concrete solution of the problem. In the following chapters we shall discuss the "how," the

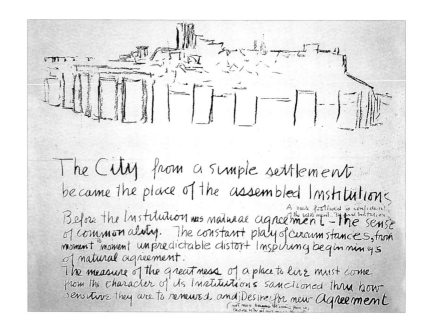

The City from a simple settlement
became the place of the assembled Institutions

Before the Institution was natural agreement – the sense
of common ality. The constant play of circumstances, from
moment to moment unpredictable distort Inspiring beginnings
of natural agreement.
The measure of the greatness of a place to live must come
from the character of its Institutions sanctioned thru how
sensitive they are to renewed. and Desire for new Agreement

*OPPOSITE: Gustave Eiffel,
Eiffel Tower, Paris, 1889.
RIGHT: Louis Kahn: "The City."*

"what" and the "where" of modern architecture in detail, and also indicate shortcomings and possible developments.

Before we continue our investigation, we have, however, to mention some dangers which have disturbed and hampered the growth of the new tradition. In general they are a result of the one-sided belief in reason and the split of thinking and feeling which stems from the Enlightenment. Obviously modern architecture was not intended as an alternative to rational technology, but rather as a complement to it. The pioneers accepted the new world, but wanted to regain the artistic dimension it had forgotten during its infancy. The Eiffel Tower remains a splendid expression of this aim. Although the pioneers succeeded in their concrete works, the methods used lagged behind. A work of art is never the result of logical analysis and cannot be understood as a compound of abstract "means of expression." It is always based on a total vision or "idea," which gathers elements that logically do not belong together. Art is essentially *irrational* and cannot be explained in scientific terms. Transferring the methods of natural science to architecture, many pseudo-modern architects killed the artistic dimension, and reduced their field to mere planning and construction. This reduction has in general taken two different directions, one stemming from the atomism inherent in analytical science, the other from the scientific belief in ordering systems. As a consequence modern architecture has degenerated to a great extent into either a neo-expressionistic play with effects, or a rigid neo-rational formalism.[65] In both cases the new vision is lost, and architecture becomes an enemy of contemporary life.

Is then a method available which can help architecture to get beyond its present state of improvisation and out of the impasse of pseudo-scientific abstraction? Indeed it is. Painters such as Klee and Kandinsky already a long time ago suggested a "phenomenological" approach to the problems of pictorial art, and some architects have taken up the same pursuit.[66] In philosophy, phenomenology has been introduced to allow for

a return to the "things themselves," through descriptions which reveal their "thingness."[67] In some cases one has also attempted to tackle problems of environment and place, and to explain spatiality as one of the basic structures of our being-in-the-world.[68] A place is thus understood as a "thing," in the original sense of the word, that is, as a "gathering" which "visits man with a world."[69] The meaning of a place accordingly consists of the world it gathers. Any world is general as well as circumstantial, and architecture should express this fact through ever new interpretations of the *genius loci*. The styles are evidently rooted in the basic structures, and represent particular sets of choices. Thus they are *exclusive*, although their general basis endows them with a timeless value. The open world, however, cannot utilize closed systems of this kind, but needs "free plans" and "open forms." To make this possible, architecture had to return to the origins that are common to the different languages of form.[70] That is, one had to abolish the styles and reconquer "the things themselves," to quote again Husserl's famous words. Phenomenology is the means to this end, but rather than developing its possibilities, the modern movement got stuck in the "scientific" impasse. It is the aim of this book to repropose the phenomenological approach, in order to make us conscious of the principles of modern architecture.

2 *the* Free Plan

The free plan is the concretization of the new conception of space. As such, it is not primarily a practical aid to accommodate various *functions* but a principle or "method" of spatial organization. Its basic aim is to help man's orientation in an open world. By the word "orientation," we do not mean only that we have to find our way around, but also the spatial relationships which form part of our actions. These relationships, however, reach beyond the immediate situation and comprise general structures such as the cardinal points and the distinction between up and down. They also comprise the structures of man's "existential space," that is, the fact that any action is related to a centre, has a direction, and takes place within a defined domain.[1] Being a point on the plan, the centre is usually understood as a vertical axis, which links the pattern of action to the sky above. The vertical direction cannot be conquered physically by man, and expresses therefore a "tension" in existential space. The horizontal, on the contrary represents a real movement, which is distinguished by one "rhythm" or another. The organization of space can always be described as a pattern of tensions and rhythms. Orientation, therefore, is general as well as circumstantial. The free plan is the result of a particular interpretation of the general structures, at the same time as it accommodates various circumstances. The mode of our being between earth and sky, which determines the free plan, stems from the new vision," and the goal is the establishment of a spatial milieu for our time.

The spatial organization of past epochs in general gave primary importance to a clearly defined centre, which represented the basic values of the form of life in question. The *axis* was also recognized as a basic existential structure, usually in direct relation to the centre.[2] Centres and axes were employed to organize distinct interior and exterior spaces, and sometimes to correlate them, as in connection with entrances or other zones of transition. This method of spatial organization naturally leads to symmetrical and static compositions, which may be more or less comprehensive. In classical Greek architecture symmetry was employed only in connection with single buildings, whereas their interrelations were solved by means of topological clustering.[3] Baroque layouts were, on the contrary, based on "infinite" geometrical patterns.

The free plan abandons the static equilibrium of central and axial symmetries. Its space is not related to dominant centres, but consists in an interaction of equivalent (albeit dissimilar) zones. The self-contained compositions of the past therefore give way to an integrated simultaneity of places in a state of dynamic equilibrium. Compositional coherence is assured by means of continuity and interpenetration rather than sequence and hierarchy. In more concrete terms we may say that the free plan implies the establishment of a new interactive relationship between inside and outside, and even the abolition of any clear distinction.[4] Thus it makes the global openness of the modern world manifest. Frank Lloyd Wright expressed this aim saying that he wanted to "destroy the box." That is, he wanted to substitute the enclosed, static spatial units of the past with a new kind of continuous totality. "Let walls, ceilings, floors, now become not only party to each other but *part of each other*, reacting upon and within one another; continuity in all . . . Instead of many things, *one* thing," he says in *The Natural House*[5] It would be wrong, however, to understand such a space as monotonous and univalent. In Wright's houses the different zones preserve their spatial identity and their character, and are also in general related to a centrally placed chimney-stack which gives the "open"compositions a hold. We shall later take a look at the means used by Wright to carry out his aim.

The free plan is thus a general concept, and cannot be reduced to any of its possible consequences, such as "flexibility."[6] Flexibility is a subordinate property of the free plan and was invented relatively late, more precisely in 1924 by Rietveld in the *Schröder House* in Utrecht.[7] Flexible, or mobile, elements can never become dominant in a free plan, as

OPPOSITE: Frank Lloyd Wright: Johnson Wax, Racine, 1936.

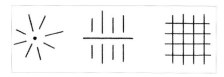

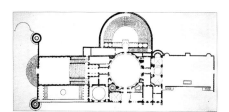

FAR RIGHT: Teatro Marittimo,
Villa Adriana outside Rome.
RIGHT: Principles of spatial
organization. Raffaello Sanzio:
Villa Madama, Rome, 1517.

freedom does not imply the abolition of identity. Freedom can only exist relative to a defined frame of reference. The free plan, therefore, has to be set into work, in each concrete case, as an interpretation of the situation, thus relating the circumstantial problem to the general vision of our epoch.

Roots of the free plan

Although the free plan is a new concept, it is rooted in the past. The development of spatial organization from the Renaissance to the Baroque points towards the birth of the free plan, and inspiration from other epochs and cultures was also important, especially the lesson of the "classical" Japanese house.[8] To understand the historical importance of the free plan and the meaning of the new tradition, it is necessary to take a look at these "constituent facts."

The idea of a continuous, isotropic space is a basic condition for the development of the free plan. It came into existence during the Renaissance, and found its precise expression in the works of Filippo Brunelleschi. Here the differentiated and hierarchical organization of the Middle Ages has been replaced by a simple addition of regular spatial units. Space is thus conceived as a continuum, which, because of its repetitive geometrical organization, was understood as the manifestation of a comprehensive divine order. The architects treated this space as a "substance" which could be structured by means of elementary geometry and described visually by means of perspective. The concept of isotropic space, however, did not prevent meaningful differentiation. Through the use of more or less "perfect" forms, sacred, public, and private buildings were distinguished. Alberti asserted that the most perfect forms, in particular the circle and the square, should be reserved for the church. A splendid example is offered by Brunelleschi's Santo Spirito in Florence (1436ff.). Here, the plan and the section are based on a square, which is repeated in regular succession (the units of the nave are four times those of the aisles). The spatial organization is visualized by means of lines in dark stone

"drawn" on the white plaster surfaces-. In spite of the additive composition, Santo Spirito appears as a differentiated and unified whole, demonstrating how variety is possible within isotropic space.

In the "Mannerist" architecture of the sixteenth century the possibility of spatial differentiation was further exploited, with the aim of recalling a wide range of natural characters. Raphael's Villa Madama in Rome (1517ff.) furnishes an important example. Here the rooms change their form and scale in correspondence with the inner and outer "forces," and the regular space of the early Renaissance is transformed into an expressive revelation of environmental qualities. Whereas the Quattrocento stressed static, isotropic order, the Cinquecento developed differentiated spatial succession. Qualitatively different places and domains were thus defined. In general, Mannerism fully regained the concrete, phenomenal character of space, combining it with the idea of an environmental continuum. The two aspects, individual place and isotropic space, are not however integrated, but rather intended as dialectical opposites.

In the Baroque architecture of the seventeenth and eighteenth centuries, on the other hand, the unification of continuous extension and local definition is fully accomplished. This is achieved by shaping the spatial elements- in accordance with their roles within the whole, and through the introduction of new methods of dynamic integration. Both possibilities were suggested by Borromini, who deliberately used spatial "cells" as the constituent elements of his compositions. The units of Borromini are, however, no longer simple geometrical figures, but complex, indivisible wholes.[9] The units moreover tend to become mutually interdependent. His organization of space is therefore simultaneously systematic and complex. In the works of Guarino Guarini the principles proposed by Borromini are worked out. Guarini composed complex plans with interdependent or interpenetrating cells, and produced forms that resemble pulsating organisms. In fact,

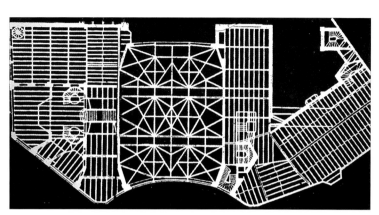
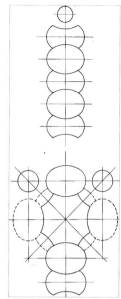

FAR RIGHT: Dientzenhofer: Principles
of "open" spatial composition (CNS).
RIGHT: Victor Horta:
Maison du Peuple, 1896-99.

Guarini considered the pulsating, undulating movement a basic property of nature, saying: "The spontaneous action of dilation and contraction . . . is present throughout the whole living being."[10] Guarini applied his principles to the solution of numerous concrete tasks, mainly churches, and in general worked out an *ars combinatoria,* which was taken over by the late Baroque architects of Central Europe, in particular the Dientzenhofers and Balthasar Neumann. The solutions of Kilian Ignaz Dientzenhofer may be described as "open" groups of interdependent spatial units which prefigure, and even out-do, the "patterns of open growth" of today.[11] Around 1750 spatial organization had thus become a matter of great virtuosity: the open, differentiated plans created by the last generation of Baroque architects integrate the single building with an "infinite" environment and at the same time preserve its particular identity.

The neo-classical architecture of the Enlightenment did not follow this approach. Rather it developed fixed types and static compositions which were intended to represent the original harmony of "natural laws." The inclusive and concrete architecture of the Baroque was thus replaced by the abstract, formalistic patterns that were to become the distinguishing mark of the Ecole des Beaux-Arts.[12] It is one of the paradoxes of history that a revolution, which should have liberated man, offered him stones for bread, not to say diagrams for places. The reason is, as we have already suggested, that architecture and art became subordinate to thought. As a result feeling degenerated into sentimentality, and was expressed by eclectic borrowing.

The free plan represents a reaction against the abstract typologies of academic architecture. During the nineteenth century it became increasingly clear that architecture had to be liberated from the official approach. In this connection it is important to remember that the architectural revolution starting with Paxton's Crystal Palace in 1851 was to a great extent accomplished by non-architects who did not feel obliged to subscribe to the academic "rules." Towards the end of the century, however, major architects also took up the challenge, aiming at an *art nouveau* which could replace the devalued symbols of eclecticism. Thus, the freedom inherent in Baroque architecture was revived and dynamic spatial layouts once again came to the fore.

In the works of architects such as Horta, Guimard and Gaudí, space regained differentiated continuity. Horta's *Hôtel van Eetvelde* in Brussels (1894-1901) may serve as an example. According to Horta a building has to be conceived as a living organism, possessing an analogous complex unity. Accordingly he created "sequences of polygonal spaces which are dynamically interrelated, optically continuous and psychologically differentiated."[13] The *Hôtel van Eetvelde* is built on one of the deep, narrow lots typical of old Belgian cities. The interior, however, appears as a magnificent succession of seemingly open, interconnected spaces grouped around a glass-covered octagon. The octagon serves as a centre for the composition, and is also axially related to the main rooms upstairs. But the entrance to the building is excentrically located at one end of the facade, from where a diagonal leads to the stairs which circulate around the octagon. A subtle play of symmetries and asymmetries is thus obtained, and the totality gains a freedom unknown even in Baroque architecture. Compositions of this kind are legion in *art nouveau* architecture, although the local character may vary.

The pre-modern architecture which came into existence about the turn of the century thus possessed the basic qualities of the free plan: continuity, transparency, interaction and differentiation, or, in short, simultaneity of place. And still, the solutions were too particular to serve as a point of departure for the new tradition. The new architecture had to start again "from the beginning," Giedion said, and in spite of its novelty the *art nouveau* did not offer any basic *principles.* It is important to recognize, however, that *art nouveau* belongs to

Frank Lloyd Wright:
Robie House, 1908

the roots of modern architecture, as does the architecture of Borromini and Neumann, and the early iron-and-glass structures. It is Giedion's merit to have uncovered these "constituent facts," in particular the relationship between the "undulating walls" of Borromini, Horta and Aalto, which in all three cases serve the purpose of spatial unification.[14] Giedion also pointed out how Wright's development of the free plan was inspired by the "romantic" one-family houses of the nineteenth century, and mentioned Charles Rennie Mackintosh as a European parallel."[15] In his houses we in fact encounter a similar wish for spatial continuity and differentiation, although the approach is less radical than in the case of Wright.

Among the roots of the free plan we also have to include the "classical" Japanese house. Once Japan was open to visitors from western countries, a keen interest in Japanese culture and art developed during the second half of the nineteenth century. Frank Lloyd Wright referred to the Japanese house as one of his sources of inspiration: "The Japanese house is a supreme study in elimination not only of dirt, but the elimination, too, of the insignificant."[16] In other words, the Japanese house confirmed Wright's idea that spatial richness does not depend on applied decoration, but rather on the handling of space itself. In the Japanese house, in fact, two of the main objectives of Wright are solved: the fluid interaction between inside and outside by means of continuous openings and projecting elements, and the dissolution of the rooms inside by means of screen-walls which direct space rather than enclosing it. Moreover, a pronounced horizontality creates a "quiet relationship with the ground."[17] The classical Japanese house is certainly related to a particular kind of society and should not be copied today.[18] Its principles of spatial organization are, however, valid and may still serve as an important source of inspiration for the further development of the free plan.

Phenomenology of the free plan

Le Corbusier's *Five Points for a New Architecture* of 1926 sum up the early development of the free plan and the open form. In general they contain two basic principles with regard to the former: the use of a regular skeleton construction (*pilotis*) which allow for the desired freedom, and the transformation of the load-bearing wall into a screen which may be placed wherever needed. These two principles are evidently interdependent, a fact which was emphasized by Mies van der Rohe.[19] Both stem from the new architecture of the nineteenth century: the concept of regular structure from the early iron-and-glass buildings, and the liberation of the wall from the early houses of Frank Lloyd Wright. The unification of the two was suggested by some of the *art nouveau* architects, but was only recognized as a new fundamental principle by Le Corbusier in his Domino project of 1914. Although the two aspects are interrelated, the liberation of the wall may be considered primary to the regular structure. It is above all the wall which directs and delineates space, and the first attempts of Wright to realize free plans took the destruction of the box as their point of departure: "I was working away at the wall as a wall and bringing it toward the function of a screen, a means of opening up space which . . . would finally permit the free use of the whole space . . ."[20] As a result, Wright transformed the box into a juxtaposition of vertical and horizontal places, which do not unify to form closed spaces, but overlap and project. Beyond the general aim of opening up space, the destruction of the box implied a continuous transition between interior and exterior, which Wright obtained through his use of projecting planes. In his houses walls, ceilings and floors continue from the inside out, and it is no longer possible to tell where interior space stops and exterior space starts. To make this continuity operant, the intervals between the planes are filled in by glazed areas, either running from floor to ceiling, or as long, horizontal strips over the parapets. However, continuity is not wanted everywhere, but mainly in connection

Gerrit Rietveld:
Schröder House, Utrecht, 1924.

with entrances, porches and terraces. The examples are legion and comprise small and inexpensive houses such as the Isabel Roberts House in River Forest and the large, luxurious Robie House in Chicago, both dating from 1908.

These two houses also illustrate the typical spatial compositions favoured by Wright. Most of his plans may be characterized as centrifugal," as the different zones are organized around a large, centrally placed chimney stack, which appears as a kind of vertical axis both in the interior and when seen from the outside. In Wright's houses we do not find any "clear structure," although he used modern building techniques to free the walls from their load-bearing function. The structural members, however, in general remain hidden. Instead the chimney stack serves as a unifying element; it rises up through the juxtaposition of planes, and keeps the composition together.[21] In general, Wright's houses are marked by horizontal extension, but the rooms also open up vertically, and a rich interplay of narrow and wide, low and high spaces is obtained. Although the compositions are mostly asymmetrical and "free," axial symmetry is used to concentrate the flux in certain points, for instance in front of the fireplace or towards the principal view. The plans may also possess a more or less worked out general symmetry, as is indicated by the concepts of "cruciform" and "windmill" plans. The Ward Willits House of 1901 is a particularly fine example of the former, while the much later residence of Herbert F. Johnson, Wingspread (1937), is a grandiose version of the windmill pattern. The interaction between outside and inside implies the abolition of the traditional facade. Wright's houses are "facadeless," and can only be understood as tridimensional totalities.

Wright's houses are distinguished by an ingenious synthesis of freedom and order, and when his early work was published in Germany in 1910, his message was immediately understood. Many architects took up his method of working with horizontal and vertical planes, for instance Walter Gropius in his model factory at the Werkbund exhibition in Cologne in 1914.

In particular the Dutch De Stijl group developed the idea, and changed it from a pragmatic means of solving the problems of the new dwelling into a symbolic expression of the new world. Inspired by the philosopher Schoenmaekers, the general method of De Stijl art became a "suspension of primary colours in orthogonal space." Schoenmaekers had in fact maintained that "the two fundamental contraries which shape our earth are the horizontal and the vertical" and that "the only colours existing are yellow, blue and red."[22] This conception was transferred to art by Mondrian and van Doesburg, and put to work by Gerrit Rietveld in the Schröder House in Utrecht (1924). The most conspicuous quality of the Schröder House is its appearance as a composition of free-standing vertical and hovering horizontal planes. These planes are throughout separated to avoid any feeling of static volume. They also lack the usual definitions of "up" and "down" by means of cornices and bases. At first glance, it may seem that the planes are juxtaposed without any discernible order. However, closer scrutiny reveals that the solution is based on a kind of centrifugal pattern with one primary room in each corner around a centrally placed stairwell. A general openness is thereby achieved, which is emphasized by projecting balconies and roof overhangs. The vertical planes which give definition to the spatial layout, are placed in such a way that they direct the movement along the house at the same time as they create an interaction with the surroundings. On all three sides, we find double-height "standing" planes which rise beyond the level of the roof. These planes evidently serve to unify the two floors and relate the configuration to the sky above. In the open areas between the primary planes dense juxtapositions of coloured, linear elements are present. Inside, the colours are extended to form large surfaces which define spatial zones and artefact. Thus the house illustrates Mondrian's words: "I became conscious that reality is form *and* space . . . space became white, black or grey, form became red, blue or yellow,"[23] and it confirms van Doesburg's more general

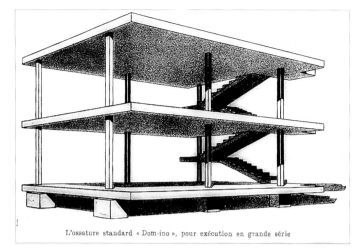

FAR RIGHT: Le Corbusier:
Open staircase in own apartment,
Paris, 1933.
RIGHT: Le Corbusier: Structural
system for "Domino" housing, 1914.

L'ossature standard « Dom-ino », pour exécution en grande série

dictum: "In contrast with the frontality which results from a fixed, static outlook, the new architecture offers a plastic richness of multi-sided, timespace activity.[24] The Schröder House, however, somehow appears as a theoretical model rather than a dwelling, reducing the "grammar" of composing with horizontal and vertical planes to its essentials. In this reduction, at a time when modern architecture had to define its basic principles, resides the importance of Rietveld's solution.

Both Le Corbusier and Mies van der Rohe evidently understood that the abstract open space of De Stijl architecture has to be "built" to become a full-grown work. Mies van der Rohe at first solved the problem by making the planes of "real" materials, such as brick, wood and concrete, reviving thus in a certain sense the approach of Wright. His "brick country house" project of 1923 may serve as an example. Later, however, he introduced a repetitive skeletal structure with the purpose of giving the free plan coherence, rhythm and scale. We understand that the clear structure did not represent an end in itself, but served to bring the free plan back to reality. When the space-defining elements are fully liberated, they need such a concrete reference. Mies's Barcelona Pavilion of 1929 offers an emblematic example. Basically this building is a composition of vertical and horizontal planes, the latter being reduced to a comprehensive podium and two flat roofs. The vertical planes are throughout treated as slabs which direct space and define zones. One long plane thus connects the two parts of the building, continuing under the roofs of both. Another plane, which embraces a pool, forms a "pocket" behind the main space. Another, completely free-standing slab defines a sitting area within the main space. The different zones are also interrelated by means of transparent or translucent partitions which are partly free-standing and partly connected with the slabs. In general, the space is conceived as a continuous flux within which subordinate zones are defined. This flux has to be understood as a progression from the entrance (which is *behind* the building) through the "interior" spaces and down

the flight of stairs to the "garden" on the other side (an analogous progression is found in the *Tugendhat House*). (In most descriptions of the Barcelona pavilion, the garden stairs are deemed to be the entrance!). The Barcelona Pavilion appears more "real" than the theoretical models of De Stijl, a fact that is also emphasized by the travertine podium, which like a symbolic "earth" unifies the whole. And still, the spatial composition as such remains too abstract to be fully accepted as a "building." The planes do not have the traditional detailing which refers to up and down and give the movement in space rhythm and scale. To solve the latter problem, Mies introduced a regular grid of cruciform, chromium-plated steel columns which carry the main roof.[25] The columnar system does not only denote "building," but also visualizes a spatial continuum into which the place-creating planes are situated. The total solution thus comprises two spatial definitions: the skeletal grid which makes the general properties of open space manifest, and the juxtaposition of planes which take care of the circumstantial situation. It is important to realize that the two definitions are interdependent: the isotropic grid becomes "alive" because of the planes, and the latter gain a general meaning because of the former. Due to its emblematic qualities, the Barcelona Pavilion is usually considered the most direct and pure visualization of the free plan.

We have already pointed out that the principles illustrated by the Barcelona Pavilion were intuited by Le Corbusier in his *Domino* project of 1914 and laid down theoretically in his *Five Points* of 1926. In the *Villa Savoye* in Poissy, which was built from 1929 to 1931, Le Corbusier himself illustrated their concrete implementation. The *Villa Savoye* is also based on a grid of regularly-spaced columns, which gives coherence to a rich and varied juxtaposition of curved and straight planes and enveloping membranes. However, here the two constituent parts take each other into consideration. Thus the columnar grid is modified at the entrance (and in some other places) to indicate that the new conception of open space is not a

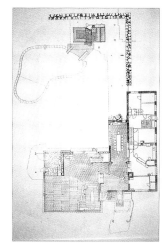

mathematical idea, but a function of life. The concrete character of the solution is also expressed by the ingenious use of the vertical dimension; the three floors evidently represent the earth (which continues under the house between the *pilotis*), the sky (which is "received" by the *solarium* on the roof), and the complex world of man in between. The levels are interconnected by means of a centrally placed ramp, which makes experiencing the house a *promenade architecturale* to quote Le Corbusier's own words.[26] In general, the house represents an answer to a concrete building task; Le Corbusier in fact describes the beauty of the situation, which ought to be respected and even enhanced by the building. In the Villa Savoye any reference to static symmetry and box-like enclosure is left behind, the house possesses an unsurpassed spatial complexity and richness. The free plan is, however, contained within an approximately square volume, and the exterior appearance is characterized by classical repose. Thus Le Corbusier could satisfy both his basic intentions: the desire for spatial freedom and the demand for elementary form.

The magnificent early realizations of Wright, Mies and Le Corbusier made the free plan come into existence as a concrete fact. All of them, however, are marked by some self-imposed limitations. Above all, the place-defining elements are almost always orthogonally disposed; only Le Corbusier sometimes employed curved or oblique partitions. When the present writer once asked Mies van der Rohe why he always used the right angle, he answered: "I have nothing against oblique angles or curved lines, if it is done well . . . The Baroque architects mastered these things, but they were the last stage in a long development."[27] In other words: the setting of the free plan in work had to proceed step by step, if the basic principles were not to be lost on the way.

A further important step was taken by Alvar Aalto. In Aalto's works there are few regular skeleton structures or free-standing partitions, and yet his buildings are undoubtedly examples of the free plan. That is, they are never closed as static, self-sufficient entities, but, without losing their identity, remain open, integral parts of a "total" environment. Aalto's sketches illustrate how he works simultaneously from the inside out and from the outside in, intending the building as an encounter with the environment. A different interpretation of the new vision is thus at work: rather than understanding the open world in geometric terms, Aalto offers a *dynamic* version. The typical Nordic relationship to nature is thereby expressed; it sees the environment as a complex interaction of "forces" rather than a manifestation of universal "harmony."[28] It is meaningful to call this attitude "romantic," in contrast to the "classic" approach of the South. Although they were not southerners, Le Corbusier and Mies were basically classicists, whereas Wright represented a synthesis of the two approaches.[29] Aalto's architecture has been labelled "romantic modernism," since his open solutions are truly modern, but certainly different from those of the "international style."[30]

'What, then, are the spatial properties of romantic modernism? Our previously used key concepts, "simultaneity," "continuity," and "interaction," are still valid. In Aalto's works, however, simultaneity is not just transparency, and continuity is not the spatial movement created by projecting planes. Here, these qualities are rather obtained through the use of forms which, while they take possession of space, change and develop.[31] The buildings may thus be compared with living organisms, and the spaces appear correspondingly alive: fanning out, contracting, sub-dividing, opening and closing. This happens rhythmically instead of following a regular "beat" as in the Barcelona Pavilion. In Aalto's Villa Mairea, the columns inside are disposed irregularly to appear as a continuation of the rhythm of the trees standing around the house. Of particular importance in Aalto's free plans, is the use of "undulating" walls. Sometimes such walls are found inside – a splendid early example is the Finnish Pavilion for the World's Fair in New York (1939) – sometimes the undulating movement takes possession of the whole building as in the dormitory for the

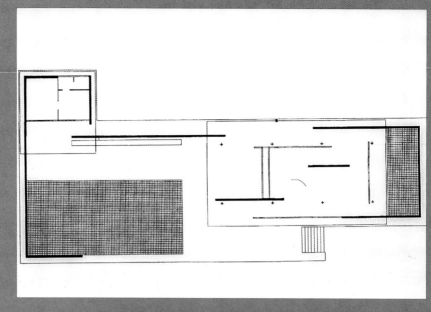

Mies van der Rohe , Barcelona Pavilion, 1929

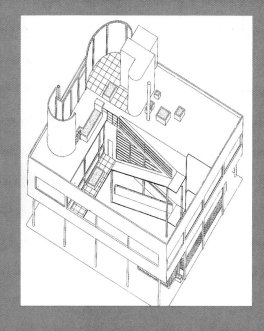

"The magnificent early realizations of Mies and Le Corbusier make the free plan come into existence as a concrete fact . . ."

Le Corbusier, Villa Savoye, Poissy, 1930

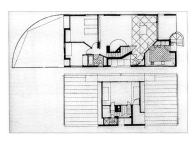

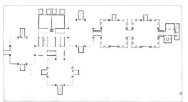

FAR RIGHT: Louis Kahn,
Richards Medical Laboratories,
Philadelphia, 1960, with plan.
MIDDLE TOP: Robert Venturi,
Vanna Venturi House,
Philadelphia, 1962
RIGHT: Robert Stern:
Lang House, Washington, 1974.

M.I.T. in Cambridge, Mass. (1947-48). The undulating wall has a greater space-creating power than the flat plane as it makes space contract and expand, and brings about a pronounced interaction between the zones it defines.[32] How, then, is unity achieved in complex organisms of this kind? Basically through a great, unitary "theme," which makes the building stand forth with conviction. Aalto's sketches prove that most of his solutions stem from such comprehensive ideas. In general, his interpretation of the free plan may be characterized as *topological* in contrast to the geometrical layouts of Le Corbusier and Mies van der Rohe.[33] The open world is, however, the common point of departure; and the new conception of space the common *credo*. Aalto's version of the free plan is important because it opens up a whole range of new spatial possibilities; in particular it makes the adaptation to local circumstances easier and more meaningful.

Since the second world war, several architects have implemented new interpretations of the free plan. Of particular interest are the "structuralist" approach which took the Richards Medical Research Building by Louis Kahn (1957-64) as its point of departure; the "field" approach developed by Paolo Portoghesi (Casa Andreis 1964-67), and the "place" approach proposed by Moore, Lyndon, Turnbull and Whitaker in the Sea Ranch north of San Francisco (1965).

The Richards Medical Research Building illustrates two ideas which would become very influential: the conception of a building as a "pattern of open growth," and the distinction between "served" and "serving" spaces. The circumstantial point of departure was the fact that scientists usually work in small groups and that the exhaust air produced by the research activities should not interfere with the work spaces. As a result, the building was designed as a juxtaposition of superimposed main spaces and a series of slender stacks containing staircases and ducts.

The cluster of towers thus created bears a certain resemblance to the densely grouped units of medieval towns, and at the same time represents an open system.[34] A free plan of a new kind is thus proposed, where openness is not necessarily achieved by means of direct transitions between inside and outside, but rather by a pattern which may be extended when needed. Identity and coherence are secured because the elements know "what they want to be." Kahn put his principles in his work in many cases, each time using different spatial units as his basic material.[35]

Kahn's ideas were taken up by numerous architects, among whom we may single out the team Candilis, Josic, Woods (Free University, Berlin 1963-73), Aldo van Eyck (Orphanage, Amsterdam 1960), Herman Hertzberger (Office Building Central Beheer, Apeldorn 1970-72), and Henning Larsen (University Centre, Trondheim 1978).[36] The danger inherent in the structuralist approach is naturally that the building becomes a mere repetition of similar elements, whereby spatial identity and human orientation are lost. When that happens, the idea of the free plan is contradicted and reduced to a mechanistic diagram.

On several occasions Paolo Portoghesi has defined space as "a system of places," and has illustrated his idea with theoretical schemes as well as executed buildings.[37] Casa Andreis in Scandriglia, northeast of Rome, is particularly illuminating. The plan of this small weekend house is organized in relation to five centres, with concentric spatial "fields." The centres are not arbitrary geometrical points, but *foci* determined by the surrounding landscape and the domestic functions. The fields therefore integrate external and internal forces. Together they form a more complex field, where zones of interaction are present. Being related to two or more centres, these zones are distinguished by tension and movement. The centres define the main places which constitute the house, whereas the fields determine the distribution of the space-defining built elements. Thus the geometric scheme of Casa Andreis does not represent abstract mathematical space but visualizes a modern simultaneity of places. On several occasions Portoghesi demon-

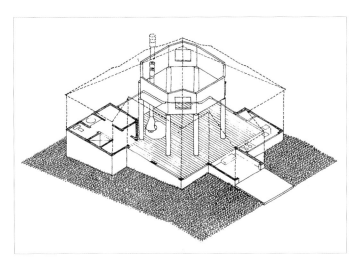

FAR RIGHT: Paolo Portoghesi:
Andreis House, Scandriglia, 1964-67.
RIGHT: MTLW, Johnson House,
Sea Ranch, California, 1966.

strated the fertility of his "method;" in particular we may recall *Casa Bevilacqua* in Gaeta (1966-71), *Casa Papanice* in Rome (1969-70), and the *church of the Sacra Famiglia* in Salerno (1969-73).[38] Portoghesi's approach to the organization of space represents a development of the juxtaposition of planes as invented by Wright and "purified" by De Stijl. The use of curved elements emphasizes the continuity basic to the the plan, and the method of geometrical integration secures unity in multiplicity. Hence we may recall Mies's words: "The Baroque architects mastered these things, but they were the last stage in a long development." Portoghesi in fact derived his interpretation of the free plan from studies of the works of Borromini and Guarini!

The word "place" is ever more coming to the fore in the architectural debate, indicating that architectural space is different from abstract mathematical space. This was evidently understood by Wright, Mies and Le Corbusier, but the epigones of the next generation tended to reduce place-making to a mere building of functional diagrams. Louis Kahn reacted against that, calling the "institutions of man" "worlds within a world," that is, "places of concentration, where man's mind becomes sharp."[39] Inspired by Kahn, several younger American architects have returned to real place-making, without however giving up the new vision and the free plan.[40] The team MLTW is of particular interest in this context. In its houses we again find the qualities described above in connection with the works of the pioneers, but in a more concrete sense than before. Space is no longer intended in geometrical terms or even as a kind of topological "organism," but is understood as an interrelationship of *built* elements: floor, enclosure and cover, or more precisely, stairs, steps, terraces, walls, windows, skylights, columns, porches, canopies and *aediculae*.[41] These "elements of place" are subject to the "order of rooms." Rooms are *unspecific spaces*, empty stages for human action, where we perform the rituals and improvisations of living. They provide generalized opportunities for things to happen,

and they allow us to do and be what we will."[42] Thus the free plan has become what originally it was intended to be, a concrete manifestation of the simultaneity of places, and thus of the modern way of life. We may in this connection quote Heidegger. "Spaces receive their being from places and not from 'space.'"[43] It would not have been possible to reach this goal, however, without the lesson of the pioneers.

Our discussion of the phenomenology of the free plan has shown that it may be subject to many interpretations which are equally valid. In some cases a particular interpretation has been worked out as a consistent "grammar" of design. This is for instance the case in the works of Mies van der Rohe, which illustrate implicit "rules" for the juxtaposition of walls, openings, and furnishings, relative to a structural skeleton.[44] A grammar which covers all the various versions of the free plan is, however, hardly possible. What is common to them all consists in the general wish for simultaneity, which implies a relationship of interaction between the various spatial zones of the interior as well as between inside and outside. Summing up, we may define the free plan as the spatial organization of a multitude of interacting places.

Actuality of the free plan
During its infancy the free plan had to be protected against forms which involved the danger of falling back on static self-sufficiency. Symmetrical units and layouts were thus "forbidden."[45] When the understanding of the phenomenology and grammar of the free plan increased, the prohibited forms came back. Already Mies van der Rohe returned to symmetrical dispositions (I.I.T), and Le Corbusier reintroduced massive walls with "holes" in them (Ronchamp). The architecture of the past was, moreover, used as a source of inspiration, and spatial forms such as rotundas and axial successions re-appeared. The danger is of course that the spatial organization closes up, as is happening in certain buildings of the "neo-rationalist" school. In the works of Aldo Rossi, for instance, the

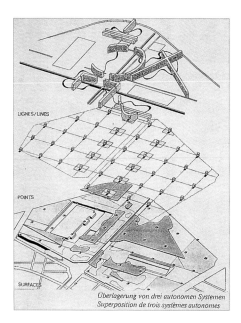

Bernard Tschumi:
Parc de la Villette, Paris, 1988.

original meaning of the *promenade architecturale* is forgotten, whereby intermediate space loses its significance. The houses of MLTW, however, demonstrate that regular spaces, such as the octagon of the Johnson house at Sea Ranch, may be included in a dynamic composition.[46] An even more radical development of the free plan is manifest in the works of Reima Pietilä, whose "natural morphology" transforms the *promenade* into a voyage through nature. In his student union building *Dipoli* at Otaniemi (1961ff.) outside and inside communicate topologically and materially, and at the same time the building represents a "station" in the extended Finnish forest. The Norwegian Sverre Fehn also gives intermediate space pride of place, as is demonstrated by his *Hedmark Museum* at Hamar (1966ff.). Here ramps and galleries lead through a continuous interior where memories of past and present appear.[47] In connection with the further development of the free plan, the concept of "layering" has been introduced. The *Parc de la Villette* in Paris by Bernard Tschumi (1982ff.) thus consists of three superimposed spatial systems which create a complex whole. It is theoretically interesting, but environmentally ineffective. The spatial manifestations of "deconstruction" are similarly dubious, since they substitute freedom with chaos, that is, spaces where the modern *promenade* becomes arbitrary and meaningless.

The free plan came into existence to make human life richer and more meaningful in a complex, open world, and that is still its purpose. One cannot become an architect today without having gone through the needle-eye of modern art, Giedion said. In the daily work of the architect that means to have understood the phenomenology of the free plan and to have been trained in the use of its "grammar." Although the free plan may be given many different interpretations, its properties are particularly well illustrated by the works of the pioneers discussed above. We might therefore add that one cannot become an architect today without knowing Wright, Mies and Le Corbusier.

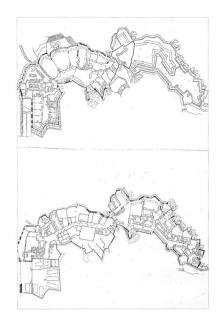

Reima and Raila Pietilä:
Mantyniemi, Helsinki, 1983-95.

3 *the* Open Form

T he *open form* is the concretization of the new conception of building. As a means of endowing man-made things with an appropriate character, it serves to help human identification with the new world. The word "identification" does not only denote the recognition of things, but also the experience of their meaning. A thing is not only meaningful because it forms part of an immediate situation, but also because of its general properties. The circumstantial and general properties with which we are concerned, consist in the relationship to earth and sky, that is, how the built form *stands, rises, extends, opens* and *closes.* These modes visualize the tensions and rhythms inherent in spatial organization. The interpretation of our being between earth and sky, which determines the open form, stems from the "new vision," and its aim is the establishment of a meaningful environment for our time.

The built form of past epochs in general was based on clearly defined choices. It could be "ground-hugging" or vertically "aspiring," or express a certain tension between such characters. It could make massive enclosure manifest, or possess skeletal openness, or visualize a state of transition. Static symmetry was usually employed to give horizontal coherence to the forms, and tripartite superimposition was a common means to reveal the basic relationship of earth, sky and the human "between" *(piano rustico, piano nobile, corona aedifici).* When ambiguities were present, as in Mannerist architecture, they appeared as disquieting disturbances of a "natural" order. In general, the built forms of the past constituted closed systems which are known as "styles." Within a style each form is related to the others, and its meaning depends on these relations.

The open form departs from this tradition. The potential simultaneity of places demands forms which make a condition of 'both-and" rather than "either-or" manifest, to use the words of Robert Venturi.[1'] The self-contained compositions of the past thus give way to collage-like ensembles in a state of dynamic equilibrium. This implies that the open form aims at the establishment of a new interactive relationship between the characters of "here" and "there." The identity of the place is not abolished, but it should not be allowed to "close" itself off as a self-sufficient world. New means of articulation were therefore developed: contradicted symmetry, inversion, displacement (relative to ordering axes), overlapping, transparency, interpenetration, fusion, metamorphosis . . . The use of these means can be more or less comprehensive; sometimes the formal ensembles may appear as thoroughly new, sometimes as a known order which is broken. Very little is in fact needed to "open up" a form. The wish for openness is already felt in the proto-modern architecture of the late nineteenth century, and even in some quasi-open compositions of historicism.[2] With the advent of *art nouveau* many of the new means of articulation were fully developed, and the "visual revolution" which took place during the first decade of the twentieth century proposed the use of a collage-like simultaneity of forms.

The open form is a general concept, and cannot be reduced to any of its possible manifestations, such as "transparency." The open form stems from the wish to make the single work of architecture belong to a more comprehensive, global world. This is not necessarily achieved by making the form very complex, but by endowing it with a potential openness, that is, a widened capacity for interaction and change. The open form has, however, like any form, to be "rooted." It ought to belong to the place, and take the circumstantial situation as its point of departure, although the "new vision" demands a manifest relatedness to what is "beyond." In general, the open form implies a return to the origins, in the sense of deriving meaning from the "things themselves" rather than from a particular stylistic system.

OPPOSITE: Dutert and Contamin: Galerie des Machines, Paris World Fair, 1889.

FAR RIGHT: Colosseum, Rome, 80.
MIDDLE: Nativity Church,
Bethlehem, c.325.
RIGHT TOP: Farm House,
Rheinland, Germany.
RIGHT BOTTOM: Farmhouse,
near Orbetello, Italy.

Roots of the open form

Although the open form is a new concept, it presupposes the expressive means of past epochs. The reaction against the styles and the wish for a return to something basic or essential, created a new interest in vernacular architecture. Even during the "international" phase of modern architecture, vernacular forms were used as a source of inspiration. Le Corbusier studied the mural buildings of the Mediterranean countries during his long voyage in 1911, and discovered the beauty of the timeless, elementary forms. Mies van der Rohe's repetitive skeletons and unitary spaces reflect early impressions of northwest German half-timbered houses, as is indicated by his own words: "Where can we find greater structural clarity than in the wooden buildings of old? Where else can we find such unity of material, construction and form? What warmth and beauty they have! They seem to be echoes of old songs. What better examples could there be for young architects?"[3] And Frank Lloyd Wright coined his motto "In the Nature of Materials," to emphasize his vernacular rootedness. In general, vernacular architecture served to clarify one's understanding of the properties of massive, skeleton structures, as well as simple, elementary volumes. It also strengthened the belief in the expressive possibilities of the materials themselves, as distinct from stylistic motifs and details.

Although the pioneers reacted against the styles, they also had to take this part of our architectural inheritance into consideration. It is also a fact that most of the pioneers of modern architecture had a classical background. "Order must exist before it can be broken," Venturi says.[4] The *classical* language is based on the qualitative abstraction of natural characters, and therefore serves to establish an accord between man and his given environment. Whereas rustication as a stylized rock visualizes natural nature, the orders represent human characters. Serlio, in fact, calls rustication *opera di' natura* and the orders *opera di mano,* By combining the two in different ways, one or another interpretation of the relationship between man and nature, that is, of the world, is made manifest. Although early modern architecture hardly used the classical language as such, its basic characters still formed an implicit point of departure, because they are an expression of our life between earth and sky. *Gothic* architecture is also related to the buildings of our epoch. This becomes immediately evident if we compare one of the Mediaeval cathedrals with the great iron-and-glass structures of the nineteenth century. Perhaps such a comparison may seem superficial, but the vision of an infinite world which is given presence as a "diaphanous" structure, is basically the same. "In the machinery hall of Contamin the French spirit has for the third time in its history after the Cathedral and the light-world of Versailles realized a grand vision of light," Hans Sedlmayr writes.[5] The transparency, layering and linearity of Gothic architecture reappear in modern buildings, whereas the stylistic details are suppressed because of their Mediaeval connotations.

The fundamental principle of simultaneity in particular relates the architecture of our time to certain buildings of the sixteenth century, that is, to the architecture of *Mannerism.* During the *cinquecento* an architecture of tension and conflict arose, which in general expressed a doubt in the ordered world of the Renaissance. The static and harmonious forms of the *quattrocento* thus gave way to dynamic and complex compositions, here classical elements are put in opposition to each other. A well-known example is the interpenetration of rustication and orders, whereby the latter appear as being "imprisoned" by the former. The motif is repeated with variations on all three floors of Ammanati's cortile in the Palazzo Pitti, Florence (1560). Sometimes Mannerism shows the elements in a state of disintegration or as unfinished. Such "disturbed" forms were in general used to attain a more intense expression, as for instance a "fight" between the forces of nature and the ordering power of man, which in Giulio Romano's *Sala dei Giganti* in the Palazzo del Tè, Mantua (1526ff.) ends with a catastrophe. The existential doubt behind Mannerist

FAR RIGHT: Benedikt Ried:
S. Barbara, Kutna Hora, 1512.
MIDDLE: Francesco Borromini:
Oratorio dei Filippini, Rome, 1637.
RIGHT TOP: Gianlorenzo Bernini,
Four Rivers Fountain, Rome, 1637.
RIGHT BOTTOM: Bartolomeo
Ammanati: Palazzo Pitti
courtyard, Florence, 1560.

architecture is related to our epoch, at least to its late post-se-ond-world war phase. As in the *cinquecento* we can no longer believe in an ordered *cosmos*, but have to face the complexities and contradictions of our everyday world. Our conflict, however, is not a split within the closed system of man and nature, but a split of thinking and feeling within an open world.

Our epoch may also be given a positive interpretation, as was done by the pioneers of modern architecture. Evidently they believed in progress and in the possibility of creating a better future. Therefore their approach was related to the "optimistic" and expansive attitude of the *Baroque*. We have already pointed out that Baroque space prepares for the free plan, although it served absolutist social systems. The same holds true for the built form. Basically the Baroque was a period of *synthesis*; one wanted to express that "everything" belongs together in a great, dynamic totality. As a result the works of art tended to become complex but integrated ensembles of multifarious elements, as for instance in Bernini's Four Rivers fountain at Piazza Navona in Rome (1650) where natural, human and abstract parts are combined to form a comprehensive *imago mundi*.[6] The wish for synthesis, that is an intimate unification of things, as opposed to Renaissance addition and Mannerist conflict, led to the development of *continuity* as a principle of composition. Baroque forms tend to grow into each other and fuse, and sometimes the same element changes to become something else, as when the cornice of Borromini's Oratorio dei Filippini in Rome (1637) turns into a volute. Borromini was in general a great inventor of "synthetic" forms, as exemplified by his window frames and gables, which combine pointed and rounded contours, and his original corners which simultaneously unite and delimit the adjacent walls. The church of Sant'Ivo alla Sapienza (1642ff.) may even be understood as a synthesis of dome and tower, that is, as a form that simultaneously embraces and rises, rests and aspires. Borromini's importance was recognized by

Giedion who, at the beginning of his book *Space, Time and Architecture* dedicated a chapter to the Italian master. In particular he stresses the importance of Borromini's "undulating" walls which prefigure the curved surfaces of modern architecture, starting with Horta's *Maison du Peuple* in Brussels (1897). "The undulating wall of Borromini's invention gave flexibility to stone, changed the stone wall into an elastic material. The undulating wall is the natural accompaniment to the flowing spaces of the flexible ground plan."[7] Giedion also points out that Borromini found inspiration in the forms of "bygone epochs" without however imitating them.[8] No wonder that architects of our epoch have taken up the possibilities suggested by Borromini!

Contrary to Baroque synthesis, neo-classical architecture represents a return to fixed types and additive principles of composition. Hence it does not show any affinity to the open form of modern architecture.[9] Again we face the paradox that the concrete manifestations of the Enlightenment contradicted its very goal: a new human freedom. The reason is evidently a confusion of thinking and feeling. Applying analytical methods to art, "enlightened" man killed the artistic dimension. In certain works of the "romantic classicism" of the nineteenth century, however, the rigidity of neo-classical typology and syntax was broken down. About the turn of the century new fascinating possibilities of expression within the classical language were revealed by Sir Edwin Lutyens, whose "open historicism" is today rediscovered as a source of inspiration.[10]

With the advent of *art nouveau* the "open form" became a reality. In the works of Horta, Gaudi, Guimard, Mackintosh, Saarinen and other protagonists the static, rational types of neo-classicism and the dubious "freedom" of historicism were substituted by a new universe of expressive means. The point of departure was again the basic properties of earth and sky, as exemplified by Otto Wagner's Karlsplatz station in Vienna (1899-1900). Here a series of quasi-vegetal, linear members emerge from a coarse granite base, rise up between smooth

FAR RIGHT: Otto Wagner:
Karlsplatz Station, Vienna, 1888.
RIGHT TOP: Hector Guimard:
Place Dauphine station, Paris, 1900.
RIGHT BOTTOM: Victor Horta:
Own House, Brussels,1898.

marble slabs, and "blossom" at the top in a crown of golden flowers and a "heavenly" arch. Without copying stylistic motifs, basic meanings of architectural form are thus revived. The composition is, however, classical in its regular symmetry, as is the contemporaneous *Secession House* in Vienna by Olbrich. In the *Maison du Peuple*, Victor Horta on the contrary developed a sensitive interplay of symmetries and asymmetries, and carried through a truly "open" facade articulation, where forms appear and disappear, unite and separate, open and close. It is incredible that what is arguably the most original manifestation of *art nouveau* was demolished in 1965. The Frenchman Hector Guimard comes close to Horta in inventive genius. Already in his *Castle Béranger* (1894-98) characteristic asymmetries and a sense of vegetal growth are present; they acquire full maturity in the Metro stations of Paris (1900) and in his own *Hôtel Guimard* in the same city (1909-12). Here is a combination of multiplicity and unity, which really proves the possibility of a "new art" based on new means of expression: continuous patterns of curved lines, translucent surfaces and freely modelled masses. As in the works of Horta, a strong sense of *image* keeps the rich details together.

In general, *art nouveau* replaced the pseudo-rationalism of the academies with empathy and poetic sentiment. Thus it went to the other extreme, rather than healing the split of thinking and feeling. That is the reason why it withered away after only a few years of life. To become truly "modern," the new architecture had to give a simpler interpretation of the origins. Now that that has been accomplished, however, we experience today a renewed interest in the complex, open forms of *art nouveau.*

Phenomenology of the open form

We have already asserted that Le Corbusier's *Five Points for a New Architecture* suggest a "theory" which comprises the free plan as well as the open form. The *pilotis* liberate the building from its traditional relationship to the ground and leave the earth free as infinite extension. The idea might seem bewildering, as it deprives the ground floor, or *piano rustico*, of' its traditional solidity, turning the building so to speak upside down. In 1926, when Le Corbusier published his "Points," the idea was by no means new. Paxton's *Crystal Palace* and Horeau's project for an exhibition hall already aimed at preserving the continuity of the earth,[11] and in the *Galerie des Machines* by Dutert and Contamin, the new openness found its programmatic expression in the elegant three-hinged arches which hardly touch the ground, although they have a span of 115 metres. Giedion justly points out that the "traditional static feeling is disrupted," and compares its "movement" with that of a dancer by Degas. He quotes the impression the building made on the sculptor Raymond Duchamp-Villon as a thirteen-year-old boy: "I remember very clearly the hallucinatory passage through the brightness of the nave in a travelling crane, above whirlpools of twisting reptilian belts, creaking, whistles, sirens, and black caverns containing circles, pyramids, and cubes."[12]

The open relationship between the building and the earth prefigured in the *Galerie des Machines* and theorized by Le Corbusier is, however, only one possible interpretation of the new world. We have already seen that Frank Lloyd Wright made his houses part of infinite space without lifting them up in the air. In fact, he stresses the importance of simultaneous rootedness and freedom, saying: "I was born an American child of the ground and of space . . ." To achieve this rootedness, he "had an idea that the planes parallel to the earth in buildings identify themselves with the ground, and do most to make the buildings belong to the ground."[13] When this belonging is achieved, the guiding walls may shoot out to open up the box. The built form of Wright therefore consists of vertical and horizontal planes of an indeterminate extension. To emphasize continuity Wright as a rule used string courses and applied horizontal strips which tie the spatial zones together.[14]

FAR RIGHT:
Charles Rennie Macintosh:
Hill House, Helensburg, 1902.
RIGHT: Antoni Gaudí:
Casa Battlo, Barcelona, 1905-7.

The guiding planes of Wright bring us back to the free plan, as developed by Mies and Le Corbusier. When the free plan is set into work, two kinds of built forms are decisive: a primary skeleton, and secondary free-standing, in-filling, or enveloping elements. In De Stijl architecture, and in particular in Rietveld's *Schröder House*, only the latter were employed. We have seen that they were treated as orthogonally disposed, coloured planes, in accordance with the ideas of the philosopher Schoenmaekers. In the *Schröder House* the general spatial definition is taken care of by white, grey and black planes, whereas the elements which constitute the "places" of the interior are coloured. Evidently the colours represent embodiments of light, as suggested by Schoenmaekers. thus the general order or the world is made visible as "form." As the coloured planes lack real substance, however, the *Schröder House* remains an abstraction.

We have already pointed out that Mies van der Rohe understood the shortcomings of De Stijl architecture and thus gave the space-defining elements concrete presence through the use of "natural" materials. In the *Barcelona Pavilion* the vertical planes have become slabs of stone, and in the *Tugendhat House* in Brno (1929-30) wood was also employed. In the latter, the materials were evidently chosen to give each "place" an appropriate character. The very "centre" of the living area is marked by a straight partition in *onyx doré*, whereas the dining alcove is surrounded by a curved wall in Macassar ebony. In spite of the materials used, the planes are essentially different from the built walls of past architecture; thus they do not really *stand* on the floor, but simply extend in space.[15] That does not, however, imply that Mies did not distinguish between up and down. The floor is in fact treated as a solid ground which belongs to the earth, whereas the ceiling is light and airy. To make this relationship evident, Mies introduced the above-mentioned system of regularly spaced, chromium-plated columns. The columns "measure" the span between earth and sky, and transform mathematical space into a concrete continuum where life may take place. In the *Barcelona Pavilion* and the *Tugendhat House*, the structural skeleton is still somewhat inarticulate. In his American works, however, Mies developed the structure into a fully integrated, regular system. Columns, beams and frames were again characterized as such, and different kinds of joints were studied to give the construction concrete presence. An early and particularly illuminating example is offered by the project for the *I.I.T. Library and Administration Building*, designed in 1944. Here the richly articulate corner clearly distinguishes between the transverse load-bearing frames with their brick in-filling and the externally stuck-on curtain walls of the lateral facades. Thus the realistic logic of the built form becomes a necessary complement to the free plan. "The structure is the backbone of the whole and makes the free plan possible," Mies said. "The free plan and a clear construction cannot be kept apart. A clear structure is the *basis* for the free plan. Without that backbone the plan would not be free, but chaotic and therefore constipated."[16] The synthesis of free plan and clear structure is also beautifully illustrated by Mies's *Farnsworth House* in Plano outside Chicago (1950).

Returning to the *Five Points* of Le Corbusier, we now understand how the *pilotis* and the *plan libre* are interrelated. What, then, is the meaning of the "free facade" and the "strip window?" First of all the free plan requires that windows and doors may be placed wherever needed, which presupposes a separation between structural and space-defining elements. But there is more to it. A "free facade" is no longer a facade in the traditional sense. The houses of Wright are, as we have pointed out, "facadeless," and do not appear as self-contained "figures." The same holds true for the houses (including the *Barcelona Pavilion*) of Mies van der Rohe. Although Le Corbusier, because of his "classical" attitude, tended to preserve the primary volumes and thereby the wall between inside and outside, he gave this wall a fundamentally new interpretation, as suggested by the concept of the "free

FAR RIGHT TOP: Le Corbusier:
Maison Suisse, Paris, 1930.
FAR RIGHT BOTTOM: Le Corbusier:
Notre Dame du Haut,
Ronchamp, 1955.
RIGHT: Walter Gropius:
Bauhaus, Dessau, 1926.

facade." A free facade is basically a function of the wish for a simultaneity of places. It cannot be read as something that unambiguously separates or links, but is open to numerous interpretations. It may of course be reduced to simple, literal transparency, as in the workshop wing of Gropius's *Bauhaus Building* (1926), hut may also become the manifestation of complex spatial "stratifications" as in Le Corbusier's *Villa Stein* at Garches (1927).[17]

In Le Corbusier's later works the possibilities implicit in the *Five Points* were further developed. The slender, somewhat insubstantial *pilotis* of the twenties thus became plastic and muscular, and the structure in general gained a new bodily presence. Already in the *Maison Suisse* at the Cité Universitaire in Paris (1930-32), the *pilotis* were given sculptural quality, and in the *Unité d'Habitation* in Marseilles (1946-52), the new plasticity is fully developed. At the same time the space-defining elements became more varied and "real." Brick, wood and *béton brut* are taken into use, and light reintroduced as an active architectural factor. At Ronchamp the hole in the wall reappears, in order to obtain a particular, meaningful relationship between interior and exterior. Because of the transformation of light that occurs in the wall, the interior of Ronchamp is characterized as a "sacred place," without ceasing to be an integral part of open space. At the same time Ronchamp offers a splendid example of the free facade, as it is impossible to reduce its form to a planar projection. In such a projection, the real quality, which resides in the actual and implied "stratifications" of the elevations, would be lost. Ronchamp does indeed make a simultaneity of environmental characters manifest! In the *High Court Building* and the *Secretariat* in Chandigarh (1951-56), Le Corbusier comes closer to the traditional facade. Even here, however, the elevations have to be understood tri-dimensionally if we want to grasp their quality as embodiments of the new conception of space.[18] In general, the new sculptural presence which characterizes the *ultima maniera* of Le Corbusier represents a more complete realization of this conception than the somewhat abstract earlier solutions. "The space-dominated, environmental continuity of the materialistically confident late nineteenth and early twentieth centuries, in which the image of man normally disappeared from architecture, was thus cast aside in favour of a new, mid-twentieth century of the embattled human presence in the world," Vincent Scully wrote in 1961.[19]

We see thus that the built form of modern architecture may be understood in terms of three categories: the structure proper (which relates the buildings to the earth and the sky through its mode of standing and its geometry), the space-defining elements (which make a pattern of life manifest in relation to the given surroundings), and the free facade (which represents a particular synthesis of the former two and thereby suggests a simultaneity of places). Some architects, like Mies van der Rohe, tend to separate structure and space-defining elements, whereas others, such as Le Corbusier, prove that they may be unified without losing modern freedom and openness.

Among those who employ a "clear structure," we may single out Pier Luigi Nervi for his fundamental contribution to the development of structural articulation. Already in the 1930s, Nervi realized built forms which visualize the "play of forces" in reinforced concrete constructions. In doing this, he arrived at solutions distinguished simultaneously by continuity and articulation.

Two factors were of decisive importance: the type of plan (centralized, longitudinal, gridded) and the need for transverse and lateral rigidity. In several cases Nervi conceived the solution in terms of repeated, prefabricated elements. As a result, the structural members grow and shrink, bend and turn, come together and fan out, interpenetrate and fuse. In doing this, however, they are neither a necessary outcome of mathematical calculation nor a direct product of sculptural modelling. Nervi himself stressed that both approaches are insufficient: ". . . confronted by a new structural problem, the mental attitude of the neo-architect is to think of a form, and

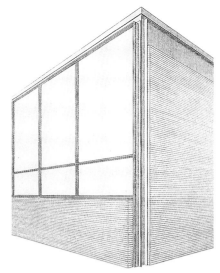

FAR RIGHT: Le Corbusier: Centre Le Corbusier, Zurich, 1963-67.
RIGHT : Mies van der Rohe: IIT Administration Building, Chicago, 1944, project.

that of the neo-engineer is to direct himself towards a fine procedure of calculation. Both forget that a structure is nothing but a system of reactions and internal stresses capable of balancing a system of external forces; and, therefore, it must be conceived as a *material organism* . . .[20] Thus, Nervi aimed at healing the split of thinking and feeling in his own way, as is shown by the motto he included in the publication of his work: "Architecture is a structural reality correctly understood and carried out with love." In our context it is important to point out that Nervi's approach gave a new bodily presence to architectural form, so that it may take part in life here and now. His limitation, on the other hand, was a less developed interest in the problems of the free plan and the free facade. Thus his buildings are characterized by a certain overall self-sufficiency.

Among the architects who managed to unify structure and space-defining elements without losing the modern openness, we may mention Alvar Aalto. Aalto's particular interpretation of the free plan could not be set into work through the usual differentiation of structural parts and secondary in-fill. Structural members are, of course, present in his buildings, but do not constitute any continuous or regular system. Rather they appear as "expressive things" which give life to the architectural organism. Columns stand "freely" and populate space; ribs rise up and fan out to embrace the room; walls open and close as if they are functions of an action taking place here and now. Non-structural parts behave in a similarly "live" way, and often it is impossible to distinguish between the two categories. As a consequence, the built forms of Aalto seem actively to take possession of space. They are truly "open" because they never constitute a finished figure and because they arouse a multitude of associations, from the memories of the local landscape to references to contemporary technology. Aalto's architecture is therefore *modern*; it has the collage-like quality of a modern work of art, and evokes a simultaneity of of environmental characters.[21] In contrast to Le Corbusier's "classical modernism," we have characterized his work as a

case of "romantic modernism." The romantic nature of Aalto's built form certainly contradicts the notion of "structural honesty" which is often presented as a basic property of modern architecture. In our opinion, the demand for full structural honesty represents an analogy to radical functionalism. "Structural honesty" can only mean that construction is reduced to its measurable aspects, and becomes a matter of analysis. Let us rather assert that formal articulation always has a structural *basis*, because construction means to "stand" between earth and sky. The visible structure may, however, be fictitious if necessary.[22] Aalto in fact composes with elements of structural derivation, in a way that is simultaneously structural and non structural.

Between Nervi's structural approach to built form and Aalto's organic one, we find the "essentialist" interpretation of Louis Kahn. For Kahn, building does not mean the expression of forces or the embodiment of environmental characters, but the uncovering of the inherent order of the world. "It is not what you want, it is what you sense in the order of things which tells you what design," Kahn said.[23] This order comprises man himself, and may therefore be understood in terms of "institutions" or basic forms of being-in-the-world. "The architect chooses and arranges to express in spaces, environment and relationships man's institutions. There is art if the desire for and the beauty of the institution is filled." "If you create the realm of spaces you make the institution alive." The means to do that are structure and light. "To make a square room is to give it the light which reveals the square in its infinite moods," Kahn says, and, "Structure is the giver of light." When structure thus determines space as the "house of an institution," it becomes a case of "inspired technology." The technological realization is thus understood as the incarnation of the institution.

Kahn's approach to building really satisfies the wish for a return to the "beginnings," which was a point of departure of modern architecture. At the same time, his built forms recall

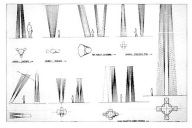

FAR RIGHT: Pier Luigi Nervi:
Structural piers and
Palazzetto dello Sport, Rome,1956.
RIGHT: Louis Kahn:
Institute of Management,
Ahmedabad, India, 1962-67.

basic solutions known from architectural history. His forms are therefore both "new and old," and open up for a creative relationship to the past. We have already referred to his versions of the free plan where traditional types of spaces constitute patterns of open growth or dynamically balanced juxtapositions.[24] Kahn's built forms analogously consist of new combinations of known elements. In the *Indian Institute of Management* in Ahmedabad (1963ff.), we find arches of various kinds, pillars and buttresses, as well as massive walls pierced by various kinds of "holes." By means of layering, overlapping and change of direction, however, these simple elements constitute complex open forms which suggest a simultaneity of spatial definitions. Of particular interest is Kahn's doubling up of the outer wall. Thus he wraps an outer "screen" around the building, which has a larger, "public" scale, the wall proper with its division in storeys. The idea was introduced in the *Salk Institute* (1959) and culminated in the *Dacca National Assembly Hall* (1962ff.). A new world is thus set into work, which at the same time seems known and reassuring. In doing that, Kahn showed that the "beginnings" are always present, although never in the same way. A beginning which is repeated is no longer a beginning, but an empty gesture.

Kahn's creative understanding of history was taken as the point of departure for a whole generation of younger architects. In particular the works of Jørn Utzon and Mario Botta are indebted to Kahn, with their emphasis on *building*, in the sense of making the natural structure of space speak (gravitation!), in connection with a meaningful use of materials and built forms. Jørn Utzon's houses at Mallorca, to which we shall return in the next chapter, thus combine the art of building with true expressive presence. A different approach was presented in programmatic form in Robert Venturi's book *Complexity and Contradiction in Architecture*, published in1963.[25] What Venturi wants is "a complex and contradictory architecture based on the richness and ambiguity of modern experience," in order to vanquish "the puritanically moral language or orthodox Modern architecture." Thus he prefers "richness of meaning" to "clarity of meaning," and an architecture of "both-and" to one of "either-or."[26] In our opinion Venturi here revives the original artistic aims of modern architecture, and his attack hits what we have called "vulgar functionalism" rather than the works of the pioneers. It is a fact, however, that modern architecture in the sixties to a great extent had become victim to mere "efficiency," and Venturi's reminder was therefore badly needed. The notion of "both-and" does not, however, imply *any* kind of richness: "An architecture of complexity and contradiction does not mean picturesqueness or subjective expressionism. A false complexity has recently countered the false simplicity of an earlier Modern architecture."[27] Instead Venturi refers to the *true* complexity found in the works of architects such as Michelangelo, Borromini and Hawksmoor, as well as Le Corbusier, Aalto and Kahn.

In order to translate his programme into architectural terms, Venturi defined several means, which are closely related to our concept of open form: the ambiguous element, the double-functioning element, the conventional element used in a new context, and the contradictory element. The architectural totality he characterizes as a "difficult whole," which is achieved through the "inflection" of the parts, that is, through their reciprocal taking each other into consideration. "Inflection is a means of distinguishing diverse parts while implying continuity. It involves the art of the fragment."[28] Venturi illustrates his ideas with numerous examples from past and present architecture, and thus his book becomes a valuable guide to the "seeing" of architecture.

The house Venturi built for his mother in Chestnut Hill on the outskirts of Philadelphia in I962 was a first setting-into-work of the new architecture of complexity and contradiction. We shall not describe the inflections present in the plan, where the different spaces are adapted to each other, but only point

Robert Venturi:
Gordon Wu Hall, Princeton, 1980.

to the treatment of the exterior which represents a new and most fascinating interpretation of the "free facade." According to Venturi the facade is where "architecture occurs as the meeting of interior and exterior forces of use and space."[29] In the *Vanna Venturi House*, the screen-like facade certainly reflects the "complexities and distortions inside," but it is also something more. The wide gable immediately signifies "house," and in particular certain wide-gabled houses of the American past. A Baroque tone is added by the break in the middle, which is echoed by the inscribed arch and the "string-course" running between the windows. The overall symmetry is contradicted by the chimney which is slightly off-centre, and by the laterally placed entrance door, as well as the walkway which is shifted to the right of the "axis."

Thus, spatially as well as formally, the facade evokes a series of simultaneous associations, and possesses the collage-like quality of a modern work of art. Moreover it adds a new possibility to the grammar of the free plan by acting as a "screen" which forms a transition between the private complexity inside and the grander scale of the public world outside. A solution to the problem of adapting a particular building to a coherent urban space is thereby suggested.

In an article published in 1978, Venturi defined architecture as a "decorated shed," saying: "To accommodate the complex and contradictory forms and structures, functions and spaces, and contexts and symbols that are realized from modern programmes, the building can end up Classical in front and Modern behind or Classical outside and Modern inside."[30] Here Venturi seems to return to that kind of eclecticism that from the outset modern architecture fought against. We may, however, recall Sullivan's idea of the possible return to "ornament" after a period of making buildings "well formed and comely in the nude,"[31] adding that this return is only meaningful if the new conception of space is preserved. In his works, Venturi has proved that it is possible to make modern buildings "clad in a garment of poetic imagery," to quote Sullivan

again. It is in fact the open form which allows for a return to ornament. Its openness no longer merely consists in openness to the given environment, but also to the memories of the past. Thus the free facades of Venturi illustrate Heidegger's dictum: "A boundary is not that at which something stops, but is that from which something begins its presencing."[32]

Our discussions of the free plan and the open form have shown that they are interrelated aspects of one phenomenon: the new architecture. A free plan demands open forms and open forms constitute the free plan. Thus a new kind of place comes into existence, which implies a simultaneity of multiple references. The interrelationship between plan and form, however, is not a one-to-one. Any free plan may be set into work by means of various built forms, such as "abstract" coloured planes or "concrete" slabs of natural materials or a combination of both. In general, the new conception of space may be given many different interpretations. Writers on modern architecture, however, often reduce "modernism" to one interpretation only, and use this reduction as a platform for one-sided criticism.[33]

The variety of possible interpretations makes it impossible to define a univocal "grammar" of modern design. Mies van der Rohe's composition with separate planes in a total enveloping space is as valid as Aalto's topological organisms. What is common, however, is the departure from the closed "figures" of past architecture. Modern architecture is "non-figurative" in the sense of being potentially open. The means to achieve this openness are common to all the various interpretations, and consist in the compositional devices indicated above, such as asymmetry, displacement, inversion, ambiguity, overlapping, interpenetration, transparency, continuity and metamorphosis. When an architect designs a building, however, he hardly says: "Here I want transparency." Instead he says: "Here I want an *open corner*." Certain concrete solutions have therefore become emblematic of the new architecture, such as cantilevered roof-overhangs, corner windows, and doors running full height between floor and ceiling. The danger involved is the use of these "motifs" without an understanding of their role as parts of a meaningful open composition. When that happens, modern architecture degenerates into a new kind of superficial play. Summing up, we may define the open form as a built embodiment of a multitude of interacting characters.

Actuality of the open form

The history of modern architecture shows that a "development" in the relationship between space and form has taken place. In the early works of Wright, space and form made up a concrete totality: space was conceived in terms of place, and form was understood "in the nature of materials." The modern architecture of the twenties favoured a more abstract approach. The wish for a return to the origins brought about a general simplification of the built form, whereby the spatial relationships gained more importance. Mies van der Rohe's slogan "less is more" must be understood in this context. It is a basic misunderstanding, however, to interpret this simplification as a wish for "monotopic" space and a case of professional blindness to consider it a "monosemantic poverty of form."[34] Later some of the pioneers proceeded beyond the stage of simplification, and gave their buildings a new bodily substance through structural emphasis and articulation. Thereby they showed how the new conception of space may be concretized as a synthesis of openness and rootedness, as already wanted by Wright. This objective is fully accomplished in the works of Louis Kahn and to some extent in those of Alvar Aalto.

With the advent of "post-modernism," which took the ideas of Robert Venturi as its main source of inspiration, the development of the open form entered a new phase. Through the reintroduction of "conventional" elements, the open form is now becoming an art of "inclusion." The danger of closing up the form is, however, manifest in the works of the neo-rationalist school, which also bear a certain resemblance to the historicism of recent totalitarian regimes. Some architects have, however, succeeded in maintaining the open form as a versatile instrument of expression and characterization. The open form came into existence to vanquish the split of thinking and feeling. It is closely related to the *collages* of pictorial art, where an analogous multiplicity of meanings is evoked. To master the open form, a thorough knowledge of modern art is therefore expedient, as well as a close study of the works of the pioneers and the actual masters of modern architecture. The idea of *collage* has in fact been adopted more or less directly by several architects. We have already mentioned Robert Venturi, and may add Jean Nouvel, who in the *Lyons Opera House* incorporated in the facade part of an existing classical building (1995). The *Hedmark Museum* by Sverre Fehn is also an eminent example of architectural collage.

Evidently, the collage entails dangers. Michael Graves started out with fascinating combinations of modern and historical elements, but in his later works unfortunately proposes a Disneyland flavour. In his case, the things themselves do not speak any more, being substituted by mere "memories."

Today, the general aim is to endow the open forms with a wider range of meanings, so that the places they constitute may give identity to the contemporary world, an endeavour that has to be interpreted in terms of the "things themselves."

BELOW: Frank Gehry:
Vitra Museum: Weil am Rhein.

4 *the* Natural House

The creation of a "dwelling" was for a long time considered the primary task of modern architecture. The modern movement in fact concentrated its attention on the dwelling and emphasized its importance: "The present development in building is undoubtedly focused on the dwelling, and in particular on the dwelling for the *common man . . .* Neither public building nor the factory is today of equal importance. That means: we are again concerned about the human being," Giedion wrote in 1929.[1] And already in 1925, at the *Exposition Internationale des Arts Décoratifs* in Paris, Le Corbusier showed a prototype apartment, which he called the *Pavillon de l'esprit nouveau.* Thus he did not demonstrate the "spirit" of the modern age by means of a didactic exhibition or a monumental symbol but with a dwelling for the common man. We may also recall his words: "Human beings are badly housed, that is the profound and real reason for the present upheavals."[2]

We have already pointed out that dwelling implies something more than shelter. How, then, does a house become a home in our uprooted epoch? Frank Lloyd Wright suggested an answer with the title of his book *The Natural House.* Dwelling today means to leave all representative forms behind and become "natural" again. The natural Wright interpreted as a new kind of informal living, in contact with natural materials, simple straightforward artefacts, and, if possible, a natural environment.[3] In short, it implies what we have called for a return to the "things themselves." To understand this aim better, it is necessary to add a few words about the house in general.

A house serves man in two basic ways: it offers him a refuge where he can feel at home and be at peace with himself, and it serves as a starting-point for his actions in the world. The two "functions" are evidently interdependent; only when the house creates a sense of belonging and protection does man gain the inner strength he needs to depart. In our open world the latter function tends to become dominant, and thus the modern house opens up on its surroundings, demanding interaction and response.

The interior of the house is different from that of other buildings. A house is used by a small group of people and its character is "personal" and "private." It is the result of a deliberate choice, and therefore represents "my world." In the house we find the things we really know and which are particularly meaningful to us. We have taken them with us and they are part of our daily life. The house therefore confirms one's identity.

This identification should, however, be prepared before entering. Among the many houses in the settlement there ought to be one we may call "mine." Standing in front of this house, should convey that it forms a link between one's private world and the public environment. As most people do not have the opportunity of determining the shape of their house, such an identification usually has to be based on a choice among existing possibilities.

In the past, houses appeared as variations on a *type.* A characteristic example is the European gable house. Here the gable signifies "house," whereas the countless variations on the theme represent adaptations to local, temporal and personal circumstances. The interior disposition was also typical, and could be understood as an interpretation of basic interrelated functions, that is, living, dining, sleeping and working.

In general the house constitutes a "microcosm" visualizing the fact that human life takes place between earth and sky. The floor represents the earth, the ceiling the sky and the walls the binding horizon. This is proved by the etymology of the words. "Floor" signifies extended flat land, a "field," a connotation which is also found in German where *Boden* means "floor" as well as "ground." "Ceiling" stems from the Latin *caelum*, "sky," whereas "wall" is derived from the Latin *valium* which means "mound." (In this connection it is interesting to note that the valley (*vallis* in Latin) gets its name from the

OPPOSITE: Jørn Utzon: Own House, Mallorca, 1971.

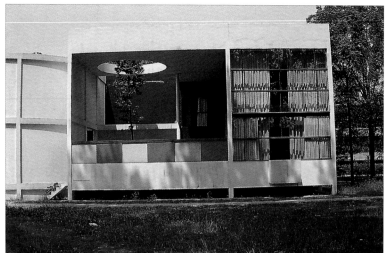

FAR RIGHT: Le Corbusier: Pavillon
de l'Esprit Nouveau, 1925.
RIGHT TOP: Pueblo housing.
RIGHT BOTTOM: Farm House,
Schwarzwald, Germany.

boundary and not from the space!) In the private interior these basic meanings may be more or less apparent, but the general meaning of *imago mundi* always remains the point of departure.

The modern house is also such an image, although it does not visualize a static, self-sufficient world. The basic functions are certainly the same, but the definition of the zones where they take place is new. Thus the modern house ought to make manifest the present world of open interaction and simultaneous events. "A dwelling should not be a retreat from space, but a life *in* space," Moholy-Nagy said.[4] The question to be answered, then, is how the modern house sets the principles of free plan and open form into work. Our previous discussion has already suggested a reply, but the problem cannot be fully understood until we have unified the two aspects of place as "house." To be able to do that, it is expedient to take a look at the roots of the modern house, that is, at those solutions which point towards its realization as an organized yet articulate simultaneity of places.

Beginnings of the modern house

The modern house, as it was realized towards the end of the nineteenth century by Frank Lloyd Wright, is the result of a gradual development, although Wright was responsible for the decisive step which made the house become "what it wanted to be." It is not surprising that the early development of the modern house took place in America. Firstly, the United States represents the new world **par excellence**, and is therefore particularly open to invention and change. Secondly, the individual house plays a more important role there than elsewhere. It should add, however, that American development was to a great extent inspired by England, where the notion "my home is my castle" has a long tradition. The differentiated, informal plan of the pre-modern house was in fact derived from mediaeval English models. Their transformation to accommodate a new way of life occurred in the United States

during the second half of the nineteenth century, as has been shown by Vincent Scully.[5]

In the projects and buildings of American nineteenth-century architects we find many elements of space and form that were later assimilated by the modern house. An asymmetrical layout adapted to the site was usual, as well as large porches (also called *piazza*) which form a transition between exterior and interior space. A general desire for horizontal extension emphasized by large eaves was also common. At an early stage in the development, the built form was characterized by exposed wooden skeletons, which make the general demand for openness manifest.[6] At a later stage, the volumes were covered with wooden shingles which unify the various volumes and create a continuous movement. Strip windows often emphasize the continuity, whereas powerful chimney-stacks anchor the picturesque totality. The plans are characterized by differentiated informality. The rooms usually constitute interacting ensembles, which open up on the surrounding porches. The spatial effect is furthermore enriched by inglenooks and bay windows. A centrally placed *hall* often acts as a focus. around which the other rooms are grouped.[7] In some cases we even find cruciform layouts which prefigure one of Wright's basic solutions. A simultaneous wish for differentiation and unity thus becomes manifest. Already Downing in his book *Cottage Residences* (1842) was conscious of the significance of some of these traits. In general he demanded that a house should "express its purpose," that is, it should look different from churches and barns. "The most prominent features conveying expression of purpose in dwelling houses are the chimneys, the windows, and the porch, veranda or piazza, and for this reason, whenever it is desired to raise the character of a cottage or villa above mediocrity, attention should first be bestowed on these portions of the building."[8] In the mature works of an architect like Bruce Price such elements gain archetypal importance and become "the massive platform, the precise posts, the solemn gable,"[9] realizing thus a new

FAR RIGHT AND RIGHT BOTTOM:
Frank Lloyd Wright:
Hanna House, Palo Alto,1936,
interior and exterior.
RIGHT TOP: Frank Lloyd Wright:
Winslow House, River Forest,1894.

interpretation of the fundamental image of man's being between earth and sky.

What, then, was the decisive step taken by Frank Lloyd Wright? In the works of his predecessors, the house was still a defined volume, or a "box," to use Wright's own word. Wright decomposed this volume and put the parts together in a new way. Some of the parts were taken over as they were; others were modified or constituted anew through the process of decomposition. Of particular importance are the separate, vertical planes which replace the traditional walls. "My sense of 'wall' was no longer the side of a box. It was enclosure of space affording protection against storm and heat only when needed. But it was also to bring the outside world into the house and let the inside of the house go outside. In this sense I was working away at the wall as a wall and bringing it towards the function of a screen . . ."[10] When the parts were recomposed the spatial organization changed. The peripherally additive plan was thus transformed into a centrifugal plan with the chimney-stack as its core. In this way the basic concept of refuge got a new interpretation. Rather than a retreat, the house became a fixed point in space from which man could experience a new sense of freedom and participation. This point is marked by the great fireplace. Hence we find at the centre an element which symbolizes the forces of nature. "It comforted me to see the fire burning deep in the solid masonry of the house itself," Wright said; and together with his use of natural materials, he thereby confirmed his wish for a "deeper sense of reality."[11] Thus, Wright's approach to natural phenomena did not consist in rationalistic observation and analysis, but in the experience of meaningful, original qualities. This implies a developed sense of nature, and a wish for rootedness. His centrifugal plans illustrate his self-identification as "a child of the earth and of space."

Wright's reinterpretation of the human dwelling remains one of the most profoundly satisfactory achievements in the history of modern architecture, because of its unique combi-nation of realism and general method. "Behind the whole development of free design ran the insistent belief that man must live as a free human being, in close contact with nature, in order to realize his own potentialities," Scully wrote, and "America consequently produced her most original monuments where one after all might have expected to find them: in the homes of individual men."[12]

The pre-modern house in Great Britain had many premises in common with the American house, but it did not arrive at a "break-through" similar to that of Frank Lloyd Wright. It is however necessary to add a few words about the English house to get a better understanding of the whole development. Since about 1750 a "picturesque revolution" had taken place in English architecture, aiming at more comfortable and natural dwellings. The main source of inspiration was the mansions and houses of the Middle Ages. These were distinguished by freely disposed, functional plans, as distinct from the representative, symmetrical layout of the Italian and French Renaissance. In the English houses the secondary rooms as a rule were related to a dominant. Often the hall is found at the intersection of the two wings of an L-shaped plan, a solution which prefigures a characteristic type of modern house. Spatial additions such as inglenooks and bay windows contribute to the varied and "human" character of the whole. During the nineteenth century these mediaeval traits were revived in combination with a new wish for natural materials and good craftsmanship.

The "romantic movement" in England may be understood as a reaction against the effects of the industrial revolution, and represented an attempt at regaining the feelings which had been pushed aside by the ruling rationalism. In contrast to the American development, it was nostalgic rather than realistic, and the resulting architectural works, such as the houses of Richard Norman Shaw, were basically eclectic in character. It cannot be denied, however, that in important respects the nineteenth-century English house paved the way

FAR RIGHT: Josef-Maria Olbrich:
Dreigiebelhouse, Darmstadt, 1903.
RIGHT: M.H. Baillie Scott:
Le Nid, 1900, project.

for the advent of the modern house. We have already mentioned its asymmetrical layout and informal interiors, and could add many details concerning the functional disposition which were described in Robert Kerr's seminal *The English Gentleman's House* (1864).

About the turn of the century some architects offered new and promising interpretations of the pre-modern dwelling, in particular C.R. Mackintosh and M.H. Baillie Scott. In addition to his works as an architect, the latter set down his ideas in a book entitled *Houses and Gardens* (1906). After discussing various "forms of plan," Baillie Scott starts his exposition of the elements of the house with a chapter on the *hall* stressing its importance as the "room where the family can meet together, a general gathering-place with its large fireplace and ample floor space . . ."

Whether it is called hall, house-place, or living room, some such apartment is a necessary feature as a focus to the plan of the house."[13] Baillie Scott thus considers the house a true dwelling, or *milieu* for family life. In his chapter on "The Soul of the House" we read: "As one enters and passes from room to room their deep and intense stillness seems eloquent with messages and blessings . . . For houses and cottages are not merely arrangements of materials to secure certain practical ends. They each and all develop . . . a personality which is either base or noble . . ." "Few things are indeed so strange as this thaumaturgic art of the builder. He places stones in certain positions – cuts them in certain ways, and behold they begin to speak with tongues – a language of their own, with meanings too deep for words."[14]

In few houses is the idea of the dwelling as an expressive work of art more beautifully realized than in Mackintosh's *Hill House* in Helensburgh near Glasgow (1902-03). Here, past and present are united in a profoundly convincing way. In general the solution represents a variation on the L-shaped plan. The exterior is simultaneously stern and picturesque and based on motifs from Scottish Baronial architecture. The gables, chim-

neys, turrets and windows are thus of local derivation, but with simple means they are transformed into a kind of open form. As an example we may point to the collage-like combination of main entrance, chimney (pierced by an opening!) and superimposed bay window. The main rooms on the ground floor are grouped around an elongated hall from where an open staircase leads to the bedrooms. Although the plan is not "free," the sense of continuity is strong, and at the same time each room has its own appropriate character. The hall receives the visitor with a "comforting" fireplace and offers an immediate sense of protection and interiority thanks to the extensive use of stained wood. As one proceeds up the staircase, coloured light penetrates, in preparation for the white luminosity of the main bedroom, where the bed is placed in an alcove under a barrel vault. Flower motifs characterize the decoration, and the interior expresses intimacy, love and happiness. The living room downstairs is also luminous, but here light relates to the exterior world, entering from a large bay window. Layers of suggested screens filter the light, creating a rich patchwork of light and shadow. In this window Mackintosh has succeeded in making the quality of Scottish light visible, with its infinite nuances. Before it was just everywhere and nowhere; now we can say: here is your light! Thus *Hill House* allows for identification and dwelling.

In Germany the independent family dwelling did not have the same tradition as in England. It was only during the *Gründerzeit* in the 1870s that a "private" bourgeois house came into existence. Its romantic character represented a reaction against the official classicism of the preceding period, but the solutions did not show much originality as to the treatment of space and form. About the turn of the century, however, a conscious attempt at creating a new "German" art and architecture was made. It found its main manifestation in the *Künstlerkolonie* in Darmstadt, where Joseph Maria Olbrich and Peter Behrens had been active as architects since 1899. As one of the members of the Vienna Secession, Olbrich

FAR RIGHT: Eliel Saarinen:
Own House, Hvittrask, 1902.
RIGHT: Peter Behrens:
Own House, Darmstadt, 1902.

subscribed to the credo: "Every age has its own sensibility. It is our aim to awaken, to encourage and to disseminate the artistic sensibility of our age."[15] In Darmstadt he had the occasion to build several houses, including one for himself. Basically these are urban dwellings rather than suburban, and the form is therefore more compact than in the contemporary American and English houses. A certain interaction with the environment is, however, present due to the asymmetrical articulation of the volumes, at the same time as a strong desire for plastic continuity is evident. The differentiated interiors are in general concentrated on a double-height hall with fireplace and staircase. A particularly impressive example is found in the large *Glückert House* (1901) where a rich geometric floral decoration makes the interior appear as the focus of a poetic natural world.

Whereas Olbrich shows a southern sense of sculptural form, Behrens is eminently Nordic in his own house, erected for the opening of the Artists' Colony in 1901.[16] The exterior is distinguished by a vibrant, expressive use of coloured lines in glazed brick, derived from the North German *Backsteingotik* of the late Middle Ages. The interiors are designed to give each room its appropriate *Stimmung.* A romantic house, indeed, but also the expression of a strong desire for composition and order. In general it illustrates Behrens' dictum: "Everything that belongs to life shall receive beauty. A rich and complex world is in fact gathered. The materials and colours, as well as the built form as such, refer to basic characters of earth and sky, and the use of undulating and crystalline decorative patterns evidently has feminine and masculine implications. The entrance door already signals a synthesis of these meanings, which are varied in each of the rooms inside, in accordance with their function. The crystal is a primary motif in the decoration, suggesting how "raw, formless life becomes beauty when it is purified by the power of artistic, rhythmical forming." In his house Behrens gave a profound interpretation of the concept of dwelling. The house is "castle" and "sanctuary," "cave" and

"balcony," place of action and intimate refuge. The gables rise up, the bay windows open out, and the niches of the interior enclose the treasures of the home. Although the general disposition is conventional and the articulation somewhat overworked, Behrens demonstrated the possibility of a meaningful modern architecture, which replaces the styles with archetypal symbols.

The wish for a "natural" life was particularly well understood and satisfied in the Scandinavian countries.[17] Having a rural rather than an urban background, the individual house naturally became the leading building task during the second half of the nineteenth century, and typologies related to American houses were developed. As a particularly important example we may single out Eliel Saarinen's own house near Helsingfors. "Hvitträsk" was built in 1902 in a typical Finnish landscape on a wooded ridge overlooking a lake. The asymmetrical layout and the use of rough stone and wood as building materials, make a profound sense of nature manifest. The interiors show a developed spatial continuity, at the same time as the various zones are differentiated as to form and character. The means employed are, however, less sophisticated than those of Behrens and rather show some affinities to Wright and Mackintosh. The later "organic" approach of Aalto and other Scandinavian architects is unthinkable without the pioneering effort of Saarinen and his contemporaries.[18]

In general the history of the pre-modern house during the second half the nineteenth century shows a characteristic wish for developing a new kind of dwelling adapted to the open world without however giving up local rootedness. Although most of the contributions were "gentleman's houses" the principles were of general importance, and in America and Scandinavia we also find solutions within the reach of the "common man." It is a paradox that the industrialized world should produce a desire for "natural" living. We ought to remember, however, that the new means of production and

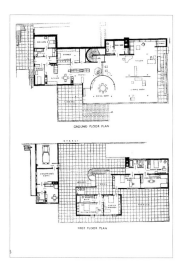

FAR RIGHT: Mies van der Rohe: Tugendhat House, Brno, 1930, plan. RIGHT: Le Corbusier: Double House, Weissenhofsiedlung, Stuttgart, 1927.

communication were not considered ends in themselves but means to obtain values which in the past were monopolized by the few. "Liberation" thus consisted in making these values accessible to everybody, without however taking over the representative pretensions of the ruling classes of the past. It was considered a basic value to possess a dwelling of one's own, and it is therefore meaningful that the new architecture took the house as its point of departure. As a result, the new house became "informal" in its inner layout as well as in its relation to the surroundings. To set the natural house into work, various means were employed. What they have in common is a sense of freedom in the disposition of the plan and a budding openness in the built form. But it was only in the early works of Frank Lloyd Wright that these ends and means were interpreted in a way which made the development of a truly modern domestic architecture possible.

The modern house
When the early works of Frank Lloyd Wright were published in Germany in 1910, the need for a new architecture was already felt. His lesson, therefore, came at the right moment, and gave the work of European architects a clear direction. The influence of Wright on architects such as Gropius, Oud, Rietveld, Dudok and Mies van der Rohe has often been pointed out. It was not possible, however, to take over Wright's typologies directly. As they were intended for suburban or rural situations, they had to be adapted to the urban environment common in Europe.[19] In general that implies that the free plan and the open form had to be combined with a certain compactness of volume and a public scale or, in short, with a more "classical" kind of order. The problem was tackled by many architects, and found its basic solution in the early works of Le Corbusier.

Already in his *Domino* project, Le Corbusier aimed at a synthesis of freedom and order, introducing amplitude: you are in the house of the purposely regular skeleton structure. His following projects, such as the seminal *Maison Citrohan* of 1920,[20] typified the free plan as a two-storey "hall"-space for living onto which the other rooms open. The model is evidently the traditional hall-house, which is more easily used in an urban context than the centrifugal layouts of Wright. In 1922 Le Corbusier added up the Citrohan type to form a block of flats called *immeubles~villas*, illustrating thus how the concept of the modern house may be transferred to the urban dwelling proper.[21] When Le Corbusier in 1927 participated in the Weissenhof exhibition in Stuttgart, he repeated the Citrohan model, this time raised over the ground on *pilotis*. At Weissenhof he also presented a very advanced double house with a flexible free plan on the main floor. Here, however, we touch upon the urban dwelling, which will be discussed in the chapter on the city. Le Corbusier's wish for a synthesis of freedom and classical order also found other sources of inspiration. The Pompeian house possesses these qualities and it is explicitly referred to in *Towards a New Architecture*: "Again the little vestibule which frees your mind from the street. And then you are in the Atrium; four columns in the middle (four cylinders) shoot up towards the shade of the roof, giving a feeling of force and a witness of potent methods; but at the far end is the brilliance of the garden seen through the peristyle which spreads out this light with a large gesture, distributes it and accentuates it, stretching widely from left to right, making a great space. Between the two is the Tablinum, contracting this vision like the lens of a camera. On the right and on the left two patches of shade – little ones. Out of the clatter of the swarming street, which is for every man and full of picturesque incident, you have entered the house of *a Roman*. Magistral grandeur, order, a splendid amplitude: you are in the house of a *Roman*. What was the function of these rooms? That is outside the question. After twenty centuries, without any historical reference, you are conscious of Architecture, and we are speaking of what is in reality a very small house."[22] What interests Le Corbusier here, is the combination

Mies van der Rohe:
Tugendhat House.

of spatial organization and richness of effect, which makes the house appear as an ordered and understood world in contrast to the "clatter of the swarming street." Thus he recognizes the nature of the house as a *microcosm*, a small world which gives the dweller his identity, in this case as *a Roman*. Le Corbusier also emphasizes that the meaning of the house does not depend on our knowing the functions; architecture "speaks" in space and form.

The lesson of the Pompeian house is only indirectly present in Le Corbusier's works, but the possibility of a dense, urban pattern of free plans was studied by Mies van der Rohe in several "court-house" projects from the 1930s. Freedom and intimacy are combined in an extraordinary way in these solutions, which represent a mature example of Mies's grammar of spatial organization.

On one occasion Mies could realize his concept of the modern house, and demonstrate the capacity of the free plan: the *Tugendhat House* in Brno (1929-30). When it was built it was considered the most radical and complete interpretation of the modern dwelling so far. [23]

The house stands on a sloping site in the northern part of Brno, from where one enjoys a fine view of the city. The access is from the upper part of the land, and accordingly the entrance is found on the top floor. The house is intimately related to the situation. Rather than being a conventional massive body, it appears as a low one-storey "wall" which extends along the street and blocks out the panorama. At a certain point, however, the wall is interrupted, permitting a framed view of the far-away castle of Brno through a passage leading from the entrance court to the terrace on the other side. So far, this view remains distant; a railing is built across the passage to tell us that it should only be understood as a "promise." A curved, translucent wall next to the passage leads the visitor to the entrance door, and a semicircular staircase carries the movement down into the large living area where the promise is fulfilled as a continuous panorama

seen through a wall of glass, which, when weather conditions permit, may disappear into the floor. The basic spatial layout is hence derived from the site, and makes the house part of an "open" world. From the garden below the two-storey volume becomes visible, but it does not appear as a unified box, as the rooms on the upper floor are set back from the facade.

The plans of the two floors are based on different, albeit related principles of spatial composition. Upstairs the bedrooms are grouped in two juxtaposed boxes, which together with the garage form a kind of free plan of three interrelated elements. The openings between the three volumes are not merely left-over intervals, but are used as primary spatial zones: one is the above-mentioned passage leading from the street to the roof-terrace, the other serves as the main entrance to the house. To emphasize and articulate the latter, the curved glass wall is introduced between the two bedroom volumes. The interaction between these is also articulated inside by means of projecting walls which make the boxes "dissolve" into the common hall.

In front of the entrance, in the hallway, and on the terrace a few cruciform steel columns appear, suggesting that the house contains a "hidden" structure within which the bedroom volumes are placed. The continuity of this structure is indicated by the flat roof which runs over the curved glass wall and the panoramic passage. The only column which carries this slab appears as a kind of "motto" or "sign" which implies spatial order as well as structural consistency. As the same column is found in the hall, outside and inside become meaningfully interrelated, beyond the continuity of the uniform travertine floor and the translucent glass wall which fills out the span between ground and ceiling.

The curved flight of stairs already offers a promise of the spatial freedom encountered in the living area. Here all reminiscences of closed boxes have been abolished; the large area appears as a spatial continuum which however comprises

Aalvar Aalto: Villa Mairea,
Noormarkku, Finland, 1939.

several distinct zones: reception, living, dining, study, and conservatory. According to their diverse character, these zones are defined by different means. For reception purposes a table and four chairs are placed in front of a translucent glass wall which appears as an "echo" of the similar wall in the hall above. Moreover its transitory character is indicated by a convex wall section which leads towards the living zone beyond. As it is made of warm-coloured wood, it also suggests that one is approaching the "inside" of the house. From the reception area it is also possible to reach the study, but the movement in this direction is somewhat hampered by a transversely placed buffet and a grand piano. The study is especially interesting as a spatial zone because it consists of both an intimate library alcove well enclosed by projecting walls on either side and completely clad in wood, and an open workspace where a large writing desk is placed in front of the glazed conservatory running all along the eastern side of the house. This winter garden links the study to the sitting room which is defined by a splendid free-standing onyx wall dividing the luminous and open zone from the more intimate study behind. Because of its position and the rich, solid material, this wall acts as the main focus of the whole spatial composition. Overlooking the landscape through the continuous, mobile glass wall, the living zone expresses a freedom unknown in any previous dwelling. The dining zone also partakes in this openness, but here the act of coming together is defined by a round table placed in a semi-circular wooden *exedra*. Behind this wall the pantry acts as a semi-open zone of transition to the enclosed kitchen and servants' quarters beyond.

The free plan of the living area is ordered by a regular succession of cruciform chrome-plated steel columns. What appeared as a "sign" upstairs here has become a complete system; the skeletal backbone of the composition is made manifest. It may furthermore be noticed that such columns appear as "echoes" in the pantry and the kitchen as well as on

the terrace which links the spatial sequence of the living zone to the garden below. Coming from the outside we are thus, on both sides of the house, met by a single column which signals the coherent order found inside. This order does not, however, represent a goal in itself. It only becomes meaningful in relation to the free plan it contains. The free plan is the "content" of the house, and our analysis has shown that it consists of several, qualitatively different zones. As a *place* the house is therefore heterogeneous, but it is given a "measure" by the homogeneous space defined by the columnar system. Thus the *Tugendhat House* illustrates the interdependence between free plan and clear structure.

Together with Le Corbusier's major houses (*Villa Stein*, *Villa Savoye*), the *Tugendhat House* represents the "international" phase in the development of the modern house. Although these houses were intentionally related to their sites, they first of all demonstrate the general principles of the free plan and the open form.

We have already mentioned that a regional version of the modern house was realized before the second world war by Alvar Aalto in his *Villa Mairea* (1939), and should add that the solution recalls the L-shaped plan so common among the "anti-classical" houses of the nineteenth century. Rather than introducing a new typology, *Villa Mairea* extends the concept of modern dwelling to comprise the identification with a local character, a wish that was strongly felt in most countries about the turn of the century, but was forgotten during the international phase. The difference between pre-modern regionalism and Aalto's locally interpreted modernism, is that the latter exploits the free plan and the open form. During the last decades the demand for regionally rooted houses has become more general, a tendency we shall, however, discuss in a later chapter.

After the second world war, the construction of one-family houses was intense in many countries. Modern typologies have been extensively used and varied, for instance in the

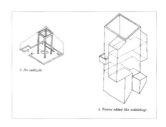

FAR RIGHT: Robert Venturi:
Carl Tucker III House,
Westchester County, NY, 1975.
RIGHT TOP: MLTW:
"Fourposter" and "Saddlebags."
RIGHT BOTTOM: Charles Moore:
Own House, Orinda, California, 1961.

numerous houses built during the late forties and the fifties by Marcel Breuer and Richard Neutra. These "late-modern" solutions did not, however, bring us any further on the way towards the realization of the "natural house." Frank Lloyd Wright's houses from the post-war period are in that sense more advanced. In spite of their qualities, the late-modern houses did not really add anything new. What, then, if anything, ought to be added?

According to post-modernism, the houses of the international phase did not fully satisfy the demand for a new dwelling, "because they did not look like houses." In other words, they lacked the quality of "image." In fact, the modern house of the twenties and thirties favoured "life in space" rather than "life with images." When modern houses became numerous, this was felt as a lack, and the desire for "recognizable" forms was felt. Thus we return to Downing's demand that a house should look different from a church or a barn.

Robert Venturi's pioneering work must be understood in this context; his designs represent important contributions to the development of solutions which are "free" and "open" at the same time as they possess a distinct identity. Thus he re-introduced "conventional" forms such as gables and hipped roofs. As an example we may mention the *Carl Tucker III House* in Westchester County, New York (1975), which is simultaneously "garden pavilion" and "tower," "home" and "balcony on the world." "If the facade at Chestnut Hill was a child's two-dimensional image of a house, here the image expands to three dimensions, for what is basic here is the sense one has of this building as an object, tall and wooden, sitting among the trees in its lush semi-rural site."[24]

To conceive the house as an image might seem bewildering, but in reality it implies a concrete understanding of the house as a "place." A man-made place is first of all something we recognize because of the characteristic form of its constituent buildings, and as subordinate places, the buildings are primary objects of our identification. Thus we return to the original aim of modern architecture: to create a new dwelling where modern life can take place.

The problems involved have been studied most significantly by Charles Moore and Donlyn Lyndon in their book *The Place of Houses*, and in numerous houses built in collaboration with William Turnbull and Richard Whitaker, the same architects have illustrated their approach.[25] It is interesting to note that *The Place of Houses* in important respects recalls the books on houses published by the pre-modern pioneers. Thus it discusses the different rooms which make up a dwelling in a concrete and detailed manner, and thereby offers a guide for the common man. In *The Place of Houses*, however, the rooms are understood as "places," and are therefore more meaningfully related to life than was the case in the earlier books on the subject. It is furthermore suggested how the sub-places of a house may be organized to form a totality which is simultaneously differentiated and united. It is also interesting to notice how the basic centrifugal and centripetal types re-appear in new interpretations. Centrifugal movement is thus expressed by rooms added peripherally "like saddlebags," whereas the centre is emphasized through the use of an aedicula or "four-poster."[26] Eminently liveable and truly modern houses are thus created, and the promise of a new dwelling is fulfilled. The Moore house in Orinda, California (1961) is in this sense emblematic: here two aediculae are inscribed within an irregular pyramid roof over a square plan, thus securing simultaneous spatial definition and image quality, while the lateral walls may be opened up to obtain interaction between exterior and interior. In the Moore House in New Haven, Connecticut (1966) the same ideas have been applied to the remodelling of an old house. Here three tower-like, perforated aediculae are disposed within a unitary space, creating a fascinating simultaneity of places, illustrating the basic tenet: "The empty stage of a room is fixed in space by boundaries; it is animated by light,

Mario Botta: House at
Viganello, Lugano, 1980-88.
OPPOSITE: Jørn Utzon:
Own House, Mallorca, 1971.

organized by focus, and then liberated by outlook."27 In general the designs of MLTW prove that a house may have a free plan and an open form and at the same time look like a house.

Actuality of the modern house

One-family houses are still built in many countries. The detached house evidently remains the ideal solution for modern dwelling, even though for practical reasons it is tending to lose in importance. The incessant growth of population and the shortage of land necessarily lead to denser types of housing. All the same, the dwelling remains the point of departure for the architecture of our time, and the lesson of the modern house is valid. How the free plan and the open form may be realized as a dwelling is still a basic problem, and can hardly be approached if one has not gone through the needle-eye of the modern house. Although Oak Park in Chicago, together with the early houses of Frank Lloyd Wright, has been declared an "historic district," the buildings themselves do not belong to the past. They are fully alive, and the new tradition which they initiated, is still growing.

It is natural in this context also to mention a house by Robert Stern: the *Lang House* in Washington, Connecticut (1972-79) is an essay in organized complexity. Symmetries are established and broken, axes are introduced and shifted, the spatial flow widens and contracts. Seen from the access, this richness is hidden behind a "formal" screen-wall which has a flavour of a neo-late-Baroque residence. Towards the garden a more freely disposed screen-wall bulges out to obtain a more intimate relationship between inside and outside. In general the *Lang House* gathers a fascinating multiplicity of spatial definitions and formal "memories" to constitute a convincingly liveable milieu.28

The modern American house is primarily semi-rural, and therefore "romantically" related to a natural environment. The European house is to a greater extent semi-urban, and as a rule more "formally" organized. Several architects of the post-modern generation have tried to give houses of this kind a satisfactory image quality. Many of them have, however, become victims of regression into closed, static compositions. Among those who have succeeded in recovering the image without giving up the new conception of space we may single out the Ticinese Mario Botta, who in a series of houses has realized a convincing synthesis.29 Botta plans mostly possess a general symmetry which is, however, broken in such a way that an interaction with the environment is accomplished. The quasi-symmetrical disposition goes together with a centripetal layout which is organized relative to a full-height vertical space in the middle. Through this space light from above radiates into the various rooms, creating a fine sense of spatial integration. The built form is very simple, consisting of solid walls in cement blocks contrasting with continuous glazed areas. The general appearance possesses a powerful image quality due to the controlled introduction of motifs which gather and distinguish the form, such as a triangular or semicircular skylight over the centrally placed vertical slit. First of all, Botta's houses look like houses; they are simultaneously new and old, and unify vernacular and stylistic memories with the lessons of Le Corbusier and Kahn.

Qualitatively unique are the two houses Jørn Utzon built for himself on the Mediterranean island of Mallorca· 30 The first house (1971) is located on an undulating "terrace" facing the sea. Above, the vault of the Mediterranean sky radiates the intense southern light. The place is elementary in the true sense of the word: stone, trees, water and sun; each element appears as if it is part of a great, universal order. The scheme consists of four buildings linked by stone walls and intimate courts. A fundamental rhythm prevails everywhere, and the scale is uniform. All units are oriented to the sea; they open to the horizon, but the view is always in keeping with the dimensions of the houses. The spaces, however, continue back to the

shaded courtyards where vegetation tells us that nature is also nearness and intimacy.

All this occurs on the platform-floor and under the series of narrow terracotta vaults that constitute the rhythmically articulate ceiling. The primary quality of the house, however, is the play of light and shadow. There are not many houses that have "understood" and grasped the Mediterranean light in this way. Thus the house is a true interpretation of the place in relation to human life.

As a *microcosm* or *imago mundi*, the modern house makes the world of private, circumstantial life visible.[31] Therefore it is basically *informal*, although it ought to comprise elements that reflect the more formal world of public institutions. A house does not offer an "explanation" in the same sense as a public building; it is directly related to life, and only indirectly symbolic. Therefore it makes "life in space" manifest. The *Tugendhat House* was used as an example to show what that implies in terms of free plan and open form. Life in space, however, remains a mere physical fact if it is not endowed with meaning through images that relate the here and now to the there and then. Meaning in general implies that the situation is understood in a mnemonic context. The authentic post-modern house allows for such a "life with images," without giving up life in space, and thus fulfils the original modern aim of a return to the "things themselves." Thus we encounter again the archetypal forms, such as the "massive platform" the "precise post," and the "solemn gable."[32]

It is in this deeper sense we have to understand Wright's demand for a "natural" house, where man as an individual may recover archetypal qualities and heal the split of thinking and feeling.

5 *the* Democratic Institution

When Le Corbusier defined the public *institution* as a "logement prolongé," or "extension of the dwelling," he implied that dwelling is not only a private function but a public one as well. Man does not only dwell in his own house, he also "dwells" when he participates in a community, and the institution makes this participation possible. The public building therefore expresses the common values and beliefs, or the "agreements" of a fellowship, to use the word of Louis Kahn.[1] Whereas the house is the image of an individual world, the institution represents the general properties of the world. We could also say that it offers an "explanation" which allows for participatory identification. The difference between the house and the public building is not, of course, absolute; an individual world always has to be a "variation" on what is common to be meaningful, whereas the public world consists of interhuman "themes." These themes do not only comprise the values of a particular society, but the general structure of man's being in the world, as well as the genius loci of the given environment. Public life is therefore not subject to continuous change, but possesses a basic order. "Order is," Louis Kahn said, and, "it is not what you want, it is what you sense in the order of things which tells you what to design."[2] At certain points of time human institutions, which until then were hidden, are discovered and bring order into the complexities of the situation. . . "Some man realized that a certain realm of spaces represents a deep desire on the part of man to express the inexpressible in a certain activity of man called monastery," Kahn said, and "somehow a light shines on the emergence of a new institution of man, which makes him feel a refreshed will to live."[3] In other words, when an institution is set into work as a public building, man experiences understanding in the sense of participation and belonging.

When we say that the public institution makes the general properties of a world manifest, it implies that its space and form are something more than mere results of functional and circumstantial adaptation. What is visualized are the basic structures of existential spatiality, in terms of centres, directions and domains, as well as modes of standing, rising, extending, opening and closing. To some extent this also applies to the private house, but what is there suggested, ought to become fully manifest in the public building. The latter, thus, has always been characterized by distinct *images* which are easily recognized and identified. As built forms, these images may be a colonnade, a pediment, a gateway, a dome, or a tower, whereas spatial images may be centralized, longitudinal or gridded halls. The spatial types allow life to take place as "togetherness," while the built images make the institution stand forth as an environmental focus or "landmark." The existence of basic typologies confirms the general nature of public buildings. It is important to emphasize that the images are not products of convention and habit (although they may be subject to habit), but visualizations of existential structures. Basically the images are atemporal, but their use is historically determined. Evidently such images are set into work "as something," that is, as a church, a city hall, or some other institution. Today the number of public institutions may seem bewildering, but the need for distinct types is still there.

The modern public building has to function as a manifestation of the new open world, at the same time as it ought to preserve the general properties of communal spatiality. It is not easy to arrive at such a synthesis. In the past, communal spatiality usually became manifest as closed, symmetrical "figures" and stylistic motifs. The new vision wanted to do away with these things, and as a result the modern public building has tended towards a certain anonymity and lack of image quality. We have, however, suggested that the "transparent," unitary halt and the "indefinite" skyscraper represent general points of departure for a new development. Topological spaces and forms, such as those introduced by Aalto, also possess figural quality without becoming closed entities. Finally

OPPOSITE: J.M.Olbrich: Hochzeitsturm (Wedding Tower), Darmstadt, 1901.

FAR RIGHT: Cathedral group,
Pisa, 1063-1118.
RIGHT: Johann Lucas von Hildebrandt:
Upper Belvedere, Vienna, 1721.

we may note that Le Corbusier's church at Ronchamp shows that a new "open" interpretation of old images such as the tower, the vault and the gateway, is possible. To give these possibilities a more precise definition, it is useful to take a look at the emergence of a new public architecture during the nineteenth century, and its historical roots.

Beginnings of the modern institution

The large iron-and-glass halls of the second half of the last century represent the first attempts at creating a modern public architecture. Many of them were solutions to entirely new building tasks, such as the factory, the railway station, the exhibition hall, and the department store. All of these allowed for the togetherness of a new mass society. But tasks such as the university, the library, and the museum were also in reality manifestations of the open world, and therefore the new concept of space also entered here, but through the back door so to speak. Labrouste's libraries in Paris with their large, transparent halls furnish characteristic examples. In some cases the hall was conceived as a pure, "modern" structure, especially in connection with temporary buildings for exhibitions; and when today we think of the beginnings of the new public architecture, solutions such as the *Crystal Palace* in London (1851) and the *Galerie des Machines* in Paris (1889) immediately come to mind. In general, however, the new halls were dressed up with historical forms in order to gain a certain "dignity." These forms were usually borrowed from classical architecture, and the temple front became a general token of civic importance. Even greenhouses were in some cases qualified in this way.[4] More original attempts at creating new symbols are also encountered, for instance in the works of H.H. Richardson and Louis Sullivan. Thus we recognize the emergence of new, meaningful "landmarks."

The questions we have to investigate are basically two: how was the hall adapted to the various building tasks, and how were the new institutions qualified as landmarks? The first question concerns the definition of public space, the second the creation of public images.

To start, let us repeat that the transparent hall is one of the great public images of our epoch. Entering a large, luminous space, seemingly without fixed boundaries, where a large number of people may gather and interact, is certainly a basic "modern" experience. As a type, the hall represents both a general coming together and openness, and is therefore a genuine case of modern *place*. Here the "open interaction" of modern society may occur, and a sense of identification with possibilities rather than finalities is experienced. The hall is therefore something more than a functional container; it is a symbolic image, and has in fact often been used where it is not strictly necessary from a practical point of view. As an example we may mention the large ground-floor lobbies of American skyscrapers, starting with the *Rookery Building* in Chicago (Burnham and Root, 1886). These lobbies do not only unify psychologically a building which consists of an "indefinite number of storeys," but make it feel part of the open world to which it belongs. In order to fulfil its role, it is important that the lobby is inside the building itself, and not added to it as a semi-independent volume.

Because of its symbolic significance and explicit image quality, the nineteenth-century hall was used in connection with numerous building tasks, and in each case it was varied to fit the situation. The process of adaptation was facilitated by the lesson of architectural history. Although the transparent hall makes the new vision manifest, it represents an interpretation of an existing type, or rather, a set of types. In general, architectural history knows three types of halls: the centralized hall, the longitudinal hall, and the gridded, *hypostyle* hall. The basic variations on the centralized hall are the rotunda, the octagon and the cube, where centralization may be emphasized by engirding ambulatories or galleries. The basic variations on the longitudinal hall are the simple, unitary *aula* and the basilica (with or without lateral galleries). The

Frank Lloyd Wright: Unity Church, Oak Park, Chicago, 1907.

hypostyle hall, finally, may be more or less isotropic depending on the geometrical pattern of the grid. We have moreover pointed out that the constituent spatial elements of all three types may be more or less interdependent.[5] The typology here outlined is not a mere matter of classification. The types represent concrete facts, because of their distinct image quality which resides in their relationship to the basic structures of existential space: centre, direction and domain. Thus, during the course of architectural history we encounter the same types, used according to the circumstances and variously characterized to make the "vision" of the epoch manifest. As examples we may recall the Egyptian hypostyle hall, the Roman rotunda, and the Christian basilica. In each case the hall is understood as an *imago mundi,* both because of its spatial properties and because of the articulation of the built form.

In pre-modern architecture we find all the basic types, which are now interpreted in accordance with the new vision. The basic aim was, as we have already pointed out, to introduce a sense of simultaneity of places. Let us mention a few of the most important examples.

The numerous conservatories and palm houses erected in various European and American cities about the middle of the nineteenth century repeat the traditional spatial types, but their quality usually resides in the general transparency of the structure rather than the image quality of the space.[6] In the great exhibition halls, however, space gains active presence. Paxton's *Crystal Palace* did not appear as a mere repetition of units, but was given unity by means of a kind of basilica section which in the transept was emphasized by a glazed barrel vault. The image quality of this solution was immediately recognized. *The Times* wrote after the inauguration on 1st May, *1851:* "Above the visitors rose a glittering arch far more lofty and spacious than the vaults of even our noblest cathedrals. On either side the vista seemed almost boundless." A new kind of public hall for a new world was thus realized. The general

quality of the *Crystal Palace* was repeated and enhanced in the longitudinal *Machinery Hall* at the 1889 Paris International Exhibition (Ferdinand Dutert and Victor Contamin). Here the grand space was unified by the continuous sweep of the large three-hinged arches which freely span the interior.

In accordance with the utilitarian character of the task, the early railway stations usually consist of a series of parallel glazed vaults resting on rows of iron columns. A new kind of hypostyle hall thus came into being, which is simultaneously gridded and directed.

Although the stations counted among the great public images of the new world, and were glorified in famous paintings such as Monet's *Gare St. Lazare*, they are today often abandoned or even demolished, as is the case with perhaps the greatest of them all: the *Pennsylvania Station* in New York by McKim, Mead, and White (1902-11).[7] To arrive there, under the glazed cross-vaults of the concourse hall, really signified to be immersed in the dynamic flux of modern life, and thus to be psychologically tuned for travelling.

Important civic functions are also fulfilled by the early market halls and department stores. The most venerated market, *Les Halles* in Paris by Baltard (1853 ff.) was unfortunately demolished some years ago. It consisted of a repetitive network of ten centralized pavilions and interconnecting "streets," all covered with a light web of iron and glass. The spatial disposition offered identity as well as freedom, and in general the building functioned convincingly as an urban focus. To buy food at *Les Halles* was experienced as a encounter with a whole world. Related to the market halls, but with a more representative function, are the glass-covered galleries of late nineteenth-century cities. The larger ones, such as the *Galleria Vittorio Emanuele II* in Milan by Giuseppe Mengoni (l865-67), appear as streets which, due to the covering, have gained the value of places. A modern synthesis of the static *piazza* and the dynamic street is thus realized. The early department stores played a less active role in relation to the

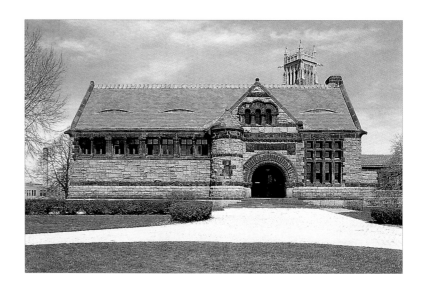

H.H. Richardson: Crane Memorial
Library, Quincy, Mass., 1880-83.

urban environment, being enclosed units. A potential open-ness was however achieved by means of "transparent" halls serving as nodes of communication. In the *Bon Marché* by Eiffel and Boileau (1876) the rich composition of stairs and galleries gave the visitor a feeling of being simultaneously in all parts of the building.

Various other building tasks were also solved as transparent halls by the pre-modern pioneers. Particularly important as architectural achievements are the *Stock Exchange* in Amsterdam by H.P. Berlage (1898-1903), the *Postsparkasse* in Vienna by Otto Wagner (1903-12), and the *National Farmers' Bank* in Owatonna by Louis Sullivan (1907-08). Of particular interest in our context are two early public structures by Frank Lloyd Wright, the *Larkin Building* in Buffalo (1903-04, de-molished in 1950) and the *Unity Church* in Oak Park (1906-07). In both cases Wright applies the idea of the unitary hall to a public task, and moreover demonstrates what the "destruction of the box" means in connection with larger structures. The *Larkin Building* represented a radical departure from the typi-cal high-rise office building developed in Chicago and defined theoretically by Sullivan.[8] It was conceived as an elongated, sky-lit hall surrounded by several storeys of subsidiary "bal-conies." The complex functions were thus interpreted as one integrated unit, a solution which was further emphasized by the open "office-landscape" on the ground floor. Although the exterior of the *Larkin Building* appeared as unified, sym-metrical form, the volume was "destroyed" by means of ver-tical slits, recesses and rows of windows. Moreover the "serving" and "served" elements of the plan were expressed as massive towers and intermediate semi-skeletal walls, thus anticipating by fifty years a basic principle of Louis Kahn.[9] The *Unity Church* is closely related to the *Larkin Building* with respect to the articulation of space and form, but with the important difference that its plan is centralized. Again a full-height, sky-lit hall is surrounded by balconies, and a sym-metrical volume is decomposed to become a juxtaposition of

standing and hovering elements. The relationship to Wright's early houses is evident, and confirms the general validity of his "method." In the *Unity Church* the new vision is set into work as "church." The means used to achieve this are very simple: a combination of central and axial symmetries, raising the main floor above the surrounding "profane" spaces of access, and a particularly expressive use of light from above. Thus the building manifests a general order, which is never in evidence in the same direct way in Wright's houses, at the same time that a more active relationship between earth and sky is suggested.

The *Unity Church* is also of particular interest because it is the first modern *church.* It has proved exceedingly difficult to give the church a new open interpretation, and the con-vincing solutions from our century may be counted on one hand. This shortcoming is certainly due to a lack of under-standing of the basic means of spatial and formal articulation, in particular the relationship between "up" and "down." From the very beginning in the fourth century, ecclesiastical architecture aimed at making the relationship between heaven and earth manifest. The point of departure was the new active role of the sky, as a heavenly realm from where divine light originates. The interior was therefore divided into two superimposed zones: a lower, earthly zone constituted by bodily elements such as columns, and a higher, heavenly zone possessing a luminous, "dematerialized" character. The history of ecclesiastical architecture is to a great extent the history of the various interpretations of the interaction of these realms.[10] In Wright's early church, the basic properties of the sacred interior are present, although the solution in certain respects appears as a first approximation.

Whereas the spatial problems of the new public architecture were quickly understood and to some extent mastered, the built form lagged behind. We have already mentioned that innumerable iron-and-glass halls of the nineteenth century were dressed up with stylistic elements to become "dignified."

FAR RIGHT: Victor Horta:
Maison du Peuple, Brussels, 1899.
RIGHT: G.Mengoni: Galleria Vittorio
Emanuele II, Milan, 1865.

Certain attempts at a recovery of basic formal images were, however, also made. In the works of H.H. Richardson and Louis Sullivan, for instance, we encounter the great, arched gateway. The motif is here used as something more than a "sign" for entering; it really becomes an image which characterizes the building as an environmental focus, or a place where a world is gathered.[11] Thus the arch with its precise, concentric form suggests that the interior space behind contains a general "explanation" which may offer man the identity he needs. (It is in this connection interesting to note that the only arch found in the Greek city of Priene marked the entrance to the *agora)* Thus the round arch entered the formal *repertoire* of modern architecture. The pointed arch and the pediment were on the contrary abolished. The reason is evidently that these forms had become emblematic of the two major styles of the European past, the Gothic and the Classical.[12] The pediment had been used thus throughout the nineteenth century in connection with classical columns, to give innumerable public buildings a symbolic "temple front," whereas the pointed arch was perceived by everybody as a token of the mediaeval church. Because of its singular importance as a public image, it was, however, not easy to replace the temple front, and we have during the history of pre-modern architecture experienced several attempts at giving it a new interpretation. We may in this connection mention the "classical" works of Olbrich, Behrens and Asplund. Although the pointed arch was abolished, the lesson of Gothic architecture was not forgotten. The transparent hall has an obvious affinity to the dematerialized, diaphanous spaces of late mediaeval churches, with the difference that the light of the latter always appears as though it is coming from above, while modern light is uniformly distributed. The skeletal structures so basic to modern architecture relate to the tracery of the Gothic wall. As an example we may mention the beautifully articulated iron front of the *Le Parisien Libéré* building in Paris by Georges Chedanne (1903-05). Buildings like this in general suggest the possibility of deriving new formal images from modern systems of construction.[13]

The tower is another conventional form which to some extent has been taken over by modern architecture. In the past, towers belonged to a few basic categories: church tower, municipal tower, defence tower and towerhouse.[14] Whereas belfries as a rule were pointed and less massive in the upper part, the municipal towers of Tuscany were given an enlarged top which made them appear as a symbolic "fortress." Characteristic images were thus formed, which acted as primary landmarks in relation to the surrounding landscape. To our knowledge, a typology of towers has never been worked out, but it would be most useful to analyze the regional variations of towers in relation to place and time. An original pre-modern interpretation of the Gothic steeple is given by Antoní Gaudí in the *Church of the Sagrada Familia* in Barcelona (1884ff.). Here an historical type is treated as a kind of open form which comprises all kinds of "memories:" geometrical patterns, natural elements, and embodied light. A pre-modern interpretation of the civic tower was attempted by Berlage in the *Stock Exchange* in Amsterdam, without however arriving at a convincing solution. More interesting is Ragnar Østberg's *Town Hall* in Stockholm (1906ff.) which takes the traditional Swedish tower as its point of departure. From the Middle Ages on, Swedish towers were characterized by a stout and massive lower part and a light, contrasting superstructure of smaller dimensions. Thus the Stockholm tower functions as an image which evokes the *genius loci.* The first full-grown modern tower, however, is the *Wedding Tower* in Darmstadt by Olbrich (1907). Standing on a symmetrical base with a splendidly decorated entrance, the tower is here characterized as an open form by means of asymmetrical openings and an original crowning feature which consists of five round arches rising to different heights. Memories of the Central European Renaissance are evoked, while at the same time certain traits typical of De Stijl architecture are prefigured.[15]

The Democratic Institution

FAR RIGHT: Rudolf Schwarz: Corpus
Cristi Church, (Frohnleichnamskirche),
Aachen, 1930.
RIGHT TOP: Gustave Eiffel:
Eiffel Tower, Paris, 1889.
RIGHT BOTTOM: Louis Sullivan:
Guaranty Trust Building, Buffalo, 1895.

In general, however, modern architecture has not managed to come to grips with the problem of the tower as a civic landmark, although its development in a certain sense started with a tower, the *Eiffel Tower* built for the 1889 Paris exhibition. The *Eiffel Tower* is *only* a tower, and thus demonstrates how a work of architecture may act as a strong and meaningful environmental image without having any defined purpose. What, then, is the "meaning" of the *Eiffel Tower*? More convincingly, perhaps, than any other building, the *Eiffel Tower* visualizes the new world. Its open, web-like structure seems to gather infinite space and unify everything it might contain into one grand, rising movement. Here logical construction transcends itself and becomes an unforgettable image of the new freedom, and thus a true expression of the unity of thinking and feeling.

The *Eiffel Tower* was a unique case, and did not inspire imitation.[16] And in any case a tower is no longer a possible landmark owing to the "rise of the skyscraper." Already in the 1890s Chicago witnessed the creation of a new building type which took the place of the tower, without however representing a substitute.[17] The skyscraper certainly makes the open world manifest, but it does not embody those values which constitute the core of human identity. It represents the conquest of space rather than an explanatory goal. Its power is great, however, as Sullivan understood when he wanted to transform the "tall office building" into a work of art: "How shall we impart to this sterile pile, this crude, harsh, brutal agglomeration, this stark, staring exclamation of eternal strife, the graciousness of those higher forms of sensibility and culture that rest on the lower and fiercer passions?"[18] Sullivan's answer was simple; he proposed to give each part of the building a form corresponding to its nature: "All things in nature have a shape, that is to say, a form, an outward semblance, that tells what they are, that distinguishes them from ourselves and from each other."[19] And, in fact, Sullivan managed to design skyscrapers which know "what they want to be," as

is shown particularly well by the *Wainwright Building* in St. Louis (1890-91) and the *Guaranty Trust Building* in Buffalo (1894-95). Here the tall office building has become a type capable of variation, and as such a true public image. It remains, however, within the limits of its symbolic content. Beyond its particular scope, Sullivan's analysis of the skyscraper is also important because it initiated that search for *principles,* which was to distinguish the next "modern" phase in the development of the new public architecture.

The modern institution

After the first world war, the need for a new kind of public architecture came to the fore. The old ways of life had disintegrated, and the abolition of traditional typologies became a necessity for the avant-garde. Even the achievements of the pre-modern pioneers were rejected, with the exception, perhaps, of the works of Frank Lloyd Wright. Architecture had to start again "as if nothing had ever been done before." During the 1920s we witness the growth of a public architecture which seems radically new. Le Corbusier's *League of Nations* project is a particularly good illustration of the new approach, and because of its explicit novelty it was not accepted for construction although it won first prize in the international competition.[20] A basic property of the solution is the differentiation of the large complex into several semi-independent units. This subdivision is in accordance with Le Corbusier's own list of "functions:" offices, assembly hall, secretariat, library, etc. Each of these is expressed as such, and then coordinated with the others to form a "group of buildings." What is here coming to the fore is the method of "functionalism," not in terms of measurable quantities, but as a desire for making the building show what it "is." The approach was, as we have suggested, introduced with Sullivan's analysis of the skyscraper. The aim was not primarily to obtain efficiency, but to transform the building into a work of art by making it "meaningful." "Meaning" was now

FAR RIGHT: Willem Marinus Dudok:
Town Hall, Hilversum, 1930.
RIGHT TOP: Walter Gropius:
Bauhaus, Dessau.
RIGHT BOTTOM: Le Corbusier:
Soviet Palace, Moscow, 1931, project.

understood in terms of *use* rather than symbolic form. As a result, the solution consists of a number of units, each having its particular identity, at the same time as they are interconnected to form a "working" totality. Thus the free plan was transferred from the scale of the dwelling to a semi-urban scale where several buildings are related to each other and to the environment. The step taken was most natural as it seemed to represent a further manifestation of the new vision. In his description of the *League of Nations* Le Corbusier, in fact, says that his project "embodies the spirit of our age."

The principle of functional differentiation was of basic importance, and was taken as a point of departure for the public architecture of modernism. It was not, however, invented by Le Corbusier, but must be understood as a natural result of Frank Lloyd Wright's "destruction of the box." Wright's influence is seen most clearly in the functionally differentiated layouts of the Dutch architects related to the De Stijl movement. In his many public buildings in Hilversum, Willem Marinus Dudok demonstrated how the free plan may be used in an urban context.[21] His work culminated with the splendid *Town Hall* (1928) where the lesson of Wright is fully understood and used to qualify a functionally differentiated complex of interacting volumes. A tall tower, asymmetrically crowned, serves as a landmark and keeps the composition together like the chimney-stacks of Wright.

The most seminal of the functionally determined, "open" buildings of the twenties, however, was the *Bauhaus* in Dessau by Walter Gropius (1926). Significantly, Gropius starts his book on the *Bauhaus* with birds-eye views, where he moves around the building by means of a series of photographs.[22] Evidently the intention is to demonstrate that the value of the *Bauhaus* does not lie in a monumental facade or a dominant motif, but in a new kind of open, many-sided totality. And, in fact, the building is not an object which, in the traditional way, may be perceived from one or more fixed viewpoints, but a facadeless

organism which demands that the movement be understood.[23] The concept of space as a container is hence substituted by a new synthesis of space and life. And the free plan is set into work on a public scale. In general, the Bauhaus consists of three functionally different wings which are joined together to form a kind of centrifugal "figure." The wings are characterized by three different kinds of transparency which visualize the spatial conditions: horizontal extension, vertical ascension and general openness. This formal differentiation illustrates Gropius's tenet that "any thing is determined by its nature," another confirmation of the essentialist approach of true functionalism. At the Bauhaus the didactic programme was in fact based on a study of the properties of material forms and structures.

Examples which illustrate the functionalist conception of the public building are legion. Le Corbusier himself worked out several other important projects, and in two cases he succeeded in having his solutions built: the *Centrsoyus Building* in Moscow (1929ff.) and the *Cité de Refuge* for the Salvation Army in Paris (1932-33). In both cases a characterizing differentiation of the various parts of the building is realized.

The functionalist approach implies a disintegration of the traditional figural form of the public building, and thus the danger of a loss of the social meaningful image. How was this danger counteracted by the pioneers of the twenties? First of all it has to be pointed out that the definition of functionally determined volumes did not imply the abolition of the basic spatial types of pre-modern architecture, the unitary hall and the repetitive grid (high-rise or horizontally extended). What happened, is that these elements were given a stronger presence as such. It is in this context that we must understand Le Corbusier's dictum: "Architecture is the masterly, correct and magnificent play of volumes brought together in light."[24] But a definition of elementary volumes is not enough to secure the quality of meaningful image, as an image implies a reference

FAR RIGHT: Alvar Aalto:
Sanatorium, Paimio, 1929-32.
RIGHT: Mies van der Rohe:
National Gallery, Berlin, 1962-68.

to the concrete structure of human actions between earth and sky. In Le Corbusier's *League of Nations* such references are, however, abundantly present: *pilotis* form colonnades and hypostyle halls, canopies and flights of stairs create "monumental" entrances, and symmetry is introduced where movement has to be directed towards a symbolic goal. At the same time a great ease reigns. "It is better that the Nations present themselves through the spirit rather than by brutality and pedantry," Le Corbusier said.[25] In his great project for the *Palace of the Soviets* in Moscow (1931), we find an analogous synthesis of freedom and order, with the difference that large, exposed constructions are used to qualify and keep the complex group of volumes formally together. A unique case in Le Corbusier's production, and possibly a concession to the Russian constructivist tradition.

It is of particular interest to note that Alvar Aalto also adopted the functionalist principle of characterizing differentiation. In his *Paimio Sanatorium* (1929-33) this is most evident, and in his later works the basic idea is never abandoned. In contrast to the other pioneers, however, he aimed at an intimate, "organic" integration of the functional units, without giving up their identity, which in fact he emphasized to obtain landmark-like qualities. Aalto's approach proved very fruitful, and found application in numerous projects for city-halls, libraries and churches. Because of its urban, local and typological implications, we shall take a closer look at Aalto's achievement in the following chapters.

Among the protagonists of modernism Mies van der Rohe was the only one who never subscribed to the principle of functional differentiation. Instead he preserved the public building as a unified, symmetrical volume.[26] Some critics have therefore been tempted to interpret his architecture as "cryptofascist." The explanation is less dramatic: Mies simply distinguishes between "informal" houses and "formal" institutions, as Alberti and many others did before him. Thus he made the 1933 Reichsbank project symmetrical without giving up his characteristic combination of free plan and repetitive construction. In the preliminary scheme for the *Illinois Institute of Technology* campus in Chicago (1939) a certain functional differentiation is present, but in the final scheme all the buildings have become regular symmetrical volumes, containing simplified free plans.[27] A serene sense of public order is thus created without relinquishing the basic freedom which is at the root of modern architecture. In his later public works Mies used an exposed primary construction to obtain a feeling of meaningful presence. As examples we may mention the project for the *opera house* in Mannheim (1952-53), the *Crown Hall* at the I.I.T. (1950-56) and in particular the *National Gallery* in Berlin (1962-68). The latter represents a last, magnificent interpretation of the theme of the transparent hall. The new conception of space is here set into work in an emblematic way, and the built form has become a powerful structure which is simultaneously "monumental" and open, thanks to the placing of the columns away from the corners. Thus the *National Gallery* may be considered one of the modern public buildings *par excellence.*[28]

Our survey of the public buildings of modernism has shown that the pioneers were fully aware of the necessity of making the institutions of the new democratic society architecturally manifest. Being conceived in terms of space rather than symbolic form, however, their buildings had some difficulty in acting as true landmarks. Functional differentiation moreover did away with the unitary halls of communal gathering.

The democratic institution today

After the second world war, the need for a "new monumentality" was strongly felt, and Mies van der Rohe's simple yet powerful buildings naturally served as an important source of inspiration. When his works and those of his followers became more numerous, however, one understood that a more varied and "expressive" architecture was needed to visualize the values of a pluralist world. The decisive step was taken by Le

Principles of Modern Architecture

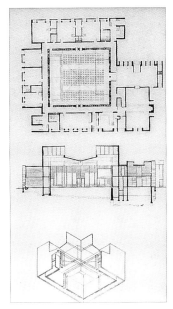

Louis Kahn:
Unity Church, Rochester, 1959-63.

Corbusier with his church at *Ronchamp* (1950-55) where the aim was to create "a vessel of intense concentration and meditation," that is, to endow architecture with a new dimension of meaning.[29]

Ronchamp's importance in the history of modern architecture can hardly be overestimated. In general it shows that archetypal meanings can be combined with the modern concept of open space. In his great public buildings in Chandigarh (*High Court*, 1951-56, *Parliament*, 1953 ff.) and in the late project for the *church at Firminy* (1960), Le Corbusier carried on his "patient search" into the possibilities of a new expressive architecture, and arrived at grandiose new interpretations of archetypal forms, such as the pillared "gateway" and canopy in the High Court Building and the truncated pyramid-cone at Firminy. His solutions, however, remain special *tours de force.* They do not really open up a public architecture of recognizable types. The late-modern works inspired by Le Corbusier's *ultima maniera* therefore mostly degenerated into empty rhetoric, such as the neo-expressionist city-halls in Boston (Kallmann, McKinnel and Knowles, 1963-69) and Dallas (I.M. Pei, 1966-78). The label "brutalism" appropriately characterizes the approach.

With the advent of Louis Kahn the problem of the modern public building entered a new phase. Rather than taking functional considerations or expressive needs as points of departure, Kahn asked what the building "wants to be."[30] This question suggests that buildings possess an *essence* which determines the solution. Whereas functionalism looked for basic principles in patterns of use, in materials and structural systems, Kahn understood the building as a manifestation of a total mode of being in the world. His approach thus represents an inversion of functionalism; the latter proceeds from "below," whereas Kahn starts from "above." Over and over again he emphasized that there exists an *order* which precedes design. In his earlier writings he used the term "form" to denote what a thing wants to be, later he preferred "pre-form." The form of

a building, therefore, is not the particular solution, but something general and "immeasurable." It is the architectural equivalent of "institution" which Kahn understood as an existential structure or mode of being in the world. The institutions stem from the "beginning," when man came to realize his "desires" and "inspirations." The main inspirations are to learn, to live, to work, to meet, to question, to express. Kahn was quite explicit about the institutions having form, and he made "form-drawings" to illustrate the spatial properties of an institution, saying: "In the nature of space is the spirit and will to exist in a certain way."[31] Whereas "form" relates to the "what," "design" answers to the "how." "Form can be detected as the nature of something, and design strives at a precise moment to employ the laws of nature in putting that into being. . ."

In his projects and executed buildings, Kahn illustrated his notion of architecture as an embodiment of man's institutions. *The First Unitarian Church* in Rochester (1959ff.) was used as an example by Kahn himself to explain his method, which here appears as a phenomenological analysis of a particular kind of "togetherness."[32] The final result is a spatial organization and a built form which visualizes this fellowship, at the same time as it is related to the general structures of our being in the world. Four "towers" rise over the main central space to receive the light of the sky. They show the course of the sun and mark the cardinal points, whereby the given situation gains universal importance. In most of Kahn's works we recognize such a meaningful relationship between the general and the circumstantial. To make this possible he reintroduced archetypal forms, which had been mostly neglected by the modern movement. It is therefore fair to assert that Kahn was the real initiator of the genuine post-modern phase in the architectural development of our time. He did not, however, abandon the free plan and the open form, but demonstrated rather that the principles defined by the masters of modernism are necessary means to the realization of buildings which explain the new world.

The Democratic Institution **69**

"The tall, standing panels are simultaneously cliff, trees and built form, while the slots between them make Finnish light manifest, as it is experienced in a stand of birch trees on a hill . . ."

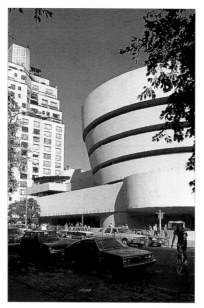

Frank Lloyd Wright: Guggenheim Museum, New York, 1959.

The post-modernists have, however, only occasionally continued Kahn's pursuit. Although they concentrate their attention on the problem of meaning and the recovery of archetypal forms, the results mostly lack depth. Fortunately there are exceptions. Let me mention here just one example of outstanding quality: Reima Pietilä's *Kaleva church* in Tampere (1960-66). With respect to both its urban context and its relation to earth and sky, it functions as a goal, but at the same time the surrounding concave wall sections communicate with the horizon. The tall, standing panels are simultaneously cliff, trees and built form, while the slots between them make Finnish cloven light manifest, as it is experienced in "a stand of birch trees on a hill," to quote Pietilä's own words.[33] Finally, the altar tree by Pietilä himself interprets verticality as growth and web. As a church, the Kaleva respects the traditional organization of ecclesiastical space, but at the same time it opens up to the qualities of the "things themselves," being thus a true *modern* work.

The development of the new institution illustrates the main phases in the history of modern architecture. The pre-modern public buildings expressed the vision of the new open world as democratic togetherness in transparent, unitary halls. The modern buildings planned and erected between the wars first of all aimed at functional differentiation within the general openness. The result was dynamic "facadeless" organisms, which could not, however, satisfy the need for stable, recognizable images. In several buildings of the last decade the image is back again. It would be a misunderstanding to interpret this as a return to the static, self-sufficient structures of the past. Now the image is conceived as part of an open composition or a complex collage. Thus modern democracy is interpreted as reciprocal respect rather than absolute order. Respect has however to be based on some kind of common understanding. In our opinion this can only consist in an "environmental awareness" which comprises the archetypal structures of our being in the world as well as the particular

genius loci. The development of a truly democratic public architecture is therefore closely related to the problems of regionalism and monumentality, which will be discussed after we have taken a look at the modern city.

RIGHT: James Stirling:
Art Museum, Stuttgart, 1977-84.
BELOW: Colin St. John Wilson:
British Library, London, 1978-98.

6 *the* Healthy City

T he city is the *problem* of modern architecture. Whereas the free plan and the open form did not imply a loss of identifiable buildings, the *ville radieuse* or "green city" represented a radical break with all traditional properties of place.[1] Thus it abolished the figural quality of the settlement in relation to the landscape, the defined urban space, and the sense of a local atmosphere or character. In short, the *genius loci* evaporated, and man was left with a kind of "non-place urban realm."[2] The loss of place evidently brings about a weakened sense of belonging and participation. Thus it is related to the human alienation so common today. When the place loses its identity, man cannot any more identify with his environment, and say: "I am Roman," or "I am a New Yorker." No wonder, then, that the current criticism of modern architecture is primarily directed against the new city.[3]

We all know that the idea of the green city was introduced to give human beings more healthy living conditions. Over and over again Le Corbusier pointed to the inhuman conditions of the historic city, which had been forced to assimilate the dense population and heavy traffic of the new industrialized society. Not without reason he called the traditional street the "street of all conflicts." In his criticism, Le Corbusier echoed comments going back to the nineteenth century, and his vision was certainly influenced by the dream of the "garden city," although he gave this idea a fundamentally new interpretation.[4] The best illustration of Le Corbusier's vision is offered by the *Maison Suisse*, the Swiss student dormitory at the Cité Universitaire in Paris (1930). Here the idea of a building on *pilotis* with a roof solarium really works. Thus the site extends meaningfully under the building between corporeal concrete piers, while the edifice rises with lightness and elegance above. An entrance hall and a living room with a "topological" form assure a more intimate adaptation to the ground.

As we have already noted Le Corbusier's point of departure was the demand for the "essential joys:" *sun*, *space* and *verdure.* This demand is primarily related to the *dwelling,* and at the outset the modern movement in fact reduced the problem of the city to the problem of the urban dwelling, without considering the place as such. "Thus the CIAM began by investigating the smallest unit, the low-cost dwelling. then proceeded to survey the neighbourhood unit found in urban settlements, and finally widened its scope to include an analysis of present-day cities," Giedion wrote in the introduction to J.L. Sert's book "Can our cities survive?"[5] We may accept the humanitarian aim of this procedure, but we understand today that it often led to the loss of the city as something more than an agglomeration of healthy dwellings, that is, as a place.

What, then, is a city? We have already mentioned Louis Kahn's definition as "the place of assembled institutions." This implies that the city is primarily a *meeting place,* a place where people come together, bringing with them their understanding of the world. We could also say that the city ought to be a *microcosmos*; it should gather the surroundings, bringing what is close and what is distant together. In this sense we may understand Alberti's definition of the city as a "large house," although the world which is gathered by the city is public and the one of the house private. In gathering a public world, the city constitutes a milieu of *possibilities*. In the city we may discover what we want to do with our lives, here we make our choice and develop our identity. When we say, "I am a New Yorker," it moreover implies that the city gives us a *common* identity (without however making us alike). This common identity consists in *having a place together,* or, in other words, in a participation which is based on openness to and respect for the *genius loci*. (It should be pointed out, however, that participation does not necessarily imply that we *use* the offered possibilities; it is sufficient to know that they are at our disposition when we need them.) Thus the city liberates because it offers the freedom of choice, at the same time as it makes us experience togetherness and cave. In the city it

OPPOSITE: Le Corbusier: Unité d'Habitation, Marseilles, 1946-52.

FAR RIGHT: Le Corbusier:
"The green city."
RIGHT: Le Corbusier:
Nemours, Algiers, project, 1934.

is possible, within a common frame, to be on the earth and under the sky in different ways.

How, then, should the city be structured to function as a meeting-place?

In some places it is still possible to experience what it means to *arrive*. We travel through the landscape and approach a settlement which, like a "thing," is there "waiting" for us. First we grasp the main outline and perhaps a dominant element, such as a church tower. As we come closer, the form becomes more articulate, and we may get an idea of what is hidden inside. And when we enter, the spaces within confirm our expectations. Depending on where we are coming from, the experience is different, but always we feel that we have reached a goal A goal cannot, however, be *different* from the environment. It is only a goal when it is related to the surrounding landscape. A goal is thus a centre where the qualities of an environment are gathered. Such a gathering may be more or less comprehensive. A village is primarily related to its immediate surroundings, whereas a capital city has to function as a focus for a whole country. A city is a meeting-place in the sense of being the gathering of a world.

As already suggested, the meeting-places of the past possessed three basic structural qualities. Firstly, they had *figural quality* in relation to the surrounding landscape, or, in other words, a clear delimitation or a dense clustering of the constituent elements. Secondly, they contained defined urban spaces, a fact which is confirmed by the very existence of words which denote these spaces: square, street, neighbourhood.[6] Finally, the settlements of the past were distinguished by a particular, local character; they possessed so to speak an individual "personality." The local character is determined by the way things *are*, that is, by what we have called the "built form." Often the built form is condensed in local motifs such as the "French window," which appears throughout Paris in innumerable variations. It is above all the spontaneous experience of the local atmosphere which makes us feel that we are "present." To

dwell in a city, does not primarily imply the use of certain buildings, but the identification with the manifest *genius loci*.

The basic structural properties of the city are apparently opposed to the free plan and the open form. When we talk about "figural quality," "defined spaces" and "local character," we refer to properties which are traditionally connected with a "closed" entity. When these properties are abolished, the city is lost. And, in fact, the green city does not deserve the name of "city." It does not represent a new interpretation of *dwelling together*, but reduces dwelling to a private function. Some writers on urban problems therefore accept the notion of a "non-place urban realm," and maintain that the city may be substituted by other means of communication, such as private television channels which allow us to "switch on" our friends when needed.[7] Evidently such "solutions" do not compensate for the loss of place, as place primarily means *presence*, in the sense of a concrete "here." *Life takes place*, and a loss of place implies a loss of life.

Is the conclusion, then, that we have to return to the traditional city? Not really. What we need, is to preserve the "idea" of the city, but, as is the case with the house and the public building, we have to give it a new interpretation. Today we understand that this cannot consist in a direct transference of the free plan to the urban scale; the free plan developed in connection with the private dwelling, and has to be modified when the scale is different. As to the open form, the problem is easier. Being a complex gathering of a world, the city always possessed a certain formal openness, in spite of its figural quality. This apparent contradiction was solved through the use of *topological* means of organization. As a totality, the city did not primarily consist of geometrically interrelated, "similar" parts, but of diverse elements which formed a less determined kind of unit, based on the Gestalt principles of proximity, continuity and enclosure.[8] The open form therefore naturally belongs to the city and expresses its nature as a meeting-place. But here also we need a new interpretation; the openness of the past

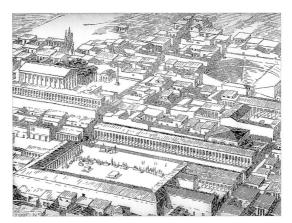

Priene, Greek settlement,
Asia Minor, 350 BC.

was in general circumscribed by the structures of a particular culture, whereas we have to cope with a global kind of interaction.

We may infer from what is said above, that the failure of the green city is due to its having been intended as a kind of blown-up modern house, where the vertical planes of the free plan have become free-standing slab-like buildings. Alberti's definition of the city as a "large house" was valid as long as both were based on the addition of defined spatial elements.[9] The new conception of space, however, demands a differentiation of the various environmental levels,[10] and thus a revision of the traditional relationship between house and city.

The basic problem is evidently to set the new conception of space into work *as a city*. To understand what that means, we may return to Kahn's definition of the city as the place of assembled institutions. If we assume that the modern "institution," be it a house or a public building, possesses a free plan, the modern city becomes an "assembly of free plans." The green city does not really constitute such an assembly, but is rather a "dispersion of free plans," or a multitude of small free plans contained within a comprehensive large-scale free plan. The resulting hierarchy is a typical manifestation of the pseudo-scientific attitude of our time, which operates in terms of "systems" rather than "visions."

As an assembly of institutions, however, the city should rather be imagined as a dense, topological ensemble of free plans, where the Gestalt principles of organization are used to secure coherence and identity. What is thus achieved is a new interpretation of the basic structural properties of the city: figural quality, urban space, and local character. Before we consider the recent development, however, we ought to take a closer look at the roots of the city, to arrive at a better understanding of what today needs to be revived.

Roots of the modern city
As a meeting-place or an assembly of institutions, a city necessarily ought to consist of qualitatively different places. The

Hellenistic city of Priene (350 BC) may serve as an example. Priene contains all the main elements of the Greek *polis*, and their location and form express the role of each within the totality. The *agora* was the public place *par excellence*. Here men came together for social life, business and politics. As an institution, it represented a democratic way of life, and its fundamental importance as the living heart of the city was expressed by its being a spatial enclosure at the centre of the urban area. This enclosure is defined by continuous porticoes. In contrast to the public character of the *agora* with its open colonnades, the houses of Priene are turned inwards, and form a tightly knit, orthogonal pattern of courtyards around which the rooms are located.

The exterior walls are continuous and practically without windows, expressing thereby the private character of the dwelling. A third kind of spatial quality is present in the sacred *temenos* of *Athena Pallas*. Within the precinct the Ionic temple is conceived as a free-standing plastic body, in contrast to the interconnected units which make up most of the fabric of the town. Thus the character it represents becomes an active force which dominated the bustling main street and *agora* below. From the theatre, which is located slightly higher up, we may contemplate the meaningful totality of temple, houses, *agora* and surrounding landscape. Finally, under the cliff to the north, the sanctuary of Demeter makes us experience the ancient forces of nature. Here the *temenos* does not contain any proud, plastic building, but a low Doric pavilion with widely spaced columns and no pediment. Like a holy grove of stone it is immersed in nature. Thus Priene illustrates how the Greek city consisted of qualitatively different places, each of which corresponded to a particular function and meaning. These meanings were visualized not only in terms of location ("at the centre," "over the houses," "next to the cliff," etc.), but also by means of an articulate built form made possible by the classical language of architecture.[11] It offered choices within an ordered world, and thereby allowed for freedom and identity.

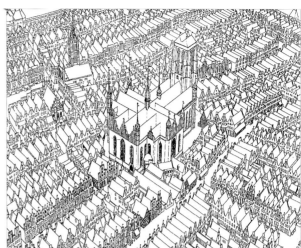

FAR RIGHT: Danzig in the
Middle Ages (reconstruction).
RIGHT TOP: Biagio Rossetti:
Street crossing, Ferrara, 1493.
RIGHT BOTTOM: Piazza, Padua, Italy.

As a structured assembly of clearly defined characters, Priene is a typical *classical* city. The mediaeval European city may on the contrary by called *romantic,* as it unites everything under one dominant theme: the relation between the human and the divine, visualized as an interaction of dwelling and cathedral.[12] Structured understanding is thus substituted by a more direct belonging. In the classical Greek city man stands below, among the gods; in the romantic mediaeval city he belongs to or yearns to find his role within a unified, sacred universe. The mediaeval city is therefore primarily an expression of *together-ness*; the topological density of its houses makes that manifest, as does the dominant centre created by the cathedral.

Urban settlements regained their importance only during the later Middle Ages, and thus in general belong to the Gothic period. Gothic details therefore mark the built forms, but the way they are employed is basically different from classical characterization. Whereas the classical language reveals the individuality of each building within the comprehensive system, the mediaeval details rather represent a "reflection" of the values embodied by the dominant church. In the "transparent" Gothic cathedral the spiritualized interior is transmitted to the entire habitat. "High Gothic architecture did delimit interior volume from exterior space yet insist that it project itself through the encompassing structure," wrote Panofsky.[13] Thus the medieval city not only makes together-ness as such manifest, but togetherness as a sharing of a common belief. The basic figural quality, or *image*, of the medieval city is in fact a towering, skeletal cathedral surrounded by a mass of similar houses. "Similarity," however, does not here mean equality; the mediaeval houses always appear as variations on a theme. In central and northern Europe this theme is mostly the *gable*-facade, which because of its formal properties also relates the houses to the pointed shapes of the church. The mediaeval city, therefore, was a *microcosmos* like its classical predecessor, but the cosmos it visualizes is one of varied integration rather than one of gathered characters.

The "ideal city" of the Renaissance aimed at a synthesis of medieval unity and classical individuation. Thus it was conceived as an integrated and mostly centralized geometrical pattern which was intended as a representation of divine cosmic harmony. Within this pattern, however, the forms were given bodily presence through the revival of classical forms. A certain abstraction from given reality was thus accomplished. We could also say that the Renaissance city was "thought" rather than imagined. Sometimes, however, its ideal form was adapted to the local circumstances, as in the extension of the city of Ferrara, planned by Biagio Rossetti after 1492. When such an adaptation happened, the Renaissance city in fact realized a synthesis of the ideal and the real. In Ferrara the street crossings are, for instance, parts of a geometrical network, but, by means of applied pilasters, Rossetti transformed them into places which are not only defined spatially, but related to a world of meanings.[14]

A characterization of this kind is evidence of the coming of Mannerism with its demand for qualitatively different places. Whereas the Greeks remained within general categories of meanings, *cinquecento* Mannerism evoked all the mysteries of nature and of man's imagination. We have already pointed out that Mannerism is related to the current interest in "complexity and contradiction," and should only add that it gave a new richness to the somewhat monotonous urban environment of the early Renaissance. The transformation of urban space into a set of characteristic places, is a result of *cinquecento* imagination, starting with Michelangelo's Piazza del Campidoglio in Rome (1536 ff.).[15] Mannerism also introduced the idea of unifying an urban and a natural environment by means of continuous "paths."[16] Exterior space thus became expressive and dynamic, and the single characteristic elements were gradually integrated into a coherent system. This implies that the space between the buildings became the most important constituent element of the urban totality, a result which was prepared for by the Renaissance concept of homogeneous space.

FAR RIGHT: Michel De Klerk:
Apartments, Henriette Ronnerplein,
Amsterdam, 1922.
RIGHT TOP: Catalan rambla.
RIGHT BOTTOM: John Wood the
Younger: Royal Crescent, Bath, 1769.

During the seventeenth century a large-scale transformation of the natural landscape took place for the first time in history. So far nature had been kept outside the *civitas*. Whereas the ideal city of the Renaissance was based on a closed geometrical pattern, a Baroque city such as Versailles shows an infinitely extended network, centred on the places of the sovereign. This network is divided into two halves by the places: on one side is the town proper; on the other nature. Thus Versailles demonstrates that the world was understood in terms of a comprehensive system of paths or directions related to a centre of meaning. Evidently the solution expresses the absolutist society of the epoch, but beyond this immediate meaning it also makes a new kind of general openness and dynamism manifest. Giedion in fact recognized how the Baroque city possessed identity because of the dominant centre, the defined urban spaces, and the meaningful relationship between built elements and nature. Thus extension, did not become dispersion, and the Baroque city demonstrates that openness and identity may be combined. In addition to urban spaces derived from older models (continuous street, enclosed piazza), Baroque urbanism also developed new types, namely the London squares, whose main element is a centrally placed garden. Terraces of buildings for urban dwelling in contact with nature were splendidly realized in Bath by John Wood the Elder and Younger (1725ff.). In Bath geometry is no longer used to relate the urban fabric to a dominant centre but to create characteristic places within an open totality. Coherence and variety are secured by means of spatial definition as well as a meaningful use of the classical language. Thus we may agree with Giedion's judgment: "It is important to notice that solutions which came out of the universal vision of the eighteenth century still remain valid long after the death of the society for which they were formulated."[17]

In spite of its valuable properties, the Baroque city could not cope with all the exigencies of the new industrial society. "Up to the nineteenth century, there had been a rough balance of activities within the city. Though work and trade were always important, religion and art and play claimed the full share of the townsman's energies," Lewis Mumford writes. "Between 1820 and 1900, however, the destruction and disorder within great cities is like that of a battlefield."[18] In general, the cities lost their defined relationship to nature, a process known as "urban sprawl," and although the spaces of the urban interior did not disappear, they became victims of the increasing traffic. In addition the new forms of production and distribution tended to break down the identity of the traditional neighbourhoods, resulting in a certain loss of the sense of place. Thus Mumford writes: "The main elements in the new urban complex were the factory, the railroad and the slum."[19] As a reaction to the destruction of the traditional urban environment, the *suburb* came into existence, and as a result the modern, one-family dwelling. Evidently, however, the suburb neither satisfied the need for *urban* dwellings nor the role of the city as a meeting-place. The same can be said about the "garden city," which was proposed as an alternative to the traditional urban settlement.[20] A garden city may of course constitute a kind of place, and therefore allow for human identification. It does not, however, gather a more comprehensive world, and therefore remains dependent on accessible cities of a traditional type.

Towards the end of the nineteenth century the *urban crisis* was a fact. The old cities seemed utterly out of tune with the new world, and it is not surprising that one tended to propose completely new utopian solutions rather than attempting a reinterpretation of their structural properties. Sant'Elia in fact talked about constructing the city *ex novo*, and his radical attitude was shared by most of the architects of the avant-garde. Official city planning, however, continued using old models, from the neo-Baroque layouts of Haussmann to the medieval picturesqueness of Camillo Sitte. The modern movement did not believe in these solutions, and Giedion in fact refers to

Hans Scharoun

"Most of these gave primary importance to the development of a new kind of semi-urban dwelling, that is a dwelling . . . that forms part of larger units, such as blocks or row houses. . ."

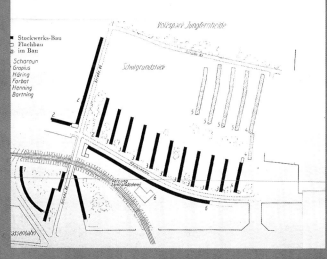

Walter Gropius

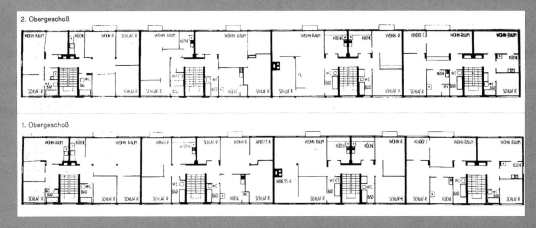

2. Obergeschoß

1. Obergeschoß

Mies van der Rohe

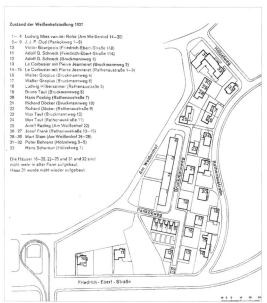

FAR RIGHT: Mies van der Rohe:
Weissenhofsiedlung, Stuttgart, 1927.
RIGHT TOP: Jacobus Johannes Peter Oud:
Row-houses, Weissenhofsiedlung, 1927.
BOTTOM: Ludwig Hilbersheimer:
Project for Berlin, 1929.

Sitte to show that "the town planner had lost contact with his period. He had become a kind of troubadour, ineffectually pitting his medieval songs against the din of modern industry."[21] Thus, from the beginning, the modern city aimed at a radical break with tradition, and rejected the lesson of history.

The modern city

Le Corbusier's concept of the *ville radieuse* has the quality of a comprehensive vision, and as such it represented a protest against the overcrowded and decayed historic cities. The idea of relating the dwelling to nature and thus to secure the "essential joys," is certainly valuable, and has in innumerable places brought about improved living conditions.[22] It is important to note that Le Corbusier's proposals were part of a general trend which comprises solutions as diverse as Howard and Unwin's garden city, Soria y Mata's linear city, Garnier's industrial city, and Wright's Broadacre city, all of which interpreted dwelling as a "natural" rather than an urban function. To the same group also belong the open patterns of slab-like blocks of flats proposed by Gropius, van Eesteren, Hilbersheimer and others. Most of these gave primary importance to the development of a new kind of semi-urban dwelling, that is, a dwelling which would offer many of the advantages and architectural qualities of the modern one-family house, although it forms part of larger units, such as blocks or rowhouses. It is symptomatic that Le Corbusier's work on the *Unité d'Habitation* started with an adding together of his *Citrohan House*, to form the *immeubles villas*. Presenting his basic "cell" as the *Pavillon de l'Esprit Nouveau* at the 1925 Paris exhibition, he emphasized the new vision, the new dwelling and the modern city. We have already mentioned that he repeated his solution at the Weissenhof exhibition in 1927. Here we also find other basic interpretations of the new semi-urban dwelling, such as the rowhouses of J.J.P. Oud and Mart Stam and the flexible apartments of Mies van der Rohe.[23] When the beginnings of the modern city are today discussed and criticized,

credit should be given to these pioneering contributions to the development of a "healthier" environment.

It is also justifiable to consider the Weissenhofsiedlung as a first step towards the recovery of certain qualities of neighbourhood and place, such as togetherness and variety. A similar result was achieved about the same time by Ernst May in his *Siedlungen* in Frankfurt a. M., and even before that by Oud at Kiefhoek in Rotterdam (1924-25). A few years later Mies van der Rohe studied the possibility of clustered courthouses, thus reviving certain properties of the Pompeian house. Even Le Corbusier, who in general rejected the medium-size dwelling unit, did not forget the problem of togetherness, defining his *unités* as "vertical villages" with "interior streets." Today we may no longer be convinced by his idea of a "vertical village," but before it is dismissed it ought at least to be compared with those villages of the past that were built on steeply sloping sites.

The weakness of the green city is evidently not the dwelling units as such, but rather their not being able to constitute a "place of assembled institutions." Two problems must be considered in this connection: firstly, the need for an urban "core" where the institutions are gathered; and secondly, the spatial definition of this gathering. The need for a core or a civic centre was soon recognized by modern architects. Bruno Taut's idea of a "city crown" (1919) thus aims at making the common values of the new society visible.[24] "We must have the same today as in ancient townscapes: the highest, the crown must be embodied in the religious structure . . . There is one word which follows rich and poor alike, which echoes everywhere and which at the same time promises a new form of Christendom: the social thought . . . If there is anything today which can provide a crown for the town then it is the expression of this thought . . ." As the "cathedral of socialism," the city crown should be a dominant structure of glass: "Infused with the light of the sun, the crystal house reigns over all like a glittering diamond which shines in the sun as a sign of the heights of plea-

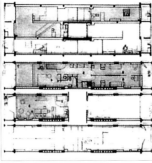

FAR RIGHT: Mies van der Rohe:
Illinois Institute of Technology,
Chicago, 1940, with plan.
RIGHT: Le Corbusier: Unité d'Habitation,
Marseilles, 1946-52, with plan.

sure and the purest peace of mind." Taut's model is evidently the transparent Gothic cathedral and the unified medieval town.

In 1929 Le Corbusier also made a first attempt at reviving the social and cultural role of the city, making a project for a *Mundaneum* or *Cité mondiale*.[25] The programme was somewhat particular, as it proposed to supplement the League of Nations in Geneva with an international cultural centre comprising a "museum of the world," various exhibition halls, a university, sports facilities and blocks of residences. The general intention was to create a "sacred place" where one could obtain a total understanding of "man in relation to time and place." The *Mundaneum* was thus intended as a true *centre* and although it did not form an urban core in the strict sense, it served as a kind of model for Le Corbusier's later designs for civic centres. The project is important for two reasons. Firstly, it shows that Le Corbusier recognized the need for places intended as an assembly of institutions and, secondly, it illustrates how he satisfied the need in terms of spatial organization. In general the *Mundaneum* consists of an orthogonally disposed "monumental" core between two freely planned park like areas containing student housing and residential blocks, respectively. A meaningful spatial differentiation is thus intended. This differentiation is due to the mode of organization (geometrical-quasi topological) rather than a contrast between true urban spaces and "green" areas. The main buildings are free-standing units, just like the residential blocks, and as such they do not enclose squares or streets of a traditional kind. A few axes of symmetry do, however, create a general coherence, and the use of basic volumetric shapes endows the ensemble with a certain monumental presence. The basic approach to public (rather than urban) space encountered in the *Mundaneum* was repeated over and over again by Le Corbusier, with the *civic centre* for St. Dié (1946) and the *Capitol* of Chandigarh (1951ff.) as primary manifestations.

Colin Rowe has pointed out that Le Corbusier's interpretation of public space represents an *inversion* of the traditional relationship between urban "figure" and urban "ground."[26] In the historical city the built matrix, the solids, formed a continuous ground on which the urban spaces appeared as "figures." In the projects of Le Corbusier, and in the modern city in general, the empty space, the void, became a ground occupied by free-standing buildings. In the traditional city we were *inside*, whereas in the modern city we always remain *outside*. "Very well," Le Corbusier might have answered, "that is exactly what I wanted; I wanted an open, green city; I wanted a healthy outside, rather than the sun and airless courtyards of the old towns!" What he lost, however, was urban space, and thus the city as a meeting-place. Rowe's analysis of the figure-ground relationship is therefore illuminating, and brings into focus the basic spatial quality of the modern city.

We could illustrate this state of affairs with numerous examples. Particularly interesting is Mies van der Rohe's 1940 plan for the *Illinois Institute of Technology*. Here we see clearly how urban space has become a continuum which is subdivided and articulated by means of free-standing built volumes, which in their juxtaposition make us remember the vertical partitions of the free plans of Mies's houses. The composition is very subtle, and makes use of symmetries, asymmetries, overlapping and changes of height to create rich nuances within a very strict and regular general organization. Because of the varied uniformity of the built form and the relatively small dimensions, a certain enclosing effect is also obtained, and a sense of urban interior is experienced, in spite of the general openness. Thus Mies's solution shows that a free plan may be transferred to the urban scale, if it is done within certain limits and with an understanding of the totality. The epigones however hardly achieved the spatial quality of Mies's compositions or the plastic presence of Le Corbusier's "monuments."[27] In their hands space simply became a series of undefined intervals, and the built form a characterless repetition which did not contribute to any sense of place. As a result, the modern city does not

FAR RIGHT: Jørn Utzon:
Fredensborg housing, Denmark, 1964.
RIGHT TOP: Jørn Utzon:
Birkehøj, Denmark, 1961, project.
RIGHT BOTTOM: Atelier 5:
Siedlung Halen, Bern, 1955-61.

invite you to "walk everywhere, as everywhere is always the same," to paraphrase Colin Rowe's words.

It is a significant fact that the reaction against the dispersed city started within the modern movement itself, and not as a criticism from outside. In 1951 the eighth CIAM conference in Hoddesdon was dedicated to the "core of the city," and the declared aim was "the humanization of urban life."[28] In his introductory address, CIAM's president, J.L. Sert stressed the need for a process of *recentralization*, and thus for "new cores," because "we still believe that the places of public gatherings such as public squares, promenades, cafés, popular community clubs, etc., where people can meet freely, shake hands, and discuss freely are not things of the past and, if properly replanned for the needs of today, should have a place in our cities."[29] After Sert's introduction, Giedion gave a historical exposé of the "background to the core," where he presented Priene, the *forum* of Pompeii, the imperial fora of Rome, Michelangelo's *Capitoline Hill* and the medieval city of Berne. History thus came back as a source of inspiration.[30] At the same conference, Le Corbusier talked about "the core as a meeting place of the arts," and illustrated his words with the projects for St. Dié and Chandigarh. Gropius talked about "the human scale," and presented his *Graduate Center for Harvard University* (1949), where a certain type of semi-urban space, the Anglo-American college yard, was reproposed. The lectures at CIAM 8 were supplemented by a discussion on Italian piazzas, and the social and historical importance of the core was emphasized. However, without exception the projects presented were of the anti-urban type with free-standing buildings in a continuous "green" space.[31] Although the need for an urban environment had been recognized, the spatial consequences were not yet understood.

During the following years, however, true urban spaces reappeared. A first seminal work was realized already in 1953 by Bakema and van den Broek with the *Lijnbaan shopping street* in Rotterdam. The message was immediately understood,

and soon a series of projects were worked out illustrating the aim of giving the pedestrian his "rights." The pursuit culminated with Peter and Alison Smithson's project for Hauptstadt Berlin (1958), where a complete network of urban streets was proposed. Towards the end of the fifties Jørn Utzon also worked out a series of housing schemes possessing figural quality relative to the landscape as well as defined public spaces. In particular we may recall his fine plan for Birkehøj (1958) which shows the place values of a village as well as a built form based on the principle of theme and variation.[32] In Utzon's projects nature is no longer a neutral ground, but a concrete reality with which the settlement interacts. Thus the basic aim of transforming the *site* into a lived *place* is reproposed. In general, Utzon's approach is rooted in Alvar Aalto's organic and regional works, but Utzon took another important step with his general concept of architecture as a "platform" under the sky, that is, as a defined space rather than a juxtaposition of built objects.

As an alternative to Utzon's organic solutions, a more rational and structural approach to the definition came to the fore about 1960. An outstanding example is the neighbourhood unit Siedlung Halen near Berne (1960) by Atelier 5. Here a number of dwellings are organized in grouped rows in such a way that the quality of a true village is regained. The built forms are simple and straightforward, in the "mood" of Le Corbusier's works.

We have already referred to "structuralism" in connection with the development of the free plan, and defined its aim as the realization of "patterns of open growth." Structuralism thus wanted to combine order (conceived as a continuous infrastructure) with freedom (conceived as varied "infill"). The approach was suggested by Louis Kahn during the second half of the 1950s and was taken up by the younger generation a few years later. As characteristic examples we may mention Kenzo Tange's plan for Tokyo (1960), Arata Isozaki's "City in the Air" project (1962), Yona Friedman's "spatial city" (1961),

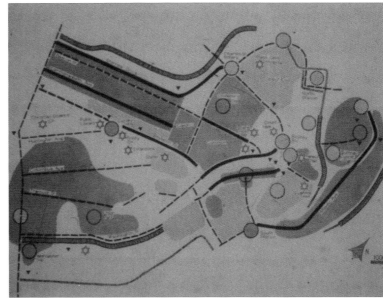

FAR RIGHT: Kevin Lynch:
Analytic diagram, Boston, 1960.
RIGHT: Park Avenue, New York.

Candilis, Josic and Woods' plan for Toulouse-le-Mirail (1962), Archigram's "plug-in city" (1964), and Moshe Safdie's "Habitat" at the Montreal exhibition (1967). Already in the seventies, however, structuralism was on the way out. Why this failure of an approach which seemed to offer so many possibilities? The simple answer is that structuralism did not really represent a new interpretation of the properties of the *city*. Again a concept developed in connection with *buildings* (for example, Kahn's *Jewish Community Center* in Trenton (1954) and Richards' Medical Research Building in Philadelphia (l957 ff.)) is "blown up" to become a city. A city, however, ought to possess a different kind of organization. As a meeting place its nature is topological rather than "structural," and its different kinds of "elements," dwellings and institutions, ought to stand forth as such, rather than being an infill subordinate to a dominant system. Structuralism therefore did not accomplish any recovery of urban space and form.[33] A pattern of open growth may, of course, be concretized as one large collage, but a city is not made that way. In the city many small collages have to be combined to form comprehensive *images* which allow for man's orientation and identification.

The modern city did not satisfy man's need for communal dwelling in a new world. Rather than developing an appropriate spatiality, it took over the free plan of the modern house. Le Corbusier thus considered the traditional city a kind of large "box" which he decomposed into a juxtaposition of free-standing elements, and the structuralists extended the Miesian concept of clear construction to comprise the urban realm as a whole. The lesson of history, however, has taught us that a city has to consist of a continuous *built* matrix rather than a comprehensive void, and that two types of places have to be present within this matrix: defined urban spaces and conspicuous landmarks. The built matrix visualizes the general togetherness of a fellowship, the urban spaces the different kinds of meeting and interaction of its members, and the landmarks their common "agreements" and values. Thus the city

becomes an *imago mundi*. Even in its late, structuralist version, the modern city did not possess this quality. Remaining in principle an "outside" or a monotonous continuum, it did not allow for qualitatively different spaces. Is, then, a modern city based on the free plan and the open form an impossibility? Not at all. The recent development proves that an "open" city is possible, not in the sense of dispersion but of potential, symbolic openness. Today we understand that the demand for a "healthy" environment also comprises the identity of place. Beyond the "essential joys," a healthy city ought to possess the qualities which facilitate human identification.

The development of the modern city

During the 1970s numerous projects and theoretical studies appeared which had the common aim of recreating the city as a meeting-place. An important point of departure was offered by Kevin Lynch in his book "The Image of the City" (1960). Lynch here proves that a city has to "facilitate image-making," that is, it has to possess an imageable form with which we can identify. Lynch moreover shows that this form has to be conceived in terms of "landmarks," "nodes," "paths" and "districts," or, in other words, as monuments, squares, streets and characteristic neighbourhoods. Thus Lynch confirms the lesson of history, and re-establishes the traditional elements of the city.[34]

It took some years before the implications of Lynch's message were understood, but today the idea of the city as place and image is again of primary concern to many leading architects. We could also say that the city is again conceived in terms of architecture, and one of the leading exponents of post-modernism, Aldo Rossi, in fact called his seminal first book *The Architecture of the City* (1966). Whereas Rossi's discussion remains general, Rob Krier aimed at a concretization of the problems in his well-illustrated study *Urban Space*, published in l975.[35] Krier here presents a balanced criticism of the modern city, a thorough analysis of the formal problems of

The Healthy City

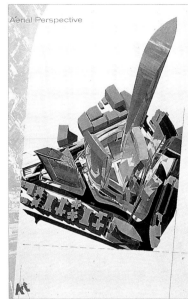

FAR RIGHT: Peter Pran: Kwum Tong
Tower, Hong Kong, 1998, project.
RIGHT: Zaha Hadid: "The Peak,"
Hong Kong, project.

urban space, and a series of valuable proposals for the reurbanization of the city of Stuttgart. The danger involved in these endeavours, however, is an unrealistic pseudo-return to the city of the past, rather than a new interpretation.

This danger is also present in the later urban works of Ricardo Bofill, such as *Les Arcades du Lac* in St. Quentin en Yvelines near Versailles (1975-80). What is lost here are the free plan and the open form, and the urban spaces are even conceived as blown-up buildings.[36] A nostalgic atmosphere therefore becomes dominant, rather than a sense of a simultaneously new and old place.

The possibility of an authentic, forward-looking post-modern urbanism has, however, been proved by certain American architects, notably Charles Moore. His *Piazza d'Italia* in New Orleans (1975-78) is a genuinely modern work in spite of its redundant use of "memories." Moore himself explains his approach thus "We are excited to encourage shapes which might make specific reference to and connect with places and times that mean something to the inhabitant, might help him to know where and when, and by extension, *who* he is." "In the United States we have for decades watched our cities die. . . Now we've discovered that we loved them after all and are trying to breathe new life into them."[37] In *Kresge College* in California (1966-74) Charles Moore and William Turnbull concretized the idea of a post-modern urbanism, creating a whole series of streets and squares, where certain elements play the role of conspicuous landmarks. The formal means employed are continuous screen-walls, broken symmetries, reverse perspectives and coloured super-graphics. Thus the free plan and the open form are set into work, at the same time as a strong identity of place is realized.

In such works the basic elements of the city, the piazza and the street, are given a new meaningful interpretation. Thus the city may again become a meeting-place where man's environmental understanding is gathered. Moore also poses the problem of regional character versus general qualities, and asks the question how we may recover an architectural "language" which enables us to keep and visualize what we have understood. Thus he says: "The spaces we feel, the shapes we see, and the ways we move in buildings should assist the human memory in reconstructing connections through space and time."[38] The city ought to satisfy these aims, but it will only be able to do so if it grows out of a true comprehension of the nature of place and of meaning. This need was already felt by exponents of the modern movement, and was posed as a demand for a "new regionalism" and a "new monumentality."

Unfortunately, however, the present city does not obey these aims. To an increasing extent it consists of corporate buildings of immense size which are architecturally independent of each other. Even if single buildings possess artistic quality, a sense of wholeness is lacking; each building only signals itself and is not related to its neighbours formally or spatially. A few architects have, however, tackled the problem in a promising way, such as the Norwegian-American Peter Pran, whose inflected high-rise structures communicate with the environment, at the same time as their bases are spatially related to the site. Distinguished by a strong sense of movement, Pran's projects moreover remain faithful to the original aims of modernism. [39]

RIGHT: "Strada Novissima,"
Venice Biennale, 1980.
BELOW: Charles Moore:
Piazza d'Italia, New Orleans, 1975-78.

7 *the* New Regionalism

Regional character is a necessary property of any authentic architecture. As all buildings form part of a concrete "here," they cannot be alike everywhere, but have to embody the particular qualities of the given place. From ancient times this quality has been recognized as the *genius loci*,[1] and historical buildings normally had a distinct local flavour, although they often belonged to a general "style." Architecture thus helped man to identify with the "spirit of the place," and offered him a sense of belonging and security.

During its infancy, modern architecture did not pay much attention to regional character. The need for establishing general principles made a certain abstraction from the circumstantial conditions necessary, and building became "international." To get rid of the devaluated symbols of historicism, the new world was taken as the point of departure. It is symptomatic that the first of the *Bauhausbücher* was called "Internationale Architektur."[2] Edited by Gropius himself, it offered a survey of new buildings from many countries, which in spite of their different origin, seemed to belong to the same "family." In the introductory text, Gropius wrote. ". . . the will to develop a *uniform* image of the world characteristic of our time, presupposes that we liberate the cultural values from their individual limitations and endow them with *general* validity."[3] Modern architecture therefore became "objective" in accordance with "international communication" and "international technology." He adds, however, that architecture also ought to remain "national." Gropius did not like the word "style," because he wanted the new architecture to be open and dynamic, but the notion of an "international style," introduced by Henry-Russell Hitchcock and Philip Johnson in 1931, was a true expression of the state of affairs at that moment. And it has ever since remained a useful label to distinguish the main current of the 1920s.

We understand, however, that a one-sided emphasis on the general aspects of architecture necessarily brings about a loss of place. A place has to possess identity, and hence a particular, local character. Considering the word "local," it becomes evident that it does not only denote the qualities of the immediate environment. In fact, we talk about a new "regionalism" rather than a new "localism," and Gropius even used the word "national." This implies that a place always has to gather a world which is larger than its proximal surroundings to be a place in the sense of a "centre." It follows that there are certain basic levels in the gathering process, which are indicated by the words "landscape," "region," "country, "world."[4] Some places gather the whole range, others only (or primarily) the "lower" levels. All places, however, must comprise the lowest level of the immediately given environment. In other words, all places must be rooted or embodied in a concrete "here." How this embodiment may happen today, is the problem of the "new regionalism." So far, we shall only point out that it implies a coming to terms with the *genius loci*, and must be understood in terms of space and form. The problem evidently also comprises the embodiment of the new conception of space.

The need for rootedness was felt quite early during the development of modern architecture. Thus, in 1930, Le Corbusier designed two houses, the *Maison Errazuris* in Chile and the *Villa Mandrot* near Toulon, where he returned to the use of "natural" materials, such as rough blocks of stone and unplaned wood.[5] In his text on the first house, Le Corbusier emphasizes that the materials do not prevent a "modern aesthetic," and in the description of the *Villa Mandrot* he points out that the composition is organized in relation to the landscape. The two houses, however, represent only a very general kind of rootedness; they relate to the landscape and they employ natural (and local) materials, but they do not really embody any regional *character*.[6] When Giedion pointed out that Aalto's architecture is *Finnish*, he evidently intended something more than adaptation to a particular site. Among the works of the first pioneers, only the houses of Frank Lloyd

Alvar Aalto: Villa Mairea.

Wright possess something of a true regional quality. Wright in fact talked about a "prairie style," and considered himself an "American" architect. Later, Aalto adopted an analogous approach. Thus we understand that the "new regionalism" implies something which goes beyond the demand for "context;" primarily it means to become part of a *tradition*, in the sense of offering a new interpretation of certain objects of human identification.

What, then, are these objects? We have already suggested the answer with the notion of *genius loci*. It follows from what has been said above that the *genius loci* cannot be understood in strictly local terms. Since the quality of a place consists in a gathered environment, the *genius loci* comprises more than that which is close at hand. "The buildings bring the earth as the inhabited landscape close to man and at the same time place the nearness of neighbourly dwelling under the expanse of the sky," Heidegger says.[7] What is gathered by a building, that is by a man-made place, is an "inhabited landscape." This landscape is brought close to us and revealed as what it is. A landscape is a space where human life takes place. It is an "inhabited space" between earth and sky. First of all it reveals itself as a certain *Stimmung*. This German word means something like "atmosphere" or "character," and moreover it says that man is *gestimmt*, "tuned," by his environment. A strong natural place, therefore, is a place where the *Stimmung* of a region is particularly evident. A *Stimmung* is, however, something intangible, and needs to be "kept" and embodied. This is done by buildings which reveal the qualities of topography, materials, vegetation, climate and light. Thus, man establishes a "friendly" relationship with his environment, and fulfils the need for "neighbourly dwelling."

How, then, is the *genius loci* kept and embodied? Basically in two ways, which we may call "visualization" and "complementarity." In some cases the buildings repeat and emphasize the qualities of the given place, and we have a case of visualization. In others, they add to the environment something that is lacking, whereby the given qualities emerge as such. Thus they complement what is given in order to establish a meaningful whole. The two modes may also be combined. Visualization is exemplified by Italian hill-top towns which reveal the inherent topographical structure, and complementarity by an enclosed man-made settlement, an "artificial oasis," in the infinite desert.[8] It is important to realize that neither mode is a case of symbolization. Visualization and complementarity produce forms which do not represent anything else, and therefore may be considered fundamental architectural acts. Vernacular architecture is in general based on these modes, but the same also holds true for the great "monuments" of the early civilizations. Thus Heidegger uses a Greek temple to show how a building opens up a world and gives to things their appearance."[9] The forms which are related to a particular region evidently possess similar properties, and become elements of a tradition or "way of building."[10] Symbolization is therefore a derivation from the original act of revelation, and a meaningful language of architecture is not an arbitrary system of conventional "signs," but an interrelated set of visualizations and complementarities. Place is therefore the point of departure of architecture, as well as its goal.

From the beginning, modern architecture wanted to return to its origins, and the question of regional rootedness sooner or later had to come to the fore. Moreover, modern architecture wanted to serve everyday life rather than the expressive needs of a particular political system. Therefore it tended towards what is "ordinary" or truly *concrete*.[11] To conquer the split of thinking and feeling means to leave the abstractions of science behind, and return to the things themselves. Things bring the world close to man, and make it palpable and real. When we say that "life takes place," we imply that life has to be related to an immediate "here." Giedion realized this when, in 1954, he published his article on "The New Regionalism."[12] Here he stressed that "all creative efforts in the contemporary arts have, as their common denominator,

FAR RIGHT: German half-timbered
house, Hamburg region.
RIGHT: German villages, typology.
(Westermans Historical Atlas).

the new conception of space, . . . but each connects it in some way with the region in which it operates."[13] This latter point he illustrated by referring to modern artists of evident regional derivation, such as Piet Mondrian and Robert Delaunay. Giedion also understood that the new regionalism is of particular importance in the "technically underdeveloped areas," or what we today call the "third world." Here meaningful traditions are swept away in no time and substituted by the worst kind of vulgar modernism. Thus Giedion advocated a "regional approach that satisfies both cosmic and terrestrial conditions," or in our terms, "sky and earth," and thus a new kind of *imagination*.[14]

The word "imagination" is certainly of fundamental importance when we consider architecture as a making of places. To keep and embody an environmental character is not an intellectual problem; it rather depends on openness to the qualities of the surroundings, and furthermore the ability to "translate" what is "seen" into meaningful *images*. We could also say that the new regionalism demands a phenomenological rather than a scientific approach. Phenomenology is concerned with what is "near," and thus it links up with the aim of giving architecture a new foundation in man's immediate being-in-the-world.

It might seem that the idea of a new regionalism is pure nostalgia. Present-day urban life is hardly related to a given natural environment. And yet it remains a fact that *life takes place*, and that a site can never die, regardless of how blind man becomes to its qualities. Any authentic architecture therefore comprises the transformation of a site into a place, and thus possesses a regional aspect.

Roots of the new regionalism
The quest for a new regionalism has brought about a keen interest in folk architecture. Being so to speak the "dialects" of building, the vernacular has to a great extent preserved man's immediate reactions to the given natural environment, and

thus the original acts of visualization and complementarity.[15] Although folk architecture was related to ways of life which hardly exist any more, its lessons in terms of space and form are still valid, and constitute an important source of inspiration in the search for "roots." The simple reason is that the regional character remains in spite of all the changes, and the vernacular discloses its properties.

A study of folk architecture reveals a series of basic typologies. The spatial layout of farms and villages in general derives from three basic modes of organization: centralization, succession and clustering.[16] Regardless of where we are in the world, we find one of these modes, or perhaps a combination of them. In Germany a thorough study of villages and farms has been carried out, and the basic types have been designated as *Rundling, Reihendolf* and *Haufendorf*. Norwegian farms show analogous forms, and corresponding names are in general use."[17] If we indicate the types on maps of the respective countries, a meaningful relationship between the layout of the settlements and the regions reveals itself. Clusters tend to belong to hilly and topographically complex landscapes; row formations are usually found in valleys (or along rivers and roads); and regular enclosures (round or square) on flat, extended lands.[18] Thus architecture visualizes and complements the spatial properties of the natural place. Today such meaningful relationships are mostly lost; buildings are scattered, regardless of the site and local tradition.

The built forms reveal an analogous correspondence. The use of massive and skeletal structures is regionally determined, and their combination is found in zones where different types of environment meet. A particularly illuminating example is offered by the varieties of half-timbered construction in central Europe. In the hilly and irregular landscape of Franconia the structure has a picturesque character with numerous subdivisions and curved members. On the open plains of Lower Saxony, on the contrary, it becomes regular and straight. Thus the built form visualizes basic regional qualities, and the

FAR RIGHT: Alvar Aalto: Technical University, Otaniemi, 1955-64.
RIGHT: Charles Rennie Mackintosh: Hill House, Helensburg, 1902.

regular structure of the north-west complements the extended land with a necessary rhythm. The site is, in other words, transformed into a place with which man can identify.

The interior spaces of folk architecture mostly represented a complement to the natural environment. The white rooms of the south offer a necessary relief in a hot, dry climate, while the "rose painted" interiors of Norwegian peasant cottages make life possible during a long, cold, colourless winter. At the same time the interiors allow the given environmental character to emerge. It would carry us too far to discuss how forms such as openings and roofs "gather" and maintain environmental qualities. Let us only suggest that modern architecture would have profited more from a study of these things, than from the abstract exercises of the Bauhaus.

Another investigation which would be of great interest as a preparation for a new regionalism is a study of the relationship between the styles and the region into which they were imported. It is a well-known fact that classical architecture changed when it moved from Italy to central and northern Europe. Classical buildings are different in Paris, London, Berlin and St. Petersburg. But these differences have hardly been described in terms of space and form, or explained in terms of the *genius loci* of the place in question. Let us only point out that the *Stimmung* of the locality evidently influences the general languages of form, just as it "tunes" the people who live there. It should be added, however, that the styles also kept their general identity, a fact which provided for a certain internationalism in nineteenth-century architecture.

Art nouveau was looking for immediate roots, and it is natural that it found inspiration in the vernacular. The different varieties of *art nouveau* are clearly inspired by local traditions, from the sculptural masses of Gaudí, the reminiscences of half-timbered gables in Guimard, to the *Kalevala-memories* of Saarinen.[19] The 1900 Paris exhibition brought all these interpretations of the new art together, and welcomed their regional roots. What has so far hardly been recognized, however, is how some of the major works of *art nouveau* visualize basic environmental characters. Let us look at just two examples. In several of his buildings Gaudí is clearly inspired by the forms of Montserrat, the sacred mountain which acts as the symbolic centre of Catalonia. In his *Palacio Güell* (1885-89), the characteristic massive pinnacles of Montserrat appear as openings in the wall. This "inversion" creates a strange feeling of having *entered* the sacred mountain, and a profound sense of belonging and understanding is evoked. A similarly meaningful experience is offered by the famous living-room window in Mackintosh's *Hill House*, described above.

In general, *art nouveau* teaches us much about the problem of "gathering" environmental qualities, and it has in fact been the subject of keen interest during recent years. Thus modern architecture returns to its origins, after its long period of "exclusion," to use Robert Venturi's word. A bridge between the inclusive works of pre-modernism and the exclusive works of the twenties is represented by Frank Lloyd Wright. In his early works, Wright took environmental qualities as his point of departure, and when he later assimilated some of the ideas of the international style, such as continuous, plain surfaces, flat roofs and large glazed areas, he still conserved his sense of place. This is admirably demonstrated by most of his houses from the 1930s, such as the splendid *Kaufmann House* in Bear Run outside Pittsburgh (*Fallingwater*, 1935) and the enchanting *Hanna House* in Palo Alto near San Francisco (1936). The house is throughout based on an hexagonal grid, which determines all the spaces and movements of the walls. Thanks to the use of 60° and 120° angles, the movement appears more "organic" than in orthogonal plans. As in Wright's early houses, a dominant chimney-stack keeps the spatial composition together. The free planning of the exterior and interior spaces is a real *tour de force*! The houses of Wright are primarily "modern," but also "American," and often regional too, due to a masterly adaptation to various types of site. In his own winter residence and studio, Taliesin West in Paradise Valley

FAR RIGHT: Frank Lloyd Wright:
Taliesin West, Phoenix, Arizona, 1934-38.
RIGHT TOP: P.V. Jensen Klint:
Grundtvig housing,
Copenhagen, 1914-1941.
RIGHT BOTTOM:
Reima and Raili Pietilä:
"Dipoli," Otaniemi, 1961-66.

(1938), he created a wonderful counterpoint to the desert landscape of Arizona and echoed Aalto's contemporaneous "Finnish" works.[20]

Beginnings of the new regionalism

When Giedion called attention to the regional qualities in Alvar Aalto's works, he introduced the discussion with a few pages on the Finnish landscape and the architectural tradition of the country. Here we read: "Finland, covered with its network of lakes and forests, suggests in its structure the days of Creation, when water and earth were first separated."[21] And, indeed, hardly any other European country has preserved a stronger sense of its origins. This sense consists not only in a love for the local landscape, but also in traditions which relate the natural environment to human life. The collection of Finnish legends published in 1835 under the name *Kalevala*, has thus remained the basic source of inspiration to Finnish artists.[22] The *Kalevala*, a poetical synthesis of cosmology and mythology, offers a "complete" basis for human identification and interaction, in the sense that it discloses regional qualities. No wonder that the Finnish art of the last hundred years has been distinguished by a singular power and unity.[23] Eliel Saarinen and Lars Sonck had already realized a truly Finnish architecture about the turn of the century, and their vision has been carried on by Alvar Aalto and his talented successor Reima Pietilä. In the works of the former, the Finnish landscape is "condensed" and visualized. His buildings are a continuation of the environment and make us see and understand, and moreover feel, that we are returning to something real and original that is not in the slightest way nostalgic.

We have already discussed Aalto's handling of space and form, and should just add here that his solutions are "rooted" in the best sense of the word. But they also possess a meaning which is valid outside the Finnish scene. Firstly, they are eminently "Nordic," and thus have something to tell all architects of the northern countries, and secondly they offer an important lesson of general importance about the topological organization of space and the possibility of using the open form to comprise local qualities. In particular, Aalto's works are important at the present time because they are modern *and* regional, and thus tell us that the desired synthesis is possible.

The works of Reima Pietilä pursue similar aims, and his results confirm the promise given by Aalto. The student union building *Dipoli* at Otaniemi near Helsinki (1961-67) was intended as a Finnish building *par excellence*. "There are two kinds of caves, caves of stone and caves of wood. The caves of wood are the dream of the people of the forest," Pietilä said, and added: "A cult is a function. The duty of a cult is to implant. The duty of a cult is to produce a local character, that is, to be something that does not exist elsewhere."[24] Thus Dipoli is dedicated to the cult of the *genius loci*. To gain his end, Pietilä rejected the usual forms of modern architecture, and found inspiration in the given environment. The general outline of the building thus repeats the movement of Finland's lakes and rocks, whereas the subdivision of the windows echoes the rhythm of the surrounding tree trunks. Exterior space enters the buildings and gradually becomes interior, and in the main rooms the image of a "cave of wood" is realized. Here an elementary sense of belonging and protection is experienced, together with the excitement of mystery and discovery offered by continuous spatial variation. A convincing synthesis of defined place and potential openness is set into work.

The regional quality of *Dipoli* becomes still more evident if we compare it with other works of the same period. Whereas Pietilä wanted to satisfy the "dream of the people of the forest," James Stirling in his buildings of the early sixties took the vision of the people of the industrialized world as his point of departure. In the *Engineering Laboratories* in Leicester (1959) and the *University Library* in Cambridge (1964) the characteristic industrial "iconography" of nineteenth-century England reappears, but it is interpreted in a new way that is truly modern.

James Stirling: Faculty of Engineering,
Leicester University, 1960-63.

Even in his first works Paolo Portoghesi wanted to re-interpret some of the basic themes of the Italian tradition. The *ENPAS-offices* in Lucca (1958-62) recall the wall articulation of a Baroque palazzo, while his *Casa Baldi* (1959-61) on the outskirts of Rome also has references to the local landscape and the traditional building materials of the region. When *Casa Baldi* was published in *L'architettura* in 1962, it was severely criticized by the editor of the magazine, Bruno Zevi. And, in fact, it was not easy to fit *Casa Baldi* into any of the architectural currents of the period. The curved walls, which form the most conspicuous elements of the house, may be understood as a further development of the vertical planes and free-standing partitions of De Stijl architecture, whereas the articulate bases and cornices and the undulating roofs have a distinct Baroque flavour. The use of tufa as the main building material relates the house to the vernacular architecture of Central Italy, while certain details, such as the ironwork and furniture, have a sophisticated flavour of *art nouveau*. *Casa Baldi* thus represents a new kind of eclecticism. Portoghesi himself explained that he wanted to design an "ambiguous building, open to many interpretations."[25] In his explanatory text he also emphasized the "value of memory," and pointed out that a true work of architecture cannot exist outside a tradition. He furthermore maintained that the historical references present in *Casa Baldi* do not consist in isolated motifs, but in methods of spatial organization and characterization which are still valid because they are "deeply rooted in each of us." He therefore calls the fear of tradition a "senile idiosyncrasy" which ought to disappear among the architects of the new generation. Together with Robert Venturi, Portoghesi was certainly one of the first to point out the need for a new relationship to place and history, and he confirmed his approach in his autobiographical sketch *Le inibizioni dell' architettura moderna*, where he shows how his works are rooted in childhood experiences of Roman streets and courtyards as well as the tufa valleys of Latium.[26]

During the 1960s and early 1970s there were many other contributions to the development of a new regionalism. In the United States a whole series of architects approached the problem. We have discussed the works of Venturi and the MLTW team, and should just add that both are eminently "American," although their importance is not confined to the national scene. The latter are particularly explicit about aiming for a "rooted" architecture, and in connection with the most successful Sea Ranch on the Pacific coast north of San Francisco (1965ff.) assert: "The *Sea Ranch* was built on a wild exposed coast. Before our arrival, the landscape was grand and very simple. The top of bluffs along the shore form a coastal plain only a few hundred yards wide. Beyond that there is a ridge of low hills . . . The cool wind from the north-east is an almost constant factor here. . . The major problem for human habitation was to get out of the wind and into sunlight . . . The isolation and haunting beauty of the land made development an awesome proposition. Houses which merged politely into the land would seem to provide little sense of security on this wild coast. Houses which stood out too strongly could emasculate those very astringencies which made the land special. What we thought was needed was a limited partnership – not a marriage – between the buildings and the land."[27] We have quoted this text because it illustrates so well the new wish for a regionally rooted architecture. And, as we have pointed out, rootedness here means something more than adapting to a site. The forms and materials used at the *Sea Ranch* evoke a wider range of American meanings, and thus make the place part of a comprehensive context.

In Japan a regionally coloured, modern architecture was also developed after the second world war. The traditional wooden structures and the classical Japanese garden are here related to the free plan and the open form. Owing to the explicit freedom of the historic Japanese house, this reinterpretation did not cause particular problems, and from the outset a natural sense of quality distinguished Japanese

FAR RIGHT: Ricardo Bofill:
Walden II, Barcelona, 1970-75.
RIGHT: Paolo Portoghesi:
Casa Baldi, Rome, 1959-62.

modernism. As typical examples we may mention the *Kagawa Prefecture* in Takamatsu by Kenzo Tange (1955-58), *the ad-ministration building for the Izumo Sanctuary* (1963) and the *Tokoen Hotel* in Yonago (1964) both by Kiyonori Kikutake. During the following years a more freely expressionistic and partly utopian approach was in evidence, and Japanese architecture was somewhat derailed from its regional development.[28]

Among the many contributions to the new regionalism in Europe we may single out the early works of the Catalan architect Ricardo Bofill. Geographically and historically Catalonia is a meeting place, where northern and Mediterranean characters interact and blend. We have mentioned the extraordinary importance of centrally-located Montserrat, which appears as a "thing" in the landscape, strong and unified and simultaneously wild and dramatic. A kind of "natural architecture" is present here; it has served as a model for the builders of Catalonia through the centuries. What are the basic properties of this architecture? In general, Catalan buildings are distinguished by a unified block-like form, to which intensely expressive details are applied. The surface thereby often acquires a vibrant appearance. Proceeding from the ground towards the sky, the expressive details gain in importance, and usually the volume terminates in a serrated silhouette. Usually the blocks contain interior spaces which appear as a kind of "habitable inversion" of the exterior world. Entering an authentic Catalan building therefore becomes like seeing things from their inaccessible "inside." In his large block of flats, *Walden 2*, Bofill has given a new interpretation of these regional and traditional characteristics. Its exterior recalls the figural quality of Montserrat and its particular way of rising towards the sky. The public courtyards are friendlier inversions of the natural image, and offer a strong feeling of meaningful place. Thus Bofill demonstrates that regional character resides in how things *are*, and that a work of architecture may bring them close to man by revealing their essence. In his book *L'architecture d'un homme* Bofill emphasizes the importance of localization, and characterizes his own work as a "brutal protest" against the international style.[29]

After our brief journey, it is natural to return to Scandinavia, where Aalto's message in favour of a new regionalism has been received with particular sympathy. After adhering to the international style during the 1930s, Scandinavian architecture has been in constant search of its roots since the second world war. In Norway the wooden architecture of the past has been used as a source of inspiration, and a "wood award" has been institutionalized to promote the development of a regionally valid modern architecture.[30] Among the winners, Sverre Fehn has distinguished himself as the author of several successful one-family houses, where the basic principles of modern architecture are given a local interpretation.[31]

The Dane, Jørn Utzon enjoys an especially important position among the Scandinavian architects of the post-war years. His fame is first of all due to his prize-winning design for the Sydney Opera House competition (1957), but several of his other works are equally important although they have remained somewhat unknown. In general, Utzon's works have an outspoken "Danish" character, being distinguished by restraint, gentleness and order. Utzon's sense of place reaches far beyond the particular tradition to which he belongs. In 1962 he published an article on "Platforms and Plateaux" where he defined architecture in terms of horizontal platforms and hovering roofs.[32] The concepts represent something much more than a metaphor of rocks and clouds. As visualizations of earth and sky, they give back to architecture its basic "dimension" as an art. The platforms of Utzon make the earth become alive as a concrete *ground*, which simultaneously offers a sense of belonging and possibilities of movement. The platform also makes the inherent qualities of the site emerge by forming a subtle counterpoint to the contours of the land. In Utzon's projects the roof also becomes a manifestation of how human life takes place "under the sky."

The New Regionalism

"The Sea Ranch north of San Francisco was built on a wild exposed coast . . . What we thought was needed was a limited partnership – not a marriage – between the buildings and the land . . ."

FAR RIGHT: Giancarlo de Carlo:
Mazzorbo housing, 1979.
RIGHT: Renzo Piano, Richard Rogers:
Centre Pompidou, Paris, 1971-77.

Utzon thus offers a general method for our understanding of the *genius loci*, and thus facilitates the development of the new regionalism. So far, his ideas have found their most complete and poetically convincing manifestation in the church at Bagsvaerd near Copenhagen (1973-76), which unifies general and local qualities.[33]

Prospects of the new regionalism

The new regionalism which developed during the 1960s, represented a complement and an alternative to the structuralism current at the time.[34] But during the last decade it has somewhat faded, and the architectural debate has rather centred on the need for a general architectural "language" based on archetypal images. The change of emphasis is understandable, but it does not imply that we have abandoned the quest for a new regionalism. When Giedion launched the idea in 1954, he had already ten years earlier published an article entitled "The Need for a New Monumentality."[35] Evidently he considered regionalism and monumentality two aspects of one general problem: the need for *meaning* in architecture. Our discussion of the nature of regional character has shown that any architectural language has to be adapted to local circumstances. A work of architecture comes into existence only when such a concrete, rooted embodiment is carried out. We have also seen that the results of the visualization and complementarity of local qualities may become elements of a tradition which transcends the immediate situation. Moreover, we have suggested that any situation has to be understood in relation to a more comprehensive whole. Regional rootedness therefore does not represent an alternative to a general "typology," but is rather a dimension of any authentic architecture.

Many of the leading architects who are active at the present time have approached the problem of regionalism, and we have centred our survey on Jørn Utzon's general understanding of architecture in terms of earth and sky. It goes without saying that any regional character may be explained in these terms, which represent a concrete version of the general concepts of space and form.[36] As the language of architecture also has to be defined by means of the same terms, we gain a common denominator which unifies the general and the circumstantial.

It is important to realize that the demand for a new regionalism came up within the modern movement itself. Representing a necessary consequence to the wish for a return to the origins, it was a natural phase in the development of modern architecture. Giedion, however, emphasizes that the new regionalism should not be confounded with the German *Heimatstil*. And, in fact, there is a basic difference. Whereas totalitarian regimes excluded the dimension of time, reducing architecture to a set of "eternal" forms, the new regionalism aims at ever new interpretations of the given environmental qualities. Giedion did not talk about a return to regionalism, but about a *new* regionalism. The new regionalism is in other words creative rather than nostalgic.[37]

This ought to be remembered when concrete problems such as the adaptation and rehabilitation of regional thinking arise today. What is intended here is not imitation or static preservation, but what we may call "creative conservation." Let me mention two examples which illustrate the idea of "creative conservation:" Giancarlo de Carlo's *Mazzorbo housing* at Burano near Venice (1979), where the urban qualities of a Venetian village are interpreted in a truly modern way, without falling into imitation and pastiche. An urban example is offered by the Centre Pompidou in Paris by Renzo Piano and Richard Rogers (1977). Here the transparent, linear structure of the French tradition gains a new interpretation; a tradition which goes back to the half-timbered houses and Gothic churches of the Middle Ages, and which reappears in certain classical buildings such as the *Grand Trianon* by Jules Hardouin Mansart (1687), and the iron-and-glass works of the nineteenth century. In this context we should recall the words of Whitehead: "The art of progress is to preserve order amid change, and change amid order."[38]

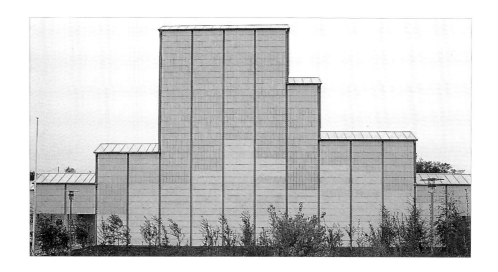

Jørn Utzon: Bagsvaerd Church, Copenhagen, 1973-76.

8 *the* New Monumentality

T he term *monumentality* implies that we expect something more from our buildings than mere "functional" fulfilment. We also want architecture to "mean" something. "The walls rise towards heaven in such a way that I am moved," Le Corbusier wrote, "That is architecture." Sigfried Giedion, who was the first to set out the demand for a "new monumentality," explained the term with these words: "Monumentality springs from the eternal need of people to create symbols for their activities and for their fate or destiny, for their religious beliefs and for their social convictions."[1] The demand for a "monumentality" thus came up within the modern movement itself, as a reaction against certain recognized shortcomings. In 1944 Giedion wrote: "In countries where modern architecture has won the battle and been entrusted with monumental tasks involving more than functional problems, one cannot but observe that something is lacking in the buildings executed. 'Something' is an inspired architectural imagination able to satisfy the demand for monumentality."[2]

Perhaps the word "monumentality" might seem puzzling, but in reality it offers an indication as to what it is all about. The Latin *monumentum* simply means "things that remind," or, in other words, things that have an enduring significance. And so there is no reason to be afraid of "monumentality." But if one prefers to use a less loaded expression, one might say "meaning in architecture." The quotation from Giedion suggests that meanings are expressed by means of "symbols," and symbolization has in fact become a primary concern of the present. As we have already pointed out, symbolization implies the need for a consistent *language* of "images."

But the nature of such a language is not at all clear. Many terms relevant to the problem are used in the present debate, but they are not given any precise definition. What is for instance the meaning of words such as "sign," "symbol" and "image" in relation to architecture, and what is the role of "memory" and "enduring significance" in a world of openness

and change? We shall return to these questions in the last chapter. Here, suffice it to repeat that the making of images is an *artistic* activity, and that the image does not offer a description of the world, but serves to "keep" a total "vision" of how things are. The poetic understanding, which is manifest in the image, is preserved in language. "Language is the house of Being," Heidegger says, and continues, "Man speaks only as he responds to language."[3]

Architecture is a language. As such it keeps the spatiality of the world. The architectural language consists of archetypal images that reveal those structures which are invariable with respect to place and time. The archetypes are not forms which exist in some distant realm as an ideal *Ding an sich.* Rather they represent basic modes of being in the world, "existential structures."[4] As a matter of fact the archetypes do not exist at all, only their various manifestations. A "typical" tower does not exist, but *towerness* is revealed in its multifarious aspects by means of ever new tower-images. Thus the work of architecture becomes "an offering to Architecture." These words of Louis Kahn[5] suggest that it is possible and meaningful to talk about architecture in general although only single works exist.

In the first chapter we asserted that architecture may be understood in terms of "space" and "form;" the first aspect permits life to take place, whereas the second embodies the situational characters involved. Architectural images are accordingly of two basic kinds: spatial or volumetric, and plastic or "built." The first category is understood in terms of geometry, although Euclidean geometry is not relevant. A spatial image becomes manifest in concrete, "lived" space with its directional differences, and therefore demands a kind of "concrete geometry" for its description. Le Corbusier intuited the importance of the spatial images when he defined architecture as "the masterly, correct and magnificent play of volumes brought together in light," but by "volume" he still meant the Platonic solids: "cube, cone, sphere, cylinder and pyramid."[6] The plastic images also become manifest in

OPPOSITE: *Le Corbusier: Notre Dame du Haut, Ronchamp, 1952-55.*

Leon Krier: "Form and content"

concrete space, and are determined by archetypal built forms such as wall, roof, column, beam, arch, pediment and opening. We have already asserted that the meaning of architectural images primarily consists in their mode of being between earth and sky, that is, by their standing, rising, extending, opening and closing. When an architectural image unites spatial and plastic qualities, it becomes an "architectural thing" which forms part of a work of architecture.

There can be only *one* architectural language, since there is only one world and one spatiality. (Analogously there is basically only one spoken language, although there are many "tongues.") The styles represent different choices within one and the same language, or, in Heidegger's terms different responses to Language. Thus we have three systems of images: *language*, which consists of basic Gestalten; *style*, which is a temporal choice among these; and *tradition*, which implies a local adaptation.[7]

Language constitutes the general basis and as such remains "hidden." It reveals itself however through the tradition of a certain locality and the style of a certain historical period. Tradition and style are interrelated; thus a style ought to change when it is translocated, whereas a tradition ought to be "coloured" by the historical period. Folk architecture illustrates well this relation between constancy and change.[8] Our discussion of regionalism showed that the vernacular is valid beyond the immediate situation, and in fact it reveals aspects of the language of architecture, just like spoken dialects, which are the "secret source of any developed language."[9] The regional tradition tells us that the language of architecture has to be set into work here and now, to engender a true work of architecture. The word "now" implies that a style is also part of any embodiment. To set into work means to reinterpret, or rather to make language speak in a way that is simultaneously new and old. The very existence of a limited number of styles demonstrates that reinterpretation is not a continuous, steady process, but happens in "waves." Certain

possibilities inherent in language are thus exploited for a period of time until they are exhausted, and a new kind of interpretation becomes necessary. The tradition, on the contrary, remains as a constant ground for these temporal changes, assuring a necessary *stabilitas loci*. It may also happen that a tradition corresponds so closely to the archetypes, that it may be used outside the place or region where it originated. The "classical" architecture of Antiquity in fact gained this general significance as a symbol system, and we may therefore with justification talk about the "classical language of architecture."

Both the styles and the traditions may be understood as systems of *types*. In order to have an existential foundation, these types ought to be variations on the archetypes of the general language. Basically a type is not a sign or a metaphor, but a relatively stable gathering of a world, which possesses the capacity for adaptation and variation. Two different explanations of the generation of types are usually given. One regards the types as something given *a priori* once and for all, whereas the other considers the types a result of generalization and historical development.[10] In a certain sense both hypotheses are correct. The archetypes are certainly invariable interworldly structures but as such they do not appear. The temporal and local types, on the other hand, are developed and changed through experience and experiment. The important point is, however, as we have already asserted, that they receive their meaning from the archetypes. That is, their *basic* meaning consists in their being variations on a "theme." A "Gothic tower" is a *tower*, but at the same time it is "Gothic," unifying thus archetype and temporal intentions. An authentic work of architecture is therefore always "old" as well as "new."

Modern architecture wanted to return to the "beginning as if nothing had ever been done before." One did not recognize, however, that this can only mean a new interpretation of the archetypes. Rather one found the "beginning" in the single, immediate situation, and history, which contains our

FAR RIGHT: Cheops pyramid,
Giza, Egypt, 2700 BC.
RIGHT: Ulm Cathedral, tower,
1502, completed 19th century.

knowledge of the archetypes, was abandoned. As a result, architecture was particularized, or reduced to a mechanical repetition of deduced "similarities." Functionalism did not accept the existential roots which give architecture its meaning. After some time, however, a sense of uneasiness arose, and the demand for a new monumentality was stated. At the same time a new regionalism was requested as a necessary complement.

Roots of the new monumentality

Architectural history discloses the language of architecture. Any authentic work of architecture makes language "speak," but some accomplish a more significant revelation than others. This becomes evident if we return to the beginning in a temporal sense. In ancient times, architecture was basically local. It arose as a response to a given environment, and the general properties of existential spatiality mostly remained hidden. In some places, however, the given situation made revelations of general importance possible. To understand what this means, it is necessary to go back to Antiquity and look at the development of the first architectural symbol systems.

In Egypt the conditions of the land itself suggest a comprehensive, "cosmic" order. Hardly any other country possesses a geographical structure of such simplicity and regularity. The life-giving Nile flowing from the south to the north and the ever present sun rising in the east and setting in the west, are the basic elements. A pair of orthogonal axes is thus indicated. The south-north direction is furthermore emphasized by the long and narrow Nile valley delimited by deserts on either side. The climate is dry and stable, and together with the regular flooding of the river, it seems to indicate eternal permanence. "Order" and "constancy" in fact denote the fundamental properties of the Egyptian world, and architecture served to give it concrete presence.[11] Stone was selected as the main building material, because it is hard and resistant to decay, and its natural character was enhanced by smooth surfaces and sharp edges. A general system of symbolic organization was developed, in which the horizontal axes are combined with the vertical direction to form a regular and uniform space. In the pyramid this understanding of the world was set into work as a balanced synthesis of vertical and horizontal forces. At the same time its incomparably massive and solid construction seems to embody strength and permanence. The pyramid, however, was the goal of a spatial sequence which comprised two other typical images: the regular hypostyle hall where orthogonal space is fixed and visualized, and the axial causeway which gives directed movement concrete presence. Finally, Egyptian architecture realized the obvious complement to the desert: the artificial oasis of the walled enclosure. A comprehensive inventory of archetypal forms is thus set into work: grid, path, centre and enclosure.

Whereas Egyptian architecture reveals the general organization of existential spatiality, Greek buildings visualize the individual character of particular places. The Greek landscape comprises a great variety of natural sites. Rather than vast expanses and general structures, it consists of defined spaces each of which possesses a distinctive individuality. Fertile plains, dominant mountains, frightening ravines and dramatic promontories seem to embody a variety of natural forces. Intense sunlight and clear air give the forms an unusual presence. In understanding these qualities, the Greeks personified them as gods, and any place with pronounced properties was experienced as the manifestation of a particular god.[12] Places where nature is dominant were thus dedicated to the chthonic deities Demeter and Hera, and places where the environment is experienced as a meaningful whole were dedicated to Zeus. Places where man had come together to form a community, a *polis*, were dedicated to Athena, and places where man put his intellect in opposition to the chthonic forces were dedicated to Apollo. Being conceived in anthropomorphic terms, the gods also represent human characters and thus constitute a bridge between man and nature.

Temples of Hera,
Paestum, 550, 450 BC.

The existential understanding which is expressed by the Greek *pantheon*, was visualized by the temple.[13] Basically, all Greek temples belong to the same "family," and may be described as plastic bodies, where the articulation and detailing determine an appropriate character. This character is "condensed" in the "order," that is, the column and its entablature. In general, Greek columns are anthropomorphic, but according to their proportion, *entasis*, capital and further detailing, the character varies. Thus the column gathers and visualizes a world; the forces of nature and the psyche of man are here interrelated, and not only as local and individual phenomena, but as parts of a meaningful totality. Standing up in space, the column in general makes character manifest as a quality of being in the world. In the temple, the order plays a constituent role, that is, the character it embodies is given a "pure," dominant presence. In other Greek buildings the orders are rather used as "characterizing elements" which do not constitute the structure, but relate it to a world of meanings. Although the orders *are* typical characters, they have to be set into work in buildings. That is, they have to be combined with spatial-volumetric types to make up a work of architecture. (Analogously the spatial types have to be "concretized" by means of the orders.) Here we return to our previous distinction between space and form; the former permitting life to take place, the latter allowing for human identification. The orders endowed Greek buildings with the concrete presence of a "thing." "Thinging is the nearing of world," Heidegger says,[14] and in his essay on "The Origin of the Work of Art" he tells us how the Greek temple opens up a world and at the same time sets this world back again on earth, which itself only thus emerges as native ground."[15] The great achievement of Greek architecture was therefore to unify the local and the general; the Greek orders are rooted in concrete places, but their meaning is universal. When we say "universal," we do not mean "complete." The Greek orders reveal certain aspects of reality, whereas others remain hidden, such as the

geometrical patterns of the Egyptians.[16] This limitation does not, however, reduce the importance of the Greek orders. Because they unite man and nature, they cover basic existential structures, and because of their everyday origin, they are easily understandable. Understanding the Greek orders, we understand basic aspects of the world, or rather, we have at our disposal a powerful means of revelation. The Greek orders correspond to the language of architecture; they enable us to "say" the world, over and over again, and from ever new points of view. They also possess the most important property of an architectural symbol-system: the possibility of translocating meanings from one place to another. The Greeks discovered truth in particular places, and by means of the orders they gathered in their *polis* what they had understood, thus making a true urban culture possible. We understand that the spatial types remain mute until they are "set back on earth" and given presence by means of the orders. Thus "the temple, in its standing there, first gives to things their appearance and to men their outlook on themselves," Heidegger says.[17]

What remained hidden in Greek architecture was to some extent disclosed by the Romans. In their buildings and urban layouts we find both a grand, comprehensive organization with some affinity to that of the Egyptians, and a meaningful use of Greek characters. In addition, the Romans developed types of spatial organization and plastic embodiment of their own. The latter has local roots, and primarily consisted in the conception of interior space as "cave-like," total rooms. In Roman architecture, we find for the first time grand internal spaces and complex groups of spaces. These spaces are covered by vaults and domes which so far had only played a secondary role in building. The local basis for the new spatial images was the ancient tradition of excavating rooms from the soft, volcanic tufa-rocks of the Roman region. The Etruscans, in fact, created entire cities for the dead using the local tufa valleys *(forre)* as "streets" along which continuous rows of facades and chambers are carved into the cliff itself. "The man who

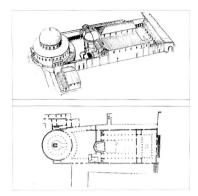

FAR RIGHT: S. Sabina, Rome, 422-32.
MIDDLE: Pantheon, Rome, c.120.
RIGHT: Holy Sepulchre, Jerusalem, 335.

excavates a space in the soft rock does not construct an "opposite" which, like the Greek temple, faces him," Kaschnitz von Weinberg wrote, "he rather penetrates into amorphous matter, and his creative activity consists in making for himself an existential space."[18] These words define well the different approaches of the Romans and the Greeks. The Romans imagined the world as a total, embracing space, organized by means of an orthogonal set of horizontal and vertical axes, and characterized by applied Greek orders. The Pantheon in Rome (120 AD) visualizes this conception in a grand and easily comprehensible way. Here an archetypal image as powerful as the Greek temple makes itself manifest, and the Pantheon therefore became one of the prototypes of western architecture. The *basilica* is another Roman type of basic importance. Here the content is not the structure of the world as such, but man's being in this world as destiny and project, understood as a path which leads him along, on the earth and under the sky. The basilica thus consists of two superimposed zones which accompany the longitudinal axis; the lower is "populated" by anthropomorphic columns while the upper is related to the sky by means of decoration and light entering from above.

In general, Roman architecture developed a coherent system of spatial types which were concretized and humanized by means of the Greek orders. Since the orders were applied rather than constituent, they lost some of their immediate presence. We could also say that they represented "memories" rather than the given here and now. Thus the Roman use of the orders demonstrates that classical architecture is a true symbol system. As such it responds to the language of architecture, and serves to reveal truth. And, in fact, the classical or *Vitruvian* tradition has survived up to the present day.[19]

It is generally recognized that Western architecture is based on two great traditions: the classical and the medieval. If we look more closely into the matter, however, it becomes evident that these traditions do not represent opposed alternatives. When Christian architecture came into existence during the fourth century AD, it took over Roman types, and by means of certain changes in articulation and decoration made them reveal new aspects of reality. The point of departure was the Roman understanding of space as an expression of man's destiny. From the very outset a few profoundly symbolic spatial structures were used for the building of churches: the concepts of "centre" and "path," which were imagined in terms of the Roman rotunda and basilica. The church proper was based on the longitudinal basilica which was interpreted as an expression of the "path of salvation," whereas a centralized space was used when the building task was a baptistery, mausoleum or *martyrium*, that is, the "before" and "after" of earthly life.[20] A pronounced interiority distinguishes all early churches. In the chapter on the public institution we have already referred to the meaningful subdivision of the lateral boundaries into a lower earthly zone, and a superimposed heavenly domain which is "spiritualized" by means of an intended dematerialization. We have also pointed out that the relationship between these realms remained the basic theme of ecclesiastical architecture through the centuries. Sometimes the two are opposed, sometimes integrated, and sometimes they interact in various ways. Thus a temporal understanding of a complete world of earth, sky, man and divinity is concretized, and architecture becomes a true *imago mundi*.

We cannot here describe the different medieval interpretations of the basic typologies, but shall only point out that Romanesque architecture worked with easily imageable compositions of volumetric units, among which the tower emerged as a significant new type. For the first time in architectural history it became an element of primary importance, expressing the existential significance of simultaneous protection and aspiration.[21] We should also add that Gothic architecture gave dematerialization general value. Here the totality of earth and sky is permeated by divine light, which reduces matter to a web of insubstantial lines. In the Gothic style the intentions of Christian architecture reached their fulfilment.

FAR RIGHT: S. Maria della
Consolazione, Todi, 1500.
RIGHT: St. Ouen, Rouen, 1318.

The spiritualized space imagined by the early Christians had finally, after a long development, become an immediate presence. The Gothic cathedral thus unifies the basic modes of spatial organization (centre and path) and the basic volumetric elements (nave and tower) into one total image, which relinquishes the opposition between earth and sky. This symbolic unity is transmitted to the community through a "transparent" structure. The church as a type thus tended towards "self-realization" through a process of variation and reinterpretation.

The "rebirth" of classical forms during the fifteenth century did not represent an abolition of the Gothic image, but rather a desire to widen its scope by reintegrating what it had left out: the anthropomorphic classical members and the elementary geometrical patterns of spatial organization. Like his medieval predecessors, Renaissance man believed in an ordered universe and in divine perfection. But his interpretation was different. The "logic" of Gothic architecture visualizes the hierarchy of parts explained by scholastic philosophy,[22] whereas in Renaissance buildings we encounter the logic of an eternal geometrical order. Perfection of form thus replaced symbolic integration. According to Alberti, the most perfect and most divine form is the circle, and centralized buildings therefore came to visualize cosmic order. The return to classicism also implied that every part of the building should appear as a clear, easily recognizable and relatively independent form. As a result, Renaissance space became homogeneous, and the buildings of the period static, self-sufficient compositions, where "nothing might be added, taken away or altered, but for the worse" (Alberti). It would carry us too far to discuss the further development during the sixteenth and seventeenth centuries. It must suffice to point out that Mannerist and Baroque architecture revealed the expressive potential of the classical tradition.[23] The basic spatial types did not really change, although new modes of organization were introduced. The classical orders were moreover used for obtaining ever new interpretations of the relationship between man, nature and the divine.[24] Thus the history of architecture from the Renaissance to the late Baroque furnishes particularly illuminating material for our understanding of typology and style.

Our brief historical survey has served the purpose of demonstrating that European architecture has always been based on spatial types as well as a generally valid system of classical forms. The architecture of the Middle Ages does not represent an exception; rather than offering an alternative to natural, anthropomorphic presence, its dematerialized forms presuppose the classical types. "An order must exist before it can be broken," and when Gothic architecture "spiritualized" bodily form, it still recognized this form as part of reality. The Renaissance and the Baroque moreover demonstrate that "classicism" and "medievalism" may be combined to form a comprehensive image, as is exemplified by the ensemble of St. Peter's piazza and church in Rome. In general, the monumentality of the past consisted in a revelation of basic interworldly structures. According to the historical situation different aspects of these structures were disclosed. This tension between the general and the circumstantial is in fact what makes a work meaningful.

Until the end of the eighteenth century the language of architecture was understood and revealed through artistic expression. A type was not considered a fixed ideal, but a kind of living, complex thing which, within certain limits, offered an infinite possibility of variation.[25] When the analytic-scientific attitude of the Enlightenment was adopted by architects and theorists, an important change took place. For J.N.L. Durand architecture became a mechanical putting together of fixed elements of a quasi-abstract nature. These parts constitute a set of models to be imitated, and are arranged with the aid of similarly abstract axes and networks. The notions of character and image are thus abandoned and superseded by mere quantification.[26] The classical orders were degraded into

*Jørn Utzon: Opera House,
Sydney, 1957ff.*

superficial decoration, and "style" became something added arbitrarily to the building *a posteriori*. "Durand's work anticipated the nineteenth century's theoretical approach to architecture: a knowledge based on history as a quarry of available material, supported by an idea of composition, elaborated and later formalized in the Beaux-Arts architectural system . . ."[27] Architectural design was thus reduced to a question of models and handbooks. It was against this degeneration that the pre-modern movement launched its attack, and as late as 1944 Giedion still mentioned Durand as a typical exponent of "paper architecture."[28] Meaning in architecture had been thoroughly devalued and a new beginning appeared necessary. We understand, however, that the modern movement did not distinguish clearly between a true existentially founded typology and the mechanistic caricature offered by the academies.

Towards a new monumentality

We have already referred to *art nouveau* as an attempt at conquering the shortcomings of academic architecture, and have pointed out that it used natural forms as well as local traditions as a source of inspiration. We have also suggested, however, that *art nouveau* did not succeed in developing a generally valid symbol system. It is significant to note that a new classicism therefore came to substitute the failing *art nouveau,* in part introduced by the *art nouveau* masters themselves, such as Olbrich, Behrens and Hoffmann. But the more radical exponents of the new architecture could not accept a revival of "styles," and aimed at a return to "origins." As a result the free plan and the open form were developed to substitute the devaluated forms of academic historicism. Our discussion of these principles has demonstrated their architectural potential and meaningful relationship to the new open world.[29] We have also shown that they are rooted in the past, and represent a further development of traditions of spatial organization and formal articulation. Thus they

respond to the language of architecture. Furthermore we have mentioned that the pioneers of the modern movement in many cases had a positive attitude to history. Le Corbusier repeatedly referred to the past in *Vers une Architecture*; Mies van der Robe praised the "wooden houses of old," and Frank Lloyd Wright was profoundly influenced by the Japanese house. Finally, Giedion, introduced the concept of "constituent fact" to show how Borromini, Guarini and other masters of the past had paved the way for modern architecture. But a basic element was still lacking: *the architectural image*. Only when modern buildings became numerous was it realized that the *pilotis*, the strip window and the guiding, free-standing wall were no real images. Le Corbusier's use of elementary volumes did not seem to help much either. A feeling of having lost something thus came about, as shown by the quotation from Giedion at the beginning of this chapter.

When the demand for a "new monumentality" arose, the first attempts at arriving at an answer led to a new kind of expressionism, initiated by Le Corbusier's church at Ronchamp, which certainly seeks to be an image and a symbol. But somehow it does not fully succeed. Ronchamp is undoubtedly a great work of art because it gathers a rich world of meanings and is capable of moving us, yet it remains a *unique* solution with no typological value. The same might be said of the various attempts of Eero Saarinen to express the "nature" of different building tasks.[30] Alvar Aalto to some extent succeeded in introducing architectural "themes" capable of variation, but here also the relation to the archetypes is weak.[31] Jørn Utzon's definition of architecture as a concretization of being between earth and sky opens up for a recovery of the archetypes, but the solutions to particular tasks still give emphasis to what is unique. Thus modern architecture has tended to oscillate between abstract generalization and atypical particularization.

What, then, is the nature of a universally valid architectural image? In general we may say that a built form becomes such

"It is undoubtedly a great work of art because it gathers a rich world of meanings and is capable of moving us, yet it remains a unique solution . . ."

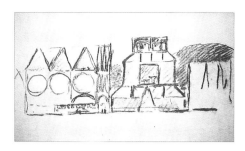

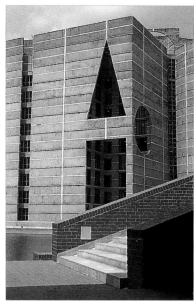

FAR RIGHT AND MIDDLE BOTTOM:
Louis Kahn: National Assembly,
Dacca, 1962ff.
MIDDLE TOP: Louis Kahn: Dominican
Sisters Convent, 1965-68, project.
RIGHT: Aldo Rossi:
"Architectural typologies."

an image when it reveals a typical way of being between earth and sky, or, in other words, a basic structure of existential spatiality. We have mentioned the pyramid, the dome, the pediment and the arch as examples of such images. They reveal general relationships between down and up, here and there, outside and inside, and are at the same time easily recognizable. A complete column with capital and base is also an image, whereas a base and a capital by themselves are only fragments of an image, or "element." We could also say that the above-mentioned forms are images because they possess a place-creating potential. Any place reveals a particular relationship of earth and sky, and is constituted by architectural images. The loss of the image therefore brings about a loss of place, and hence a "loss of life."

The first architect of the post-war period who attempted a recovery of authentic architectural images was Louis Kahn. Kahn used to say that the only volume of an encyclopedia that really interested him was "volume number zero." He also said that he loved beginnings." It seems fair to interpret these statements as expressions of a desire for a return to the archetypes, that is, for a return to what was there "before" history and "before" the styles.[32] And in fact, in his works many of the basic images reappear in a kind of "original" state. Sometimes we are reminded of Egyptian structures, and often of Roman buildings stripped bare of their Greek characterization. Thus we fully agree with Vincent Scully, who, in his early monograph on Kahn, wrote: "The impression becomes inescapable that in Kahn, as once in Wright, architecture began anew."[33] In certain works such as the project for a Convent for the Dominican Sisters in Media, Pennsylvania, we really feel that ancient themes have been given a new, valid interpretation.

Yet still something is lacking. Kahn's images are certainly related to the archetypes, and they are easily recognizable, but they do not constitute a symbol system which responds to the language of architecture. They do not, like the Greek

orders, allow for variation, combination and translocation of meanings.

Two architects have contributed in a particularly decisive way to the recovery of the typical image: the American Robert Venturi and the Italian Aldo Rossi. We have already discussed Venturi's use of "conventional elements" and his conception of the building as a "decorated shed." We have moreover pointed out that his return to imagery represents a new interpretation of the open form, and hence a further development of *modern* architecture.[34] Let us add only that Venturi does not treat the basic forms of the past as fixed models. To him they are true types open to reinterpretation. Not only does he use them in a new context, but transforms the image into a sign of itself. Venturi thus asserts that "we cannot construct historical architecture today," but, "we can represent it through appliqué or sign." The resulting independence of form and function is in the interest of a more effective functionalism, because our "allowing form and function to go their separate ways permits function to be truly functional," at the same time as we do not have to "falsify" structure. What is here advocated bears a certain analogy to the use of characterizing "fictitious" orders in Roman, Renaissance and Baroque architecture, and Venturi in fact considers himself an "architect who adheres to the classical tradition of western architecture."[35]

Some of those who have taken up Venturi's approach have succeeded in realizing an architecture where the language of architecture is again "speaking."[36] Common to all of them is the recovery of basic types of spatial definition and plastic articulation in connection with modern collage-like openness. Thus they do not copy the historic elements, but as a matter of principle give them a new appearance through devices such as inversion, augmentation, stylization and erosion. A sense of nostalgia is therefore hardly present in their works, but rather the courage to face the interrelated realities of past and present.

Frank Gehry: Solomon Guggenheim Museum, Bilbao, 1997.

Rossi and his followers, on the contrary, represent a radical break with the modern tradition. Rossi deliberately shuns the *plan libre* and returns to neo-academic compositions based on abstract, elementary volumes. His point of departure is a desire for a typology which is commonly understandable and which may help us to recover the city as a "work of art."[37] We cannot but agree with this aim, and with his correct distinction between "type" and "model." Thus he says: "The type is the very idea of architecture, and constitutes what is closer to its essence."[38] In his works he therefore uses cubes, prisms, triangular prisms, cylinders, cones, semi-spheres and pyramids as elementary "pieces." Although some of them are given slight overtones of local memories, they are not articulated with reference to earth and sky. Rather they seem to exist in a realm which is outside time and place. In spite of his use of basic images, Rossi's architecture therefore appears strangely unreal. The embodiment in the here and now is almost entirely lacking, and thus his compositions do not allow for orientation and identification, and for life to take place. Rossi's approach has undoubtedly a certain affinity to the "typical" architecture of the totalitarian regimes of our century, which also excluded the temporal dimension, and visualized a nostalgic dream of an ideal past, not to say a lost paradise.[39]

In general, the antinomy between the approaches of Venturi and Rossi stems from the split of feeling and thinking of our epoch. Venturi represents the artistic side, and aims at expressing those complexities and contradictions which can be grasped only by means of the work of art. Rossi, on the contrary, carries on the pseudo-scientific attitude which stems from the Enlightenment, and which led to the academic architecture of the nineteenth century. In fact, Rossi and his followers call themselves "neo-rationalists."[40] Architecture cannot, however, be based on mere reason. Typology is not architecture, and before it can become a useful aid in our pursuit of meaning, it has to be freed from the rationalists' world of abstractions and brought back to the concrete world of

phenomena. This does not mean that we consider the language of types a matter of mere feeling, but rather that it ought to have an existential foundation, where thinking and feeling are united through a phenomenological understanding of the world which relates the given to the archetypes. On the basis of this understanding the new monumentality may become a true embodiment of the archetypes in the here and now.

Such an embodiment also implies a meaningful relationship to the given environment. That is, a certain regional tone should be present, at the same time as the institution should form a continuation of the urban tissue. To repeat: "monumentality" and "regionalism" belong together and make up the dimension of *meaning* in architecture.

Today, however, we experience a different approach: the institutions are becoming monuments to the architect who designed them, rather than expressions of common agreements and values. The competition organized in 1996 by the Vatican for "The Church of the Jubilee – Year 2000" on a site in Rome, may serve as a typical example (cf. *Ecclesia* 6/96). None of the six entries bears any relation whatsoever to the *genius loci* of Rome, and certainly not to the basic spatiality of the church. An incredible degeneration in architectural understanding hence becomes manifest, a degeneration promoted by the Roman Catholic church itself! The only project which possesses spatial qualities is the one by Frank Gehry, whose somewhat conventional plan is organized within his characteristic twisted volumes. In this case the strained forms may have a certain meaning, contrasting with the schematism of the adjacent blocks of flats. However, since Gehry, uses the same kind of distorted volumes everywhere regardless of place and task, the meaning dissolves into nothingness. His personal exhibitionism culminated with the *Guggenheim Museum* in Bilbao (1997), which is a *tour de force* of arbitrary invention.

9 *the* New Place

The aim of modern architecture is the creation of a new *place* where modern life may "take place." During the nineteenth century the industrialized world was becoming a fact. New means of production, new demographic patterns and new socio-political structures were coming into existence. In short, a new way of life had to be accepted and mastered. New forms of understanding and participation were thus needed, in addition to the solution of practical problems. To dwell does not mean only shelter, but a sense of belonging and meaning. To experience existence as *meaningful* may in fact be considered the basic human need; and meaningful existence presupposes a meaningful place which is commonly shared.

Modern architecture from the very beginning was concerned about meaning. Early pioneers such as Frank Lloyd Wright, Henry van de Velde, Adolf Loos and Hendrik Petrus Berlage, denounced the "lies" of historicism, and demanded a new, authentic architecture. The point of departure of the modern movement, therefore, was not primarily problems of function and technology, but the demand for "honesty." Thus Giedion wrote: "According to the easy explanation that was advanced later, the movement developed as the application of two principles: the abandon of historical styles, and consequent upon this the use of 'fitness for purpose' as a criterion. The explanation is correct, inasmuch as both these factors were involved, but it does not go far enough. The movement took its strength from the moral demands which were its real source. The cry went up, 'Away with this infected atmosphere!'"[1]

As a consequence, the modern movement gave much attention to questions of "honesty" and "morality," and in general aimed at the recovery of authentic and original forms which could substitute the "devalued symbols" of historicism. Thus the movement developed the general principles of "functionalism" and "structuralism" believing that the expression of function and structure would generate new meaningful forms.

To some extent the promise was fulfilled. On closer scrutiny, however, it becomes evident that the successes of modern architecture were not due to functional analysis and structural innovation. What is valid in modernism rather stems from a new artistic vision which grasps the basic qualities of the new world.[2] Giedion understood that, and asserted that the "new sensibility" was the real source of modern art. The new sensibility, however, is a rather vague concept, and needs to be substituted by a more precise theory of meaning. In the past, meaning was a matter of language, style and tradition, and hence a commonly shared possibility. The modern movement, on the contrary, believed that meaning would arise spontaneously from the single situation, and the "new tradition" was intended as a "method" rather than an interpretation of the language of architecture. Today we realize that meaning demands a more general understanding of the world, as well as a language of forms for its expression.

Post-modern architecture therefore concentrates its attention on the problem of meaning. So far, it seems to be generally agreed that meaning has to do with *images* rather than functional or structural forms. A form is meaningful because it "represents" something, because it tells us something, and because it helps our orientation in an identification with the world in which we live. The nature of the image is, however, hardly understood. Many post-modernists regard it as a "sign," that is, an arbitrarily chosen element which "signifies" something else. According to semiological theory the language of architecture becomes "a system of agreed-upon rules to communicate."[3] Evidently, architectural forms may function as signs, but their meaning cannot be reduced to a mere matter of "agreement," and their purpose to interpersonal communication. Basically, an image is not a sign. An image reveals rather than communicates; it illuminates and explains.

Human understanding implies *stability*. One cannot understand without recognizing, and one only "stands under" if the things are known. In fact, we have pointed out that man has

OPPOSITE : Ricardo Bofill: Pyramid, Le Perthus, Catalonia, Spain, 1976.

*Giglio Castello, Island of
Giglio, Italy (medieval village).*

to "keep" the transient world of phenomena to which he belongs, and we have suggested that the total "vision" of how things are, is kept by works of art. Art therefore "opens up" a world and enables man to "dwell." We have also asserted that art fulfils its task by means of images, which are complex and unanalyzable totalities. Let us repeat Heidegger's words: "Only image formed keeps the vision. Yet image formed rests in the poem."[4] What, then, is such a vision? In general it recognizes a thing as what it is, that is, in its "thingness." With this term we do not intend a generalized concept or an archetypal *idea*, but the gathering of a world, which means the relationship of the thing to other things. When the thingness of things is disclosed, the world becomes meaningful; what was there as transitory impressions is kept and explained. A vision, a perception, in the widest sense of the word, needs an image to become "real." Rilke understood that when he said that the "things that live only in passing, . . . look to us for rescue," and that we are therefore here to "say" them.[5] Our task as humans is to keep the world by means of images. Thus we "rescue" the things that constitute the world, and find our own identity. Human identity consists in what one has "seen," and "kept" in the "image formed." Hence the image reveals a world.

An explanation, however, is never complete. When an image reveals certain aspects of a thing, others remain hidden. Truth, thus, is simultaneously disclosure and concealment, as the Greeks recognized in their concept of *alétheia,* and not an adequation between perception and object. "When I paint a sea shell on a gravel bank," Andrew Wyeth says, "it is all the sea – the gull that brought it there, the rain, the sun that bleached it there by a stand of spruce woods."[6] Thus the image makes a world visible. Another painter would have revealed different aspects of this world. In general the image keeps what has been seen, and is therefore a *recollection*.

The Greeks understood the true nature of the image. To them, *Mnemosyne,* memory, was the mother of the Muses,

with Zeus as the father. Zeus thus needed memory to bring forth art. Mnemosyne herself was the daughter of the earth and the sky, which implies that the memories which give rise to art are our understanding of the relationship between earth and sky, and our own being in this "between." Neither earth alone nor sky alone produces a work of art. Being a goddess, Mnemosyne was both human and divine, and her daughters were hence understood as the children of a complete world: earth, sky, humans and divinities.[7] The poetic image is therefore truly integral, and radically different from the analytic categories of logic and science.

We understand moreover that an image is something different from a "sign." When Wyeth painted the shell, he did not make a sign for something. His image does not signify "shell," and still less "sea or gull." Rather it evokes a world. In a certain sense, it *is* its world. A world becomes present in the image, directly and without any mediation. Whereas a sign is part of a code, that is, a system which may be constructed or dissolved *ad libitum*, the work of art speaks to us without our knowing any particular man-made code. The world, as a world, is therefore only known as art. Art embodies truth. "*Was bleibt aber, stiften die Dichter,*" Hölderlin says, "what remains is founded by the poets."[8] Everything else is an abstraction from reality. A system of signs is based on abstraction, and serves communication rather than revelation. The artistic image, therefore, cannot be understood semiotically, and it is deplorable that the present discussion on "meaning in architecture" has got stuck in the impasse of semiology.[9] We also ought to emphasize that the image does not "imitate" reality. The work of art "is" reality. The ancient theory of *mimesis*, in fact, does not explain the image as a gathering, and therefore fails in making us comprehend the nature of imagery.

In *The Thinker as Poet* Heidegger offers the necessary explanation with the help of a poem:

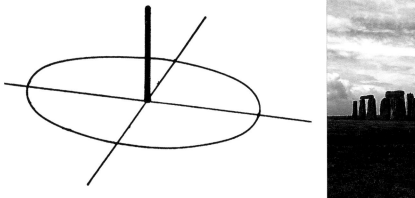

FAR RIGHT: Stonehenge,
Salisbury Plain, England
RIGHT: The structure of
existential space (CNS).

Forests spread
Brooks plunge
Rocks persist
Mist diffuses
Meadows wait
Springs well
Winds dwell
Blessing muses.[10]

Here language speaks. It speaks about the world and reveals its nature. Fortunately it is possible to make many true statements about forests, brooks and rocks, and Heidegger's words are therefore selective. But they are not arbitrary, and they do not abstract from the given phenomena. Rather they penetrate to their core, and reveal basic and easily understood *meanings*. Thus they make the things stand forth as such, and by bringing them together in a poem, each of them helps the others to emerge. We have called this emerging of things by means of images "visualization."

When man makes language speak about things, however, he usually does not tell only how they are, but also how they *could be*, that is, how he would like them to be at that moment. In speaking about things thus, a "dream" or "project" is generally present. To reveal how things could be, means to add something they are "lacking." A lack, however, is not foreign to the thing, but rather something which belongs to its hidden nature. Image-making therefore does not mean only visualization, but also "complementarity." It is what the situation lacks, which sets the historical process in motion, and makes ever new interpretations necessary.

We have used the word "spatiality" to denote the mundane structure which is visualized and complemented by architecture. The basic lack in the spatiality of the world is the empty space between earth and sky. That is where architecture occurs. Although this in-between space is empty, it is structured. The structure is determined by earth and sky, and is general as well as local. The general aspects are the archetypal pattern of spatial organization (topological, geometrical) and the archetypal characters (*Stimmungen*) of localities. The local structures are variations on the archetypes. To allow human life to take place in this structured emptiness, architecture has to adapt to the spatiality of human life itself. Also here we have to do with general as well as circumstantial structures, the latter being temporal. The general aspects consist of the archetypal patterns of spatial behaviour (centre, path) and the archetypal sentiments (*Stimmungen*) of the psyche. The temporal structures are variations on the archetypes.

When a work of architecture visualizes the structure of earth and sky and complements what is lacking, a total world is brought into presence, and the site is transformed into a *place*. That is the meaning of Heidegger's words: "The buildings bring the earth as the inhabited landscape close to man and at the same time place the nearness of neighbourly dwelling under the expanse of the sky." What is brought close, what is revealed, is not just a landscape, but an "*inhabited* landscape." The place which is constituted by the buildings thus comprises man, not only in the sense that it allows him to act, but because it embodies his being-in-the-world.[11] Thereby the momentary action becomes part of *life*, it gets a "measure" and a meaning, and man may say that he *dwells*. To create places which permit dwelling is the profound task of architecture. It can only be fulfilled when architecture is intended as an *imago mundi.*

Place as image

Human life takes place. Its taking place, however, does not occur in infinite kinds of places. Basically, there are three major categories of such places, which correspond to three basic modes of being in the world. We may call these modes private or personal life, public life, and collective life, and the corresponding places "house," "institution" and "city." In previous chapters we have discussed the fundamental properties of these categories and should just add a few words about how they may gain the quality of place, that is, of *imago mundi*. In addition we should also discuss how the three categories are interrelated, and how they relate to the language of architecture. Finally, we have to consider the findings in relation to the ends and means of modern architecture.

The house serves daily, personal life. Its nature is circumstantial, and its form is related to local and temporal conditions. This does not mean, however, that all houses are entirely different. Any situation represents a variation on the general structures of the world, and it is therefore meaningful to consider the house an *imago mundi*. We have already referred to the original connection between floor, ceiling (roof) and wall on the one hand, and earth, sky and horizon on the other. The earth, the sky and the horizon which are visualized by the house are local rather than general. Thus the house primarily complements the deficiencies of the *site* and makes what is close at hand emerge. It constitutes a concrete, individual "here," and allows life to take place "now." In the past, however, the concrete "here" became *typical*, because "neighbourly dwelling" implied the sharing of a site and a way of life. Vernacular houses therefore appear as variations on types, and visualize a particular "inhabited landscape." Together they make up a meaningful place, and their constituent parts – floor, roof and wall – possess the quality of images.

In general a domestic image is simultaneously an image of the spatial structure of man's being-in-the-world and of the given environment. It grasps correspondences (*übereinstimmungen*) between the two structures, or adds what is lacking, to create a "friendly" interrelationship. On the human side we find the simultaneous needs for refuge (shelter) and point of departure. The first need is in general satisfied by enclosure, and generous embracing roofs have in fact always been distinctive of human dwellings. The shape of the roof varies in relation to the given environment, and serves to adapt the house to its surroundings through visualization or complementarity. Inside the houses, refuge may for instance be expressed by means of the vertical axis of a centrally placed hall, which may be given emphasis by a set of posts visualizing the symbolic "core."[12] It may also be expressed by the simpler means of alcoves (sometimes vaulted), and inglenooks and fireplaces. The chimney is a particularly important exterior image of the dwelling, because of its gathering of domestic fire and vertical axis. The expression of the house as an existential point of departure is for instance taken care of by images such as projecting roofs, verandas and bay windows. The latter may also be understood as a simultaneous embodiment of shelter (alcove) and opening (projection). The double-function refuge-point of departure demands windows which are small as well as large, that is, a varied and "irregularly" distributed set of openings.[13] The domestic floor, finally, should simultaneously unify the house with the ground and indicate possible centrifugal movements.[14] The reason why the *gable* has served as a domestic image *par excellence* in many parts of the world, is probably that it unifies embracing shelter and potential openness. A pyramid, on the contrary, primarily means shelter, or a final point of arrival. The gable also indicates the cardinal points, and was in ancient times related to the concepts of *cardo* and *Irminsul*.[15] In general, the image of the house is distinguished by a certain informality and complexity. The general structures of spatiality (regular symmetries and rhythms) are only suggested, and the character is local and personal. When a house is directly related to a natural site, the echoes of a general order are primarily found inside, whereas an urban dwelling may show a measure of exterior public order and a more informal interior.[16]

As a place, the house offers a sense of rootedness; it belongs to the locality and makes it emerge as what it is. Today, the typical "neighbourly dwelling" has lost most of its meaning. The houses of a modern suburb do not form any community, and the single unit either expresses the private "dreams" of the owner, or is a standardized solution which could have been located anywhere. And yet all sites possess distinct properties, and each person is subject to the basic patterns of being-in-the-world. A phenomenological understanding of these factors ought therefore to help the coming into existence of meaningful domestic images, even in our time.

The public *institution* serves the agreements of a fellowship. That is, it is not just a functional container, but should offer an "explanation" which relates the way of life of the community to the general structures of the world. The institution is therefore an *imago mundi* in a very significant sense. Not only do its floor, ceiling and wall represent the earth, the sky and the horizon, but these parts ought to be treated and interrelated in a systematic and expressive way. The word "landmark" indicates well the explanatory focal function of the institution within the built environment. When institutions are added to the dwellings, what is merely suggested becomes significantly and clearly revealed, and the place emerges as a forum for the life of a fellowship. Although the public institution ought to possess a certain measure of local character, it is not primarily a function of the site and circumstantial life. Rather it relates to the immediate "here" to a more distant "there," and makes the locality become part of the world. To satisfy this aim, the institution ought to possess a conspicuous place-creating image quality.

Like the house, the public institution is simultaneously an image of existential spatiality and of the given, local environment. Here, however, the general properties of centre and path ought to be emphasized rather than their situational adaptation. And at the same time the built form ought to visualize basic mode of standing, rising, extending, opening and closing. Thus the institution reveals the fundamental structure of spatiality. Our brief historical survey in the last chapter showed how the Egyptians concentrated their attention on systematic, geometrical organization, the Greeks on local and individual characters, and the Romans on space as

an "interior." In Early Christian architecture, finally, man became a partaker, and what so far had been a disclosure of the environment as such, was transformed into a *lived* space. Thus the concept of place as the embodiment of a complete world of earth, sky, humans and the divine was set into work. No wonder that the church remained the public institution *par excellence* for centuries, and that its image became synonymous with place and civilization.

The basic images of the institution are, as we have already pointed out, the great unitary hall (centralized, longitudinal or gridded), and the distinct volume, such as the tower and the dome. In the past, public buildings were generally conceived as compositions of such volumes. As an example we may point to the larger Romanesque churches.[17] One of the reasons why modern public buildings have lost much of their meaning is certainly that they are conceived in terms of functional pattern and "expressive" structure rather than volumetric image. It is the image, however, which visualizes the general spatiality of the world, and thus gives the institution its quality. We do not have to expand on what has already been said about the modes of standing, etc., but should emphasize that the articulate built form of the public institution reveals how an historical epoch understands its being between earth and sky.

The *city* gathers the various existential interpretations of a collectivity. It is therefore pluralist rather than unitary, and when we say that it constitutes a goal in existential space, it is because it offers *possibilities* rather than a particular explanation. As an *imago mundi* it is complex and even contradictory, and makes man realize that life consists of choice and project. But it also has to be rooted in a locality and constitute a centre which makes a region emerge as what it is. In the past, the regional qualities were more pronounced than today, but even then the city always made a more distant world manifest. Because of its local rootedness, the city may be considered a "large house" (Alberti), but this definition does not convey its quality as a meeting-place.

Michelangelo:
Capitol Hill, Rome, 1536ff.

The image of the city is already a generally known concept, thanks to the studies of Kevin Lynch. Lynch has shown that a conspicuous image quality is necessary to make the city fulfil its function. Thus it ought to possess figural quality in relation to the landscape, that is, have a defined delimitation and a coherent fabric, and it has to consist of identifiable urban spaces which are related to explanatory "landmarks." Traditionally, the city wall, the continuous street, and the enclosed square (market) were the primary images which constituted the city as a place. Sometimes the urban spaces may become explanatory elements in their own right, and thus fulfil the function of a public institution. Michelangelo's *Capitoline Square* is an early and significant example.[18] Most of the traditional images of the city are lost today, with a loss of the place as a "milieu of possibilities" as a result. To recover the image of the city is therefore an urgent task.

As an assembly of institutions and dwellings, the city visualizes the relationships between the different categories of buildings. We have suggested that the houses and the public institutions ought to belong to the same "family," in the sense of formal appearance, with the latter serving as explanatory foci. To avoid misunderstandings, we should add that the city certainly also comprises buildings which do not directly belong to the categories mentioned above. Places for work are particularly important among these. The kind of togetherness which is here taking place may be understood as an extension of the dwelling, without however gaining the quality of an agreement. A meaningful relationship between various categories of buildings presupposes a common language of forms, which refer to the general, local and temporal aspects of the world which are gathered by the city. By means of this language, meanings are translocated and brought together to form the complex gathering which is the essence of the urban place. The images which constitute the architectural language are in part atemporal, and some of them have been described above. Atemporal images are necessarily abstract, and have to

be adapted to the here and now. This also holds true for the classical language of forms, which, although it possesses a certain measure of concreteness, ought to be subject to ever new interpretations. It is hardly reasonable to believe that "human freedom" would benefit from a dissolution of the traditional city.[19] Freedom does not consist in being nowhere, but in the possibility of choice. We therefore ought to emphasize that human identity and fellowship depend on the recovery of the image of the city.

In addition to the concrete images of house, institution and city, any epoch also possesses a more general "conception of space," which may be considered an image in its own right. The conception of space in fact "keeps" the existential spatiality of the epoch, and may therefore become an end in itself. In other words, the basic qualities of house, institution and city are left out and the work of architecture is intended as a mere illustration of the general conception. Evidently this generalization brings about a loss of contact with the reality of the here and now. That is what to some extent happened to modern architecture, particularly when the free plan was transferred from the house to the city. We understand, therefore, that a conception of space or place becomes truly meaningful only when it is set into work "as something."

The new tradition

When Giedion presented the ideas and the development of modern architecture in his influential book *Space, Time and Architecture*, he used as the sub-title "The Growth of a New Tradition."[20] The modern movement wanted to do away with the historical styles, and also rejected the notion of a new "international style" although this term has, with some justification, become common usage.[21] The "new tradition," on the contrary, was intended as a line of development of a different kind. The point of departure was the new conception of space, and the "growth" of the tradition consisted of the gradual implementation of this conception, in connection with

Antoni Gaudí:
Parc Güell, Barcelona, 1900-14.

the various building tasks of the new world.[22] Because of its universal significance, the new conception of space is usually regarded as a kind of "method" of spatial organization. A method cannot, however, constitute a tradition. A tradition is set into motion by a particular "vision" of the world, and becomes manifest as a set of images which are capable of variation and reinterpretation. The new conception of space is such a vision, and the new tradition consists in the images it has generated. To become part of life here and now, these images have to relate to the *genius loci*, and be set into work as something, that is, as house, institution or city. The growth of the new tradition is the history of how that happened. Although an historical development is always complex and comprises many interwoven trends, it is meaningful to distinguish between three major creative phases: the pre-modern period starting in the second half of the nineteenth century and lasting until about 1914; the modern period proper taking up the interval between the two world wars; and the post-modern period of the present. Between these phases we find transitory episodes characterized by "expressionistic" experimentation. What, then, were the basic aims and results of the three periods?

Pre-modern architecture concentrated its efforts on the substitution of the devalued symbols of historicism with *art nouveau*, and in many respects it succeeded in creating new meaningful images. The image of the house was recovered with many significant local variations. Let us remember the "massive platform," "precise post" and "solemn gable" of the pre-modern American house, and recall the embracing, articulate roofs and varied openings of Olbrich's houses, the fireplaces, inglenooks and bay windows of Mackintosh, and the powerful chimneys of Lutyens and Voysey. We could add innumerable examples, and may conclude that the pre-modern house succeeded in offering man a meaningful place for his private life. Moreover, we have seen that pre-modern architecture created significant images related to the public life of

the new world, such as the transparent, unitary hall and the dominant skyscraper. Both were quickly understood, and were taken as the point of departure for a development which is still going on. As to the image of the city, pre-modernism introduced many new ideas, and in a few cases, such as the late housing developments of the Amsterdam School,[23] contributed significantly to the imagery of the urban environment. In general, pre-modern architecture demonstrated the possibility of truly new interpretations of the archetypes. The modes of standing, rising, extending and opening were thus exploited in fascinating ways, and related phenomenologically to the world of natural forms and processes.[24]

As an example we may mention the extraordinarily rich and poetic world of Gaudí's *Parc Güell* in Barcelona (1900-14). Here Gaudí reveals the essence of natural place, "on earth under the sky." From the marine underworld at the entrance with its white tiles, touches of blue and images of sea life, we rise up to a chthonic hypostyle hall with "terrible" pseudo-doric columns, and from there we proceed to the terrace above (the so-called Greek Theatre), where we may settle under the sky, surrounded by an undulating rim of colour, the glazed tiles of which seem to have been scattered into fragments by the light of the sun. Or we may approach the terrace from the upper side, coming out from the landscape with its images of rocks and forest to behold the distant sea. A multitude of archetypal spaces and characters are thus brought together to form one total, albeit articulate, image which reveals the phenomena of nature as perhaps never before in the history of architecture. It is significant to know that this great and profound *imago mundi* was conceived as the focus of a garden community comprising some sixty dwellings, but only two houses were built. Gaudí himself went to live in one of them in 1906.[25]

Considering the richness and significance of pre-modern architecture, we may again wonder why it came to a sudden end before the first world war. Superficially it may seem that

Gunnar Asplund: Woodland
Cemetery, Stockholm, 1935-40.

the development was interrupted by the war, and that the aus-
tere post-war years were no longer congenial to the exuber-
ance of *art nouveau.* In reality, however, *art nouveau* had lost
its impetus already by 1905, and at the same time the "visual
revolution" of Cubism took place. What happened, therefore,
was that *art nouveau* was abandoned because it did not give
due attention to the *new conception of space.* Its world was
still primarily the traditional one of natural forces and human
sentiments, whereas the new world of openness, mobility,
interaction and simultaneity played only a secondary role.[26]
The main exception was the architecture of Frank Lloyd
Wright, and his works therefore came to play the role of cata-
lyst for the next phase in the growth of the new tradition.

Modern architecture did away with pre-modernism, as a
son rejects his father, because it wanted to be "truly modern."
Rather than offering a reinterpretation of a world of
"known" phenomena and memories, it aimed at visualizing
the hard and even frightening realities of the new world, in
order to master it emotionally. Therefore it concentrated its
attention on the setting into work of the new conception of
space. As a result, the principles of the free plan and open
form were developed. When set into work, however, these
principles proved to be something more than a "method."
The *Barcelona Pavilion* is an image of the spatiality of the
modern world, as are the *Villa Savoye* and the Bauhaus.
Modern architecture therefore succeeded in keeping the
"new vision" by means of new images. It also to some extent
succeeded in incorporating certain images of house and institution, such as qualitatively different domestic zones and
the unitary public hall. At the environmental level of the city,
however, the quality of image was almost entirely lost. In
general, we may also assert that modern architecture left out
the image quality of how something *looks.* Spatial images
are not sufficient; man also needs for his identification conspicuous and recognizable built forms. In short, a house ought
to *look* like a house, and nothing else.[27]

Modern architecture, however, *tended* towards a recovery
of the built image. The growth of the new tradition certainly
implies that development should not stop with the setting into
work of the new conception of space. The next steps to be
taken were, as was clearly understood by Giedion, the inclusion of regional characters and "monumental" symbolism. An
example from the late 1930s may be quoted to indicate the
beginning of this third phase of the new tradition. Gunnar
Asplund's *Woodland Cemetery* in Stockholm (1935-40) is a
genuine piece of modern architecture, but it also possesses
certain qualities which were rare at the time of its construction, and which suggest a possible synthesis of the phenomenological approach of pre-modernism and the general principles of modernism.[28] What strikes the visitor to the *Woodland
Cemetery,* is its profound quality of *place.* The layout does not
simply represent a setting-into-work of a functional pattern,
but consists of expressive forms and qualitatively different
spaces, which comprise natural as well as man-made parts. The
natural elements are of archetypal value: the gently rising,
extended lawn, the crowning mound, the friendly grove of
birch trees, and the more sinister forest of firs. The characteristics of this landscape are visualized and counterposed by
equally archetypal architectural forms; the delimiting and
guiding wall, the open hypostyle hall which gives measure to
space, the centrally placed tetrastyle light-core within the hall,
the cavelike embracing interior of the main chapel with its
anthropomorphic columns, the flight of steps, and, last but
not least, the elementary sky-related enclosure for meditation
on the top of the mound. A large, free-standing cross acts both
as a "sign" and a focal point to the composition. As a whole,
the *Woodland Cemetery* is something more than an exhibition
of archetypes; it is above all an *imago mundi* where architecture relates nature and human life. The free plan is used to
make the various places interact meaningfully, without forming
static, axial symmetries. The different parts of the crematorium are
moreover juxtaposed in an open collage-like way. Thus the

Gunnar Asplund: Woodland Cemetery, Stockholm, 1935-40.

Woodland Cemetery demonstrates how modern architecture may become truly meaningful through a recovery of the origins.

Like the works of Alvar Aalto from the late 1930s, the architecture of Asplund pointed towards the third, *postmodern*, phase of the new tradition.[29] Without giving up the new conception of space, the aim is to widen the scope of modernism to comprise regional (natural) characters and archetypal ("monumental") meanings. In the works of Asplund and Aalto the new contents were understood in quite general terms, while the recent development makes more direct references to particular traditions or "memories." Thus the image quality becomes more "concrete." Today known forms reappear, albeit in new interpretations, and man's need for identification and participation is hence strengthened. The role of classical forms in this development has already been discussed. We should add, however, that "classicism" forms only one component of post-modern architecture. Today, as in the past, the role of classical forms is above all to "humanize" the more abstract archetypes.

A convincing example of the new synthesis of volumetric image and meaningful memories is offered by Ricardo Bofill's *Pyramid* at Le Perthus on the border between Catalonia and France (1976).[30] The building task in question was the creation of a national symbol, that is, a structure which would make manifest the identity of Catalonia in space and time. During the elaboration of the project, the striking image of a pyramid emerged. What has this solution to do with the place, and what is its meaning? At Le Perthus the landscape consists of a continuous series of hills, one behind the other. Most of these hills have a kind of pyramidal shape. The pyramid of Bofill therefore does not look foreign to the place, but rather appears as a more precise variation on a given theme. It reveals the "hidden geometry" of the land, and makes us recognize one of the basic properties of the situation. In general the pyramid expresses how the earth of Catalonia rises towards the sky. But there is more to the solution. At the centre of the principal face of the volume, a flight of steps leads towards the top. The steps are almost two feet high, and make the way up a "hard journey." But a thrilling goal is visible from below: a small "temple" consisting of a *cella* and four pillars *in antis*. Climbing the steps, the twisted and truncated form of the pillars gradually become apparent, and close to they stand out dramatically against the sky, their red colour and semi-organic form contrasting with the prismatic, yellow *cella*. But even the temple does not represent a final goal; between the two middle pillars, within the *cella*, another flight of stairs rises up towards infinity. What does this piece of architecture mean? The truncated pillars symbolize the mutilated fingers of the medieval hero Vifredo el Velloso, who, before dying, pulled them across his shield, shouting: "Here is your banner!" And the flag of Catalonia is four red stripes on a golden ground. The yellow cella hence represents the golden shield. But the symbolism is something more than a depiction of an historical event. By putting the "banner" on the top of the pyramid, Bofill made the eternal soil of Catalonia emerge as the stage where history takes place, and since the pyramid also acts as a symbolic centre, the importance of the particular event is given due recognition. When the golden shield is transformed into a man-made space, the historical moment becomes part of the world of human endeavour. The flight of steps leading up towards the unknown evidently symbolizes another structure of this world. As a counter-movement, heavy drops of blood roll down on both sides of the main stairs, in the form of discs of red brick. Thus the pyramid at Le Perthus makes manifest a world. At the same time, it recounts what being in this world implies: to reveal what is general and eternal through the historical moment and at a particular place. Finally, it shows how architectural forms may function as "signs," although their principal meaning rests on a different level.

Together, pre-modern, modern and post-modern architecture make up the new tradition. The first phase gave primary

Louis Kahn: Kimbell Art Museum, Fort Worth, 1967-72.

importance to a reinterpretation of the phenomena of nature and human life by means of *art nouveau,* at the same time as the new conception of space was emerging. The second phase concentrated its attention on the setting into work of this conception in terms of free plan and open form. In order to do that, the phenomenological approach of the first phase was somewhat neglected. and replaced by a study of the properties of materials and structures. The second, modern, phase therefore tended to degenerate into "late-modern" structural expressionism, at the same time as the free plan was reduced to "functional patterns" and the city to a mere question of "planning."[31] In order to overcome these shortcomings and recover some of the values of pre-modern architecture, the third, post-modern, phase of the new tradition has aimed at a return to the phenomenological approach, and, moreover, has added a new concern for past "memories." This does not imply a revival of the academic approach, but simply the desire to become once again a part of history.

The expected recovery of the language of architecture makes it possible to replace the ever new inventions which are dominant today with creative work within a living tradition. Since language is the "house of being" and thus contains "everything," it may in fact be used directly to reveal previously hidden aspects of reality, or, if one prefers, to offer reinterpretations of reality. This process is not dependent on functional demands but may take place within architecture itself. In the past architecture was to a great extent subject to "stylistic development."[32] In this sense it possesses a certain "autonomy," but of course always remains part of the world. But the new tradition does not really correspond to the styles or the traditions of the past as it is of neither a temporal nor local nature.[33] Rather it shows how modern architecture is "on the way to language."

From space to place
The loss of the image is a major characteristic of the present environmental crisis. This proposition may not appear con-

vincing to everyone, since we are no longer used to thinking of architecture in terms of images. For too long we have been giving exclusive attention to function and structure. Without images, however, our environment is reduced to a mere spatial container. Thus we are deprived of those things which constitute our everyday world, and we are also deprived of the memories which relate this world to human life. It would be unfair, however, to make modern architecture responsible for this state of affairs. Modern architecture came about to heal the split of thinking and feeling which has caused the loss of the image. In principle it succeeded, but the success was never fully implemented. A false modernism, known as radical or "vulgar" functionalism, became dominant, and architecture degenerated into the "built diagrams" so common today. We cannot accept, however, that this implies the "failure" of modern architecture. Neither can we support the view that post-modernism necessarily represents a break with the new tradition. Post-modernism rather evolves out of modernism, and its success depends on its being able to combine the free plan and the open form with the meaningful image.

The advent of post-modern architecture is also due to changes in the new world itself. Until recently out technological potential seemed to offer the possibility of freedom and prosperity for all. What was a promise, however, has become a frightening menace. Technology no longer appears as a means to an end, but has become an end in itself, and even threatens to put an end to everything. It is tempting in this situation to find escape in nostalgia and superficial stimuli. The present demand for stimuli, however, proves the need for art. Dwelling presupposes an authentic relationship with the world, which is made possible only by art. When the modern world becomes overwhelming and frightening, it is more important than ever to master it emotionally, and to learn to grasp it through what we have called a "poetic vision." Only through such a vision can man develop a new love and respect for things, and thus be able to "save the earth."[34] In terms of

Louis Kahn: Kimbell Art Museum, Fort Worth, 1967-72.

architecture this means the creation of true *places,* and thus the recovery of the built *image*. We could also say that today we are moving away from a quantitative conception of dwelling towards a qualitative one. Quality in architecture implies a return to a concrete "here," that is, to the place, both in terms of constancy and change. The *genius loci* therefore ought to become part of the new tradition, in order to give it roots.

We have suggested that the recovery of the place as a concrete "here" which gathers a world, presupposes a phenomenological attitude. This attitude is synonymous with that unity of thinking and feeling which was the original aim of the modern movement. A phenomenological attitude takes the unity of subject and object as its point of departure, or, in other words, understands man as being-in-the-world. Today the study of environmental problems tends to be split in two: psychological and sociological studies on the one hand and semiological "analyses" of architecture on the other. We may safely say that social research has failed to provide a basis for architectural practice, and that semiology remains foreign to the language of architecture. Since existential spatiality comprises the social as well as the linguistic dimensions, a phenomenological investigation of man's being-in-the-world will offer a realistic basis for the effort to equip him with a new place.

What is here advocated is a return to what is *concrete*. Our daily environment consists of *things*, rather than abstractions such as molecules and atoms.[35] Present-day education is almost exclusively based on abstraction, and as a result we have lost the sense of things and the ability to keep them by means of images. This does not, however, imply a rejection of science and technology. To the Greeks *techne* meant "bringing-forth," and belonged to *poiesis,* revealing. "The essence of technology is by no means technological," Heidegger says, because "technology is a mode of revealing. Technology come to presence in the realm where revealing and unconcealment take place, where *alétheia,* truth, happens."[36] A phenomenological

approach may give back to technology its true significance, and thus restore architecture as *building,* in the true sense of the word. Thus Heidegger says: "Only when we are capable of dwelling, only then can we build."[37] Here "dwelling" means a poetical or phenomenological relationship to the world, or what Heidegger calls *Andenken*. Literally *Andenken* means to think in a devoted way, with *Andacht*. I repeat, therefore, that an attitude of devotion and love is necessary if we want to penetrate to the meaning of things. To adopt such an attitude may seem impossible at a time when everything is questionable or even frightening. If it is taught from childhood, however, it will become a natural basis for man's understanding of his being-in-the-world. Thus he will no longer be alienated from his environment, but possess that "environmental awareness" which is a presupposition for meaningful building. Phenomenology, in the sense of environmental awareness, therefore ought to become the "gathering middle of education."

At the beginning of this book, we asked the question: "How is orientation and identification possible in a world of interaction and change?" On the basis of the discussion which followed, we may answer: orientation and identification means dwelling.

Dwelling presupposes a poetic, phenomenological attitude to everything. The understanding which is obtained through this attitude must be kept in images. By means of images, space must be transformed into place, and dwelling is thus accomplished. The new tradition indicates the way towards the new place, in particular through the expression of openness and mobility. The post-modern quest for the image also belongs to its growth. The new place is new as well as old, in the sense that it presents a new interpretation of the archetypes of existential spatiality. On the urban level the new place will be varied and pluralistic, on the domestic level varied and familiar, and on the institutional level explicitly symbolic.[38] Common to all levels is the quality of place as a gathering of images which keep an understood world, or, in short, the quality of *imago mundi*.

OPPOSITE AND RIGHT TOP: Villa Busk, Bamble, 1990.
BELOW LEFT AND BOTTOM: Glacier Museum, Fjaerland, Norway, 1990.
BELOW RIGHT MIDDLE: Hedmark Museum, Hamar, 1979.

Sverre Fehn, works, 1979-90

Pritzker Prize, 1997

FAR RIGHT AND MIDDLE:
Patrick Berger:
Parc Citroën, Paris, 1995.
RIGHT: Bernard Tschumi:
Parc de la Villette, Paris, 1982ff.

The creation of true places is on the way, although it may seem that the results are drops in the ocean. It is also important to distinguish the true places of the present from the pastiches of superficial post-modernism. The reconquest of the image does not imply a mere application of historical motifs, or a return to the styles of the past. Rather true post-modernism wanted a return to meaningful forms, not in the sense of semiology, but as gatherings of disparate contents, forming synthetic wholes.

Louis Kahn was the first who understood architecture in this way, and we remember Vincent Scully's words: "In Kahn architecture began anew." In general, Kahn aimed at creating places which correspond to the "institutions" of human life. His buildings, therefore, form part of an environmental whole, a fact he himself confirmed when he defined the city as "the place of assembled institutions." In a particularly poetic way, his approach becomes manifest in the *Kimbell Art Museum* in Fort Worth (1966-72).[39] Here the environs are taken in by the vaulted porches on either side of the entrance. They do not, however, lead directly to the doorway; before entering one has to cross an open court with coarse gravel on the ground. Water and a grove of low trees accompany the *promenade*. The porches have the same covering as the interior spaces and thus unite outside and inside, and stand forth as the "theme" of the whole building. Whereas outside the vaults are closed at their apex, inside they open up to let in light, in accordance with Kahn's dictum that all interior space must have natural light. With its repetitive but significantly varied structure, the Kimbell makes us understand Kahn's words: "Order is."

In Paris the *Parc Citroën* by Patrick Berger et al. (1995ff.) stands out as a similarly fine place, where environmental and architectural qualities are united. Here the ultimate "contents" of the composition are not works of art, but plants The large greenhouses by Berger originate from the surrounding nature and bring us back to it in a more intimate way, making us experience the "inside" of what is given. A truly poetic interpretation. Coming from the significant Parc Citroën, Bernard Tschumi's *Parc de la Villette* (1982 ff.) appears as a joke. Spatially it possesses a certain complexity and reproposes the theme of the architectural promenade, but the depth of meaning is lacking. This lack is recognized by the architect himself when he calls the red pavilions dotting the park, *folies*. In fact, they do not have any content, but make "insane" nothingness manifest. But since it is impossible to express nothingness, the *folies* rather represent a world of arbitrary stimuli. The Parc de la Villette and Parc Citroën thus demonstrate the difference between mere stimulus and the genuine "thing," the latter in the original sense of *gathering*.[40]

The two Parisian parks belong to the city, but they are not urban places in the usual sense of the word. The recovery of urban space has, however, been given considerable attention since the *Strada novissima* exhibition at the Venice Biennale in 1980.[41] The facades presented there were mostly post-modern pastiches, but the urban problem as such was posed, not only in spatial terms, but also as an interplay of past and present. In general, we may assert that an urban place is not a function of separate buildings, but a *gestalt* in its own right, which the facades have to obey. Intermediate space is the real problem, and we should point out that the street has always had this quality.

Modern architecture has given intermediate space pride of place. Now the public spaces are communicating with the interior of buildings as well as the surroundings, and a truly "open" place comes into being, where the ideals of equality and freedom may be enacted. Sverre Fehn's prize-winning project for the extension of the *Royal Theatre* in Copenhagen (1996) offers a significant illustration.[42] Here an existing street is transformed into a covered promenade, which links the old and new auditoria on either side. The grand and varied space is covered by large concrete vaults, which have a certain resemblance to the wings of a bird. The free plan and the

FAR RIGHT: Sverre Fehn: Royal Theatre, Copenhagen, 1996, project. RIGHT: Le Corbusier: Tower of Shadows, Chandigarh, 1956ff.

expressive structure are united to form a true place (rather than a building), and the potential of modern architecture has again proved adequate to the task in question.

At the beginning of this book, we asserted that modern architecture came into existence to help man feel at home in a new world. We also maintained that this aim presupposes a healing of the "split of thought and feeling" which has dominated Western civilization since Descartes. Finally, we pointed out that the means to this end is the creation of a *new place*. Having considered the basic principles and the development of modern architecture, we may return to these assertions. And we should ask whether the aims have been fulfilled.

The answer is yes and no. Modern architecture has indeed proven able to help man's identification with the present world. In a practical sense it has given him the new dwelling demanded at the outset of the movement, and artistically it has united thought and feeling in valid syntheses. A development has also taken place, from the basic, but somewhat reductive, insights of the pioneers, to the varied and "inclusive" works of the present generation. Giedion was right in considering modernism a "new tradition." Today, however, the positive results appear as drops in the ocean. More than ever poverty reigns, and extensive slums are appearing everywhere. A new eclecticism has become the mode of expression of the well-to-do, an eclecticism which lacks even the stylistic basis of the parvenue architecture of the nineteenth century. For several reasons our cities are losing their quality of place, and nature is becoming subject to pollution and senseless exploitation. Hence, the situation which at the turn of the century led to the advent of modernism, is rife again, and in an even more accentuated form. It is no surprise, therefore, that the "death of architecture" has been announced.

It is my hope that this book will prove that architecture is still alive, and that modern architecture remains the only authentic expression of our time. It is also my hope that a better understanding of its principles and development may restore our belief in the "new tradition." In order to ensure that it continues, we have to master the "grammar" of the free plan and the open form, remembering that "freedom" and "openness" imply something more than formal properties. Thus the abolition of any closed stylistic system is needed, in favour of an open interaction of identities. Le Corbusier understood this when he wanted to base our endeavours on *objets aux reactions poetiques*, and when he built the *Tower of Shadows* at Chandigarh, a tower whose only function is to show how light creates potential presence from morning to evening. It is located close to the *Open Hand*, another work of his which expresses the unity of the things themselves and man's being-in-the-world.

Footnotes

Chapter 1: The New World

1. "Secure" does not refer here to social conditions, but to the quality of being "known."

2. Le Corbusier: *Towards a New Architecture*, London 1927, pp. 12, 210.

3. Le Corbusier: op.cit. p. 9.

4. Mies van der Rohe in *G. No. 1*, 1923. Quoted from P. Johnson: *Mies van der Rohe,* New York 1947, p. 183.

5. Hannes Meyer in *Das Werk,* Vol. VII, 1926. Quoted from Tim & Charlotte Benton, Dennis Sharp: *Form and Function,* London 1975, pp. 106ff.

6. Antonio Sant'Elia in *Nuove Tendenze*, 1914. Quoted from Benton & Benton, Sharp: op.cit. p. 71.

7. S. Giedion: *Bauen in Frankreich,* Leipzig/Berlin 1928, p. 41.

8. Mies van der Rohe in *Die Form*, 1930. Quoted from P. Johnson: op.cit. p. 190.

9. The word "spatiality" (*Raumlichkeit*) was introduced by Martin Heidegger to denote that "what is within-the-world . . . is also within space." See *Being and Time*, New York 1962 (1927), pp. 83, 135.

10. L. Moholy-Nagy: *The New Vision*, New York 1947 (1928), p. 56.

11. W. Gropius: *The New Architecture and the Bauhaus*, London 1935, p. 20.

12. S. Giedion: *Walter Gropius,* Teufen St. Gallen 1954, p. 63.

13. See C. Norberg-Schulz: *Baroque Architecture*, New York 1971, pp. 9ff.

14. See H. Sedlmayr: *Verlust der Mitte,* Salzburg 1948.

15. As an example we may refer to the "compositions" of J.N.L. Durand. See S. Giedion: *Architecture, You and Me*, Cambridge, Mass. 1958, p. 29.

16. S. Giedion: "Napoleon and the Devaluation of Symbols," *Architectural Review* No. 11, 1947.

17. S. Giedion: *Architecture, You and Me*, p. 18.

18. Giedion: op.cit. p. 26.

19. Voltaire: *Traité de Metaphysique*, 1734.

20. Locke: *An Essay concerning Human Understanding*, 1690.

21. K. Lankheit: *Der Temple der Vernunft,* Basle 1968. After the French Revolution many churches, among them Nôtre Dame in Paris and the cathedrals of Chartres and Strasbourg were transformed into "temples of reason."

22. See Hans M. Wingler: *The Bauhaus,* Cambridge, Mass. 1969.

23. Giedion: op.cit. p. 7.

24. Giedion: op.cit. p. 7.

25. Giedion: op.cit. p. 11.

26. M. Heidegger: "The Thinker as Poet," in *Poetry, Language, Thought* (ed. A. Hofstadter), New York 1971, p. 7.

27. M. Heidegger: "The Thing," in op.cit. p. 163ff.

28. The term the "things themselves" stems from Husserl. See E. Husserl: *Die Krisis der europäischen Wissenschaften,* 1936.

29. Quoted by C. Giedion-Welcker: *Schriften 1926-71,* Cologne 1973, p. 299.

30. P. Mondrian: *Plastic Art and Pure Plastic Art,* New York 1945, p. 17.

31. This is particularly the case after the second world war.

32. G. Kepes: *The New Landscape,* Chicago 1956, p. 22.

33. It is to misunderstand Gestalt theory to believe that organization comes "afterwards;" the world is *given* as Gestalts.

34. The new way of seeing and understanding was also called the "new sensibility" (Giedion) and the *"esprit nouveau"* (Le Corbusier).

35. L. Sullivan: "Ornament in Architecture" (1892) in *Kindergarten Chats and Other Writings,* New York 1947, p. 187.

36. Le Corbusier: op.cit. p. 141.

37. Gropius: op.cit. p. 20.

38. Mies van der Rohe in *Bau und Wohnung*, Stuttgart 1927.

39. Has it ever been explained what "follows" means in this statement?

40. Reprinted in H. Meyer: *Bauen und Gesellschaft,* Dresden 1980, p. 40.

41. Adolf Max Vogt: "Woher kommt Funktionalismus?" in *Werkarchithese* 3, 1977.

42. See C. Norberg-Schulz: *Genius Loci*, London/New York 1980.

43. The word "mood" is also used as a translation of Heidegger's concept of *Befindlichkeit,* which more appropriately denotes a general state of being in the world. See *Being and Time*, pp. 172ff.

44. Le Corbusier: op.cit. p. 141.

45. Le Corbusier: op.cit. p. 31.

46. Le Corbusier: *Oeuvre Complète* I, Zürich 1937, pp. 128-9. We prefer to translate *plan libre* as "free plan" rather than "open plan," as openness is only one possible property of the *plan libre*.

47. We have adopted the term "open form" to indicate that the modern built form possesses a basic "openness" to various contents.

48. The term was introduced by Henry-Russell Hitchcock and Philip Johnson in 1931.

49. Frank Lloyd Wright: *The Natural House,* New York 1970 (1964), p. 16.

50. C.R. Ashbee: "Frank Lloyd Wright, eine Studie zu seiner Würdigung" in *Frank Lloyd Wright,* Berlin 1911.

51. Werner Gräff in *Bau und Wohnung*, Stuttgart 1927.

52. See Klaus Döhmer: *"In welchem Style sollen wir Bauen?,"* Munich 1976.

53. P. Beaver: *The Crystal Palace,* London 1970, p. 37.

54. Sullivan: op.cit. p. 203.

55. See Le Corbusier: *La Maison des Hommes*, Paris 1942.

56. Le Corbusier: *Propos d'Urbanisme*, Paris 1946.

57. See C. Norberg-Schulz: *Louis Kahn, idea e immagine*, Rome 1980.

58. See CIAM 8: *The Heart* of *the City*, London 1952.

59. Giedion: *Architecture, You and Me,* pp. 48ff.

60. Regionalism, however, should not be confused with the *Blut und Boden* policy of the Nazis.

61. S. Giedion: *Space, Time and Architecture*, 5th ed., Cambridge, Mass. 1967, p. 620.

62. Giedion: *Architecture, You and Me*, p. 145.

63. Giedion: *Space, Time and Architecture*.

64. See C. Norberg-Schulz: *Genius Loci*.

65. See Charles Jencks: *Late-modern Architecture*, London 1980.

66. We may point to Jørn Utzon and the MLTW team.

67. See in general C. Norberg-Schulz: *Genius Loci*.

68. Norberg-Schulz: op.cit.

69. Heidegger: "The Thing."

70. The relationship between the original, the local and the temporal is discussed in Chapter 8.

Chapter 2: The Free Plan

1. See C. Norberg-Schulz: *Existence, Space and Architecture*, London 1971. In *Towards a New Architecture* Le Corbusier writes: "An axis is perhaps the first human manifestation; it is the means of every human act." (p. 173).

2. See D. Frey: *Grundlegung zu einer vergleichenden Kunstwissenschaft*, Vienna/Innsbruck 1949.

3. See C. Norberg-Schulz: *Meaning in Western Architecture*, London/New York 1975, Chapter II.

4. See Frank Lloyd Wright: *The Natural House*, p. 45.

5. Wright: op.cit. p. 19.

6. Cf. Peter Blake's superficial discussion in *Form follows Fiasco*, Boston/Toronto 1974.

7. See T.M. Brown: *The Work of G. Rietveld Architect*, Utrecht 1958.

8. See Giedion: *Space, Time and Architecture*, p. 405.

9. See R. Wittkower: *Art and Architecture in Italy 1600-1750*, Harmondsworth 1958, pp. 130ff.

10. G. Guarini: *Placita Philosophica*, 1665.

11. See C. Norberg-Schulz: *Kilian Ignaz Dientzenhofer e il barocco boemo*, Rome 1968.

12. See A. Drexler (ed.): *The Architecture of the Ecole des Beaux-Arts*, London 1977.

13. P. Portoghesi in *GA 42*, Tokyo 1976.

14. Giedion: *Space, Time and Architecture*, pp. 110ff.

15. Giedion: op.cit. p. 399.

16. Giedion: op.cit. p. 405.

17. Wright: op.cit. p. 17.

18. Cf. again Blake's superficial discussion in op.cit. p. 32.

19. C. Norberg-Schulz: "Rencontre avec Mies van der Rohe," *L'architecture d'aujourd'hui*, No. 79, 1958, p. 40.

20. Wright: op.cit. p. 33.

21. Wright's houses also possess a "hidden" geometrical order, which is sometimes shown in the floor pattern (Hanna House, etc.).

22. M.H. Schoenmaekers: *The New Image of the World*, 1915.

23. Mondrian: op.cit. p. 13.

24. Quoted in Brown: op.cit. p. 68.

25. He later called this a "clear structure."

26. Le Corbusier: *Oeuvre Complète* II (1929-34), Zürich 1935, p. 24.

27. Norberg-Schulz: "Rencontre . . ."

28. It is particularly well expressed in the Finnish legends *Kalevala*. See Norberg-Schulz: *Nightlands*, Cambridge, Mass.

29. See Norberg-Schulz: *Genius Loci*.

30. See P.D. Pearson: *Alvar Aalto*, New York 1978, p. 151. The character of Aalto's work is on the contrary misunderstood by D. Porphyrios in *Sources of Modern Eclecticism*, London 1982.

31. We may in this connection recall the metamorphoses found in the works of Borromini.

32. Again we may refer to the works of Borromini, as did Giedion in *Space, Time and Architecture*.

33. On topology in architecture, see Norberg-Schulz: *Existence, Space and Architecture*.

34. An open but defined system of this kind had already been developed by Kahn in his project for the Trenton Jewish Community Center (1954).

35. See R. Giurgola, J. Mehta: *Louis I. Kahn*, Boulder 1975.

36. On structuralism in general, see A. Lüchinger: *Strukturalismus*, Stuttgart 1981.

37. See C. Norberg-Schulz: *The Works of Paolo Portoghesi and Vittorio Gigliotti*, Rome 1975.

38. All in collaboration with Vittorio Gigliotti.

39. See Norberg-Schulz: *Louis Kahn*. Also Norberg-Schulz: "Kahn, Heidegger and the Language of Architecture" in *Oppositions* 18, 1979.

40. Robert Venturi has in fact offered important contributions to the further development of the free plan and the open form.

41. See C. Moore, G. Allen, D. Lyndon: *The Place of Houses*, New York 1974.

42. Moore, Allen, Lyndon: op. cit. p. 82.

43. Heidegger: *Poetry* . . . p. 154.

44. A particularly good example is the 1935 Hubbe House.

45. We may compare this with Arnold Schönberg's restrictive rules for the "composition with twelve tomes."

46. See G. Allen, D. Lyndon, C. Moore: *The Place of Houses*.

47. C. Norberg-Schulz: *Sverre Fehn, Opera completa*, Milan 1997.

Chapter 3: The Open Form

1. R. Venturi: *Complexity and Contradiction in Architecture*, New York 1966, p. 23.

2. As an example we may mention the country houses by Sir Edwin Lutyens. See D. O'Neill: *Sir Edwin Lutyens, Country Houses*, London 1980.

3. Mies van der Rohe: "Inaugural Address as Director of Architecture at Armour Institute of Technology," 1938. In P. Johnson: *Mies van der Rohe*, p. 192.

4. Venturi: op.cit. p. 47

5. H. Sedlmayr: *Verlust der Mitte*, p. 53.

6. R. Wittkower: *Bernini*, London 1955, p. 34ff.

7. Giedion: *Space, Time and Architecture*, p. 113.

8. Giedion: op.cit. p. 121.

9. The same holds true in certain works of "post-modern classicism."

10. See L. Weaver: *Houses and Gardens by E.L. Lutyens*, London 1914.

11. Inside the Crystal Palace even trees were left standing!

12. Giedion: op.cit. p. 270.

13. Wright: *The Natural House*, p. 16.

14. See *Global Interior: Houses by Frank Lloyd Wright* 1, Tokyo 1975.

15. Mrs. Tugendhat reports that Mies insisted on having doors which ran the whole height between floor and ceiling. See W. Tegathoff: *Mies van der Rohe, die Villen und Landhausprojekte*, Essen 1981, p. 91.

16. Norberg-Schulz: "Rencontre avec Mies van der Rohe."

17. See C. Rowe: *The Mathematics of the Ideal Villa and other Essays*, Cambridge, Mass. 1976, pp. 167ff.

18. For the relation between facade and space in Le Corbusier's works see Le Corbusier: *The Modulor*, London 1954.

19. V. Scully: *Modern Architecture*, New York 1961, p. 45.

20. P.L. Nervi: *New Structures*, London 1963, p. 7.

21. As we have already pointed out, D. Porphyrios in *Sources of Modern Eclecticism* does not understand this quality in Aalto's works.

22. The concept of fictitious structure is discussed in Norberg-Schulz: *Intentions in Architecture*, Oslo/London 1963.

23. See Norberg-Schulz: "Kahn, Heidegger and the Language of Architecture."

24. The latter case may be exemplified by his project for a Convent for the Dominican Sisters in Media, Pennsylvania (1965-68). See Giurgola-Mehta: op.cit.

25. In his introduction, Vincent Scully says that it is "probably the most important writing on the making of architecture since Le Corbusier's *Vers une Architecture* of 1923."

26. Venturi: op.cit. p. 23.

27. Venturi: op.cit. p. 25.

28. Venturi: op.cit. p. 91.

29. Venturi: op.cit. p. 88.

30. Venturi: "Une definition de l'architecture comme abri décoré," *L'architecture d'aujourd'hui*, 197, June 1978, pp. 7ff.

31. Sullivan: "On ornament."

32. Heidegger: op.cit. p. 154.

33. A characteristic example is Porphyrios: *Sources of Modern Eclecticism*.

34. Porphyrios: op.cit.

Chapter 4: The Natural House

1. S. Giedion: *Befreites Wohnen*, Zürich 1929, p. 9.

2. Le Corbusier: *La maison des hommes*.

3. See Wright: *The Natural House,* passim.

4. Moholy-Nagy: *The New Vision*, p. 59.

5. V. Scully: *The Shingle Style,* New Haven 1955 (2nd ed. 1971).

6. The so-called "stick style."

7. Scully calls this type of plan "peripherally additive."

8. Quoted from Scully: op.cit. p. xxxii.

9. Scully: op.cit. p. 127.

10. Wright: op.cit. p. 33.

11. Wright: op.cit. p. 32.

12. Scully: op.cit. pp. 162-3.

13. M.H. Baillie Scott: *Houses and Gardens*, London 1906, p. 18.

14. Baillie Scott: op.cit. pp. 38ff.

15. *Ver Sacrum,* January 1898.

16. C. Norberg-Schulz: *Casa Behrens*, Rome 1980.

17. Including Finland.

18. Such as the Finn Lars Sonck and the Swede Lars Israel Wahlman. Norberg-Schulz: *Nightlands.*

19. At the beginning southern Europe was excluded from the development.

20. The name "Citrohan" was chosen because its sounds like *Citroën*!

21. An analogous "urbanization" of rural dwelling types took place in the Middle Ages.

22. Le Corbusier: *Towards a New Architecture*, p. 169.

23. See C. Norberg-Schulz: *Casa Tugendhat*, Rome 1983.

24. Paul Goldberger in *GA* 39.

25 C. Moore, G. Allen, D. Lyndon: *The Place of Houses*, New York 1974.

26. Moore, Allen, Lyndon: op.cit. p. 52.

27. op.cit. p. 82.

28. See *Robert Stern* (introduction by V. Scully), London 1982.

29. See *Mario Botta, Architetture e progetti negli anni '70*, Milan 1979. *Mario Botta 1978-82*, Milan 1982.

30. *Utzon*: *Mallorca*, Copenhagen, 1996.

31. C. Norberg-Schulz: "The Dwelling and the Modern Movement," *Lotus* 9, Milan 1975.

32. Scully: op.cit. p. 127.

Chapter 5: The Democratic Institution

1. Norberg-Schulz: "Kahn, Heidegger and the Language of Architecture."

2. Norberg-Schulz: op.cit. Also: Norberg-Schulz: *Louis Kahn, idea e immagine*.

3. Norberg-Schulz: op.cit.

4. For instance the temperate Palm House in the Royal Botanic Garden in Edinburgh (1858). See S. Koppelkamm: *Glasshouses and Wintergardens of the Nineteenth Century,* London 1981, p. 76.

5. See Norberg-Schulz: *Meaning in Western Architecture.*

6. See Koppelkamm: op.cit.

7. Demolished in 1964.

8. L. Sullivan: "The Tall Office Building Artistically Considered" (1896), in *Kindergarten Chats . . .*

9. H.P. Berlage visited the building a few years after its completion and wrote: "I went away with the conviction of having seen a genuinely modern

work, and with respect for the master able to create things which had no equal in Europe." Quoted from G.C. Manson: *Frank Lloyd Wright to 1910*, New York 1958, p. 154.

10. See Norberg-Schulz: *Meaning in Western Architecture.*

11. The motif is already fully developed in Richardson's Sever Hall at Harvard University, 1878-80.

12. The round arch was kept because of its *general* character.

13. The history of architecture shows that forms always have a structural basis.

14. Towerhouses are found throughout Europe, from Italy in the south to Scotland in the north.

15. "Baltic" memories are however hardly present, as suggested by Kenneth Frampton in *GA Document*, Special Issue 2, p. 151.

16. Some "copies" were nevertheless made, for instance on the Petrin Hill in Prague.

17. See C.W. Condit: *The Chicago School of Architecture*, Chicago 1964.

18. Sullivan: op.cit. p. 202.

19. Sullivan: op.cit. p. 207.

20. There were 377 entries in the competition. See Le Corbusier *Oeuvre Complète* I, p. 160.

21. See *Willem M. Dudok*, Amsterdam 1954.

22. W. Gropius; *Bauhausbauten Dessau*, Bauhausbücher 12, Dessau 1930.

23. C. Norberg-Schulz: *Bauhaus,* Rome 1981.

24. Le Corbusier: *Towards a New Architecture*, p. 31.

25. Le Corbusier: *Oeuvre Complète* I, p. 168.

26. Thus he reversed the dictum "form follows function," saying: "We construct a practical and economical space into which we fit the functions." Norberg-Schulz: "Rencontre avec Mies van der Rohe."

27. See P. Johnson: *Mies van der Rohe*, pp. 132-34.

28. Compare its explicit "monumentality" with the simpler post office at the Federal Center in Chicago (1958-64).

29. Le Corbusier: *Oeuvre Complète* VI 1946-52, p. 72.

30. Norberg-Schulz: "Kahn, Heidegger . . ."

31. See Norberg-Schulz: op.cit.

32. See "Louis Kahn," in *Perspecta* 7, New Haven 1961, pp. 14ff.

33. R. Pietilä: *Intermediate Zones in Modern Architecture*, Helsinki, 1985.

Chapter 6: The Healthy City

I. Le Corbusier: *La Ville Radieuse*, Boulogne 1934.

2. The term stems from the American urbanist Malvin Webber. See M.M. Webber: "Urban Place and Nonplace Urban Realm" in *Explorations into Urban Structure*, 1964.

3. See for instance the writings of Jane Jacobs, Colin Rowe and Rob Krier.

4. The modern criticism of the industrialized city originates in the writings of Engels.

5. J.L. Sert: *Can our Cities Survive?*, Cambridge, Mass. 1944.

6. See K. Lynch: *The Image of the City*, Cambridge, Mass. 1960.

7. Webber: op.cit.

8. See Norberg-Schulz: *Intentions in Architecture.*

9. The definition does not, however, fit all historical epochs; the Greek city had a basically different spatial organization from the Greek house. Alberti's definition is a typical idea of the Renaissance.

10. The concept of "environmental level" is introduced in Norberg-Schulz: *Existence, Space and Architecture*, London 1971.

11. The origin of the classical language of architecture is disclosed in V. Scully: *The Earth, the Temple and the Gods*, New Haven 1962.

12. See W. von den Steinen: *Der Kosmos des Mittelalters*, Berne 1959, p. 5.

13. E. Panofsky: *Gothic Architecture and Scholasticism*, Latrobe 1951, p. 44.

14. It is tempting to make a comparison with Venturi's concept of the "decorated shed."

15. Norberg-Schulz: *Meaning in Western Architecture*, p. 270.

16. For the first time in Villa Montalto in Rome by Domenico Fontana (1570).

17. Giedion: *Space, Time and Architecture*, p. 709.

18. L. Mumford: *The City in History*, London 1961. p. 446.

19. Mumford: op.cit. p. 458.

20. Mumford. op.cit. pp. 487ff.

21. Giedion: op.cit. p. 778.

22. For instance in many Scandinavian cities.

23. See *Bau und Wohnung,* Stuttgart 1927.

24. B. Taut: *Die Stadtkrone*, Jena 1919. Quoted from Benton & Benton, Sharp: *Form and Function*, pp. 82ff.

25. Le Corbusier: *Oeuvre Complète* I, pp. 190ff.

26. C. Rowe, F. Koetter: *Collage City*, Cambridge, Mass. 1976, p. 62.

27. In Mies's own Detroit housing, however, urban space is completely lost.

28. CIAM 8: *The Heart of the City,* London 1952.

29. op.cit. p. 6.

30. Giedion had throughout his career been looking for "constituent facts," starting with his book *Spätbarocker und romantischer Klassizismus*, Munich 1922.

31. Works by Sert, Tange and others were presented.

32. See *Zodiac* 5, 1959, p. 102.

33. See Lüchinger: op.cit.

34. Lynch op.cit.

35. R Kner: *Urban Space,* London, 1979 (1975).

36. Bofill has in fact taken plans of Baroque churches (!) as models for his urban spaces.

37. "The Work of Charles Moore," *A+U* 1978, pp. 9-10.

38. op.cit. p. 13.

39. *Peter Pran*, London, 1998.

Chapter 7: The New Regionalism

1. See C. Norberg-Schulz: *Genius Loci*, Milan, London, New York 1979.

2. W. Gropius: *Internationale Architektur*, Munich 1925.

3. Gropius: op.cit. p. 7.

4. See Norberg-Schulz: op.cit.

5. Le Corbusier: *Oeuvre Complete* II, pp. 48, 58.

6. Even Mies van der Rohe related the Tugendhat house to the landscape!

7. M. Heidegger: *Hebel der Hausfreund*, Pfullingen 1957, p. 13.

8. See Norberg-Schulz: op.cit.

9. M. Heidegger: "The Origin of the Work of Art" in *Poetry, Language, Thought*, pp. 41ff.

10. The German *Bauweise* has no English equivalent.

11. Charles Moore and Robert Venturi both stress their wish to be "ordinary."

12. S. Giedion: "The New Regionalism" in *Architectural Record* 1954. Reprinted in *Architecture, You and Me*, pp. 38ff.

13. Giedion: op.cit. pp. 143-44.

14. Giedion: op.cit. pp. 148-51.

15. Compare Heidegger's statement that the dialects are the "source" of any developed language. See Hebel p. 7.

16. See Norberg~Schulz: *Existence, Space and Architecture*.

17. See Norberg~Schulz: op.cit.

18. These relationships are not to be understood as "rules." See in general Norberg-Schulz: *Genius Loci*.

19. The varieties were well presented at the Paris exhibition in 1900.

20. See *GA* 15.

21. Giedion: *Space, Time and Architecture*, p. 622.

22. The legends were collected by the writer Elias Lönnrot. An enlarged edition was published in 1849.

23. We may in this connection recall the works of the painter Gallén-Kallela and the composer Sibelius.

24. R. Pietilä, "Dipoli," *Arkkitekti* 9, 1967.

25. *L'architettura*, 1962.

26. P. Portoghesi: *Le inibizioni dell'architettura moderna*, Rome.

27. Moore, Allen, Lyndon: *The Place of Houses*, p. 32.

28. See the first edition of this book.

29. R. Bofill: *L'architecture d'un homme*, Paris 1978.

30. See D. Rognlien (ed.): *Treprisen*, Oslo 1978.

31. Sverre Fehn: *Opera completa*, Milan, 1997.

32. *Zodiac* 10, Milan 1962.

33. *GA* 61, with an introduction by C. Norberg-Schulz.

34. In the works of the Danish architect Henning Larsen regionalism and structuralism are combined.

35. Giedion: "The New Monumentality" in *New Architecture and City Planning* (ed. P. Zucker), New York 1944. Reprinted in *Architecture, You and Me.*

36. See in general Norberg-Schulz: *Genius Loci.*

37. Giedion: op.cit.

38. A.N. Whitehead: *Process and Reality*, New York 1929, p. 515.

Chapter 8: The New Monumentality

1. Giedion: *Architecture, You and Me*, p. 28.

2. Giedion: op.cit. p. 32.

3. M. Heidegger: "Language" in *Poetry, Language, Thought*, pp. 189ff.

4. The term "existential structure" was introduced by Heidegger in *Being and Time*.

5. See Norberg-Schulz: "Kahn, Heidegger and the Language of Architecture."

6. Le Corbusier: *Towards a New Architecture*, p. 31.

7. These terms are mostly used without any clear distinction.

8. In Norway the vernacular building types remained constant from the thirteenth to the nineteenth century.

9. Heidegger: Hebel . . . p. 7.

10. The latter is usually combined with the semiological understanding of language as a system of conventions.

11. See Norberg-Schulz: *Meaning in Western Architecture*, Chapter 1.

12. See Scully: *The Earth, the Temple and the Gods.*

13. Scully: op.cit.

14. Heidegger: "The Thing," *Poetry* . . . p. 181.

15. Heidegger: "The Origin . . . ," *Poetry* . . . p. 42.

16. Greek layouts, however, reveal basic *topological* properties.

17. Heidegger: op.cit. p. 43.

18. G. Kaschnitz von Weinberg: *Mittelmeerische Kunst*, Berlin 1965, p. 513.

19. See E. Forssman: *Dorisch, Jonisch, Korintisch*, Uppsala 1961.

20. Norberg-Schulz: *Meaning in Western Architecture*, Chapter 4.

21. Norberg-Schulz: op.cit. Chapter 6.

22. Panofsky: *Gothic Architecture and Scholasticism.*

23. Norberg-Schulz: *Meaning in Western Architecture.*

24. Forssman: op.cit.

25. See R. Moneo: "On Typology," *Oppositions* 13, Cambridge, Mass. 1979.

26. Moneo: op.cit. p. 29.

27. Moneo: op.cit. p. 31.

28. Giedion: *Architecture, You and Me*, p. 29.

29. Today they are often misunderstood, for instance in the writings of Peter Blake and Demetri Porphyrios.

30. See *Eero Saarinen on his Work* (ed. A.B. Saarinen), New Haven.

31. Cf. his libraries and churches.

32. "Before" is not used in a temporal sense here.

33. V. Scully: *Louis I. Kahn*, New York 1962, p. 25.

34. Venturi in fact says that his own architecture "evolves out of" modern architecture. *Architectural Record*, June 1982, p. 118.

35. Venturi: op.cit. pp. 116, 118.

36. Such as Charles Moore, Robert Stern and Michael Graves.

37. A. Rossi: *L'architettura della città*, Padua 1966, p. 30.

38. Rossi: op.cit. p. 33.

39. See in general *Rational Architecture*, Brussels 1978.

40. op.cit.

Chapter 9: The New Place

1. Giedion: *Space, Time and Architecture,* p. 293.

2. Thus we have repeatedly referred to the works of Frank Lloyd Wright, Le Corbusier, Mies van der Robe and Louis Kahn.

3. M. Gandelsonas: "On Reading Architecture" in *Signs, Symbols and Architecture* (ed. G. Broadbent, R. Bunt, C. Jencks), Chichester 1980. p. 244.

4. Heidegger: "The Thinker as Poet" in *Poetry* . . . .

5. R. M. Rilke: *Duinese Elegies IX*.

6. W.A. Corn: *The Art of Andrew Wyeth*, San Francisco 1973, p. 55.

7. The ancient idea of the world as a "fourfold" is revived in Heidegger: "The Thing," op.cit. p. 179.

8. The lines conclude the poem *Andenken*.

9. In general see Broadbent, Bunt, Jencks: op.cit.

10. Heidegger: "The Thinker as Poet," in *Poetry* . . . p. 14.

11. A certain correspondence (*Übereinstimmung*) between man and his environment therefore exists.

12. We may recall the Pompeian tetrastyle atrium, and the "fourposters" of MLTW.

13. See for instance Olbrich's houses.

14. As was so often convincingly done by Frank Lloyd Wright.

15. J. Trier: "Irminsul," *Westfälische Forschungen* IV, 1941.

16. The formal exterior of Palladio's Villa Rotunda is according to his own explanation a function of the site.

17. Such as St. Michael in Hildesheim (1001).

18. Norberg-Schulz: *Meaning in Western Architecture*, p. 270.

19. Today we experience in fact a general wish for the recovery of the city.

20. First edition 1941.

21. Walter Gropius repeatedly rejected the concept of "style," although it had been reintroduced by Hitchcock and Johnson in 1931.

22. See Giedion: *Space, Time and Architecture*.

23. In particular the apartment blocks at the Henriette Ronnerplein in Amsterdam by Michel de Klerk (1921-22).

24. Thus August Endell wrote: "Nature seems to live and we begin to understand that there really are sorrowing trees and wicked treacherous branches, virginal grasses and terrible gruesome flowers . . . This is the power of form upon the mind, a direct, immediate influence without any intermediate stage, by no means an anthropomorphic effect, but one of direct empathy." A. Endell: "The Beauty of Form and Decorative Art" (1897-98), reprinted in Benton & Benton, Sharp: *Form and Function*, p. 21.

25. C. Martinell: *Gaudí*, Barcelona 1975, pp. 86, 180.

26. This fact does not, however, lessen its constituent importance.

27. In *The Language of Post-modern Architecture* (London 1977) Charles Jencks presents a series of "metaphors of Ronchamp" which "interpret" the church as a duck, a pair of folded hands, a ship, a hat, and a mother with child.

28. *GA* 62. The landscaping was done in collaboration with Sigurd Lewerentz.

29. In fact today we experience a renewed interest in the works of Asplund. See S. Wrede: *The Architecture of Erik Gunnar Asplund*, Cambridge, Mass. 1980.

30. See R. Bofill: *L'architecture d'un homme*.

31. Various "design methods" also derive from these trends.

32. This happened in Romanesque and Gothic architecture, as well as within the classical tradition.

33. It comprises, however, temporal and local aspects.

34. The expression stems from Heidegger. See *Poetry* . . . p. 151.

35. See Norberg Schulz: *Genius Loci*, p. 6.

36. Heidegger *Basic Writings*, New York 1977, pp. 287, 295.

37. Heidegger: *Poetry* . . . p. 160.

38. One might ask how such a meaningful whole is possible in our time of super-dimensions. Using the language of architecture intelligently, the large buildings may for instance appear as a "neutral" backdrop to smaller, but more articulate (and more significant) structures, a relationship which is already becoming apparent in American cities.

39. J. Lobell: *Between Silence and Light*, Boston 1985, pp. 94ff.

40. B. Tschumi: *Le Parc de la Villette*, Seyssel 1987.

41. P. Portoghesi (ed.): *The Presence of the Past*, Venice 1980.

42. *Sverre Fehn, opera completa*.

Bibliography

DOCUMENTS

Alvar Aalto Skisser (ed. G. Schildt), Helsingfors 1973

Architecture rationelle (ed. R. Delevoy), Brussels 1978

Baillie Scott, M.H.: *Houses and Gardens*, London 1906

Bau und Wohnung, Stuttgart 1927

Bayer, H., Gropius, W., Gropius, I.: *Bauhaus 1919-1928*, New York 1938

Benton,T., Benton, C., Sharp, D.: *Form and Function*, London 1975

Bloomer, K.C., Moore, C.W.: *Body, Memory and Architecture*, New Haven 1977

Bofill, R.: *L'architecture d'un homme*, Paris 1978

CIAM Dokumente 1928-1939 (ed. M. Steinmann), Basle/Stuttgart 1979

CIAM 8, The Heart of the City (ed. J. Tyrwhitt, J.L. Sert), London 1952

CIAM '59 in Otterlo (ed. O. Newman), Stuttgart 1961

Conrads, U.: *Programme und Manifeste zur Architektur des 20. Jahrhunderts*, Berlin 1964

Cook. P.: *Architecture: Action and Plan.* London 1967*

Doesburg, T. van: *Grundbegriffe der neuen gestaltenden Kunst*, Munich 1925

Friedman, Y.: *L'architecture mobile*, Tournai 1970

Gropius, W.: *Internationale Architektur*, Munich 1925

   Bauhausbauten Dessau, Munich 1930

   The New Architecture and the Bauhaus, London 1935

Häring. H.: *Fragmente*, Berlin 1968

Hilbersheimer. L.: *The New City*, Chicago 1944

Hommage à *Giedion* (ed. P. Hofer), Basle/Stuttgart 1971

Howard. E.: *Garden Cities of Tomorrow*, London 1946 (1898)*

Johnson, P.: *Writings*, New York 1979*

Krier, R.: *Urban Space*, London 1979 (1975)

   On Architecture, London 1982

Le Corbusier: *Vers une architecture*, Paris 1923*

   Urbanisme, Paris 1925

   Précisions, Paris 1930*

   La ville radieuse, Paris 1935*

   La maison des hommes, Paris 1942*

   Le Modulor, Paris 1950*

Loos, A.: *Ins Leere gesprochen*, Paris 1921

   Trotzdem, Innsbruck 1931

Meyer, H.: *Bauen und Gesellschaft*, Dresden 1980

Moholy-Nagy, L. Von: *Material zu Architektur*, Munich 1928

   Vision in Motion, Chicago 1947

Moore, C.W.; Allen, G.; Lyndon, D.: *The Place of Houses*, New York 1974*

Nervi, P.L.: *Aesthetics and Technology in Building*, Cambridge, Mass. 1965

Portoghesi, P.: *Le inibizioni dell'architettura moderna*, Rome 1974

Rossi, A.: *L 'architettura della citta*, Padua 1966

Roth, A.: *Begegnungen mit Pionieren*, Basle/Stuttgart 1973

Saarinen, E.: *Search for Form*, New York 1948

Scheerbart, P.: *Glasarchitektur*, Berlin 1914

Schwarz, R.: *Vom Bau der Kirche*, Würzburg 1938

   Von der Bebauung der Erde, Heidelberg 1949

   Wegweisung der Technik, Berlin 1979 (1926)

Sert, J.L.: *Can our Cities Survive?*, Cambridge, Mass. 1944

Ungers, O.M.: *Architecture as Theme*, Milan 1982

Velde, H. van de: *Zum neuen Stil,* Munich 1955

Venturi, R.: *Complexity and Contradiction in Architecture*, New York 1966*

   Learning from Las Vegas, Cambridge, Mass. 1972*

Wachsmann, K.: *Wendepunkt im Batien*, Wiesbaden 1959

Wagner, O.: *Die Baukunst unserer Zeit,* Vienna 1914

Werkbund (ed. L. Burckhardt), Venice 1977

Wingler, H. M.: *Das Bauhaus*, Cologne 1962

Wright, F.L.: *The Natural House*, New York 1954*

   On Architecture, New York 1941*

GENERAL WORKS

Alexander, C.: *Notes on the Synthesis of Form*, Cambridge, Mass. 1964*

Argan, G.C.: *Progetto e Destino*, Milan 1965

Bacon, E.N.: *Design of Cities*, New York 1967*

Banham, R.: *Theory and Design in the First Machine Age*, London 1960*

Benevolo, L.: *History of Modern Architecture*, I/II, London 1971 (1960)*

Bohigas, O.: *Arquitectura modernista*, Barcelona 1968

Broadbent, G.; Bunt, R.; Jencks. C.: *Signs, Symbols and Architecture*, Chicester 1980

Collins, P.: *Changing Ideals in Modern Architecture*, London 1965

Condit, C.: *The Chicago School of Architecture*, Chicago 1964

Cook, J.W.; Klotz, H.: *Conversations with Architects*, London 1973*

De Stijl 1917-1931, Visions of Utopia (introd. H.L.C. Jaffé), Oxford 1982

Dizionario Enciclopedico di Architettura e Urbanistica (ed. P. Portoghesi), Rome 1968-69

Döhmer. K.: *"In welchem Style sollen wir Bauen?,"* Munich 1976

Drew. P.: *Die dritte Generation,* Stuttgart 1972

Drexler, A.: *Transformations in Modern Architecture*, London 1980

   The Architecture of the Ecole des Beaux-Arts (ed.), London 1977

Ein Dokument deutscher Kunst I-V, Darmstadt 1977

Frampton, K.: *Modern Architecture, a Critical History*, London 1980

   Modern Architecture 1851-1919, *GA Document Special Issue* 2, Tokyo 1981*

   Modern Architecture 1920-1945, *GA Document Special Issue* 3. Tokyo 1983*

Frampton, K.: *Studies in Tectonic Culture*, Cambridge, Mass. 1995

Gayle, M.; Gillon, E.V.: *Cast-Iron Architecture in New York*, New York 1974

Giedion, S.: *Bauen in Frankreich*, Leipzig 1929

    Space, Time and Architecture, Cambridge, Mass. 1941 (5th ed. 1967)*

    Mechanization Takes Command, London 1948*

    Architecture, You and Me, Cambridge, Mass. 1958

Grube, O.W.; Pran, P.C.; Schulze, F.: *100 Years of Architecture in Chicago*, Chicago 1973

Hitchcock, H.-R.; Johnson, P.: *The International Style*. New York 1932*

Hitchcock, H.-R.: *Architecture, Nineteenth and Twentieth Centuries*, Harmondsworth 1958

Jacobs, J.: *The Death and Life of Great American Cities*, New York 1961*

Jencks, C.: *Modern Movements in Architecture*, London 1973*

    The Language of Post-Modern Architecture, London 1977

    Late-Modern Architecture, London 1980

    The Architecture of the Jumping Universe, London 1995

Jencks, C.; Baird, G. (eds.): *Meaning in Architecture*, London 1969

Joedicke, J.: *Geschichte der modernen Architektur*, Stuttgart 1958

    Architektur im Umbruch, Stuttgart 1980

Kepes, G.: *Language of Vision*, Chicago 1944*

Klotz, H.; Bofinger, H. and M.; Paul, J.: *Architektur in Deutschland*, Stuttgart 1981

Klotz, H. (ed.): *Vision der Moderne*, Munich, 1986

New York Architecture, Munich, 1989

Kopp, A.: *Ville et revolution*, Paris 1967

Kurokawa, K.: *Metabolism in Architecture*, London 1977

Lampugnani, V. M.: *Encyclopedia of 20th Century Architecture*, London 1986

Luchinger, A.: *Strukturalismus in Architektur und Städtebau*, Stuttgart 1981

Lund, N.O.: *Nordisk Arkitektur*, Copenhagen, 1993

Lynch, K.: *The Image of the City*, Cambridge, Mass. 1960*

Macleod. R.: *Style and Society*, London 1971

Macmillan Encyclopedia of Architects I-IV, New York 1982

McCoy, E.: *Five California Architects*, New York 1975

Mumford, L.: *The City in History*, London 1961*

    Roots of Contemporary American Architecture, New York 1952

New Chicago Architecture (eds. M. Casari, V. Pavan), New York 1981

Nesbitt, K. (ed.): *Theorizing a New Agenda for Architecture*, New York, 1996

Noever, P. (ed.): *Architecture in transition*, Munich 1991

    The End of Architecture, Munich 1993

Norberg-Schulz, C.: *Intentions in Architecture*, Oslo/London 1963

    Existence, Space and Architecture, London 1971*

    Meaning in Western Architecture, London 1975 (1974)

    Genius Loci, London 1980 (1979)

New World Architecture, New York 1988

The Art of Place, New York 1988

Nightlands, Cambridge, Mass. 1996

Nordic Classicism 1910-30 (ed. S. Paavilainen), Helsinki 1982

Pehnt, W.: *Expressionist Architecture*, London 1973

Platz, G.: *Die Baukunst der neuesten Zeit*, Berlin 1927

Porphyrios, D.: *Sources of Modern Eclecticism*, London 1982

Portoghesi, P.: *Postmodern*, Milan 1982

Posener, J.: *Anfänge des Funktionalismus*, Berlin 1964

Postiglione, G.: *Funzionalismo Norvegese*, Rome 1996

Quilici, V.: *L'architettura del costruttivismo*, Bari 1969

Robinson, C.; Bletter, R.H.: *Skyscraper Style*, New York 1975

Roth, A.: *La nouvelle architecture,* Zürich 1940

Rowe, C.: *The Mathematics of the Ideal Villa*, Cambridge, Mass. 1976

Rowe, C.; Koetter, F.: *Collage City*, Cambridge, Mass. 1978

Russell, F. (ed.): *Art Nouveau Architecture*, London 1979*

Scully, V.: *Modern Architecture*, New York 1961*

    American Architecture and Urbanism, New York 1969

Sedlmayr, H.: *Verlust der Mitte*, Salzburg 1948

Service, A.: *Edwardian Architecture and its Origins*, London 1975

Siegel, C.: *Strukturformen der modernen Architektur*. Munich 1960*

Stern, R.A.M.: *New Directions in American Architecture*, New York 1969

Tendenzen der zwanziger Jahre, Berlin 1977

Yorke, F.R.S.: *The Modern House*, London 1934

Zevi, B.; *Storia dell'architettura moderna*, Torino 1950

MONOGRAPHS

Aalto, Alvar

Alvar Aalto, Bauten I-III (ed. K. Fleig). Zürich 1963-78

Gutheim, F.: *Alvar Aalto*, New York 1962

Neuenschwander, F.: *Atelier Alvar Aalto 1950-51*, Zürich 1954

Pearson, P.D.: *Alvar Aalto and the International Style*, New York 1978

Schildt, G.: *Det vita bordet*, Helsingfors 1982

Schidt,G.: *Moderna Tider*, Stockholm,1985

    Den manskliga faktoren, Stockholm 1990

Asplund, Erik Gunnar

Ahlberg. H.: *Gunnar Asplund Arkitekt 1885-1940*, Stockholm 1943

Caldenby, C., Huttin, O.: *Asplund*, Stockholm 1985

Wrede, S.: *The Architecture of Erik Gunnar Asplund*, Cambridge, Mass. 1980

Behrens, Peter

Hoeber, F.: *Peter Behrens*, Munich 1913

Cremers, P.J.: *Peter Behrens. Sein Werk von 1909 bis zur Gegenwart*, Essen 1928

Norberg-Schulz, C.: *Casa Behrens*, Rome 1980

Bilancioni, G.: *Il primo Behrens*, Florence 1981

Berlage, Hendrik Petrus

Singelenberg, P.: *H.P. Berlage, Idea and Style*, Utrecht 1972

Bofill, Ricardo

Taller de Arquitectura, Ricardo Bofill (introd. by C. Norberg-Schulz), Tokyo

Botta, Mario

dal Co, F. (ed.): *Mario Botta, Architetture 1960-85*, Milan 1985

Mario Botta (introd. by E. Battisti, K. Frampton), Milan 1979

Mario Botta 1978-1982 (introd. by P. Nicolin, F. Chaslin), Milan 1982

Mario Botta, La Casa Rotonda (ed. R. Trevisiol), Milan 1982

Mario Botta (introd. by C. Norberg-Scbulz), Tokyo*

Emozioni di Pietra, Milan 1997

Cinque Architetture, Milan 1996

Boullée, Etienne-Louis

Kaufmann, F.: *Three Revolutionary Architects: Boullée, Ledoux, Lequeu*, Philadelphia 1952

Rosenau, H.: *Boullée and His Revolutionary Architecture*, London 1976

Lankheit, K.: *Der Tempel der Vernunft*, Basle/Stuttgart 1968

Vogt, A. M.: *Boullée's Newton-Denkmal*, Basle/Stuttgart 1969

Breuer, Marcel

Blake, P.: *Marcel Breuer*, New York 1949

Jones, C.: *Marcel Breuer: Buildings and Projects 1921-1961*, New York 1962

de Carlo, Giancarlo

Brunetti, F.; Gesi, F.: *Giancarlo de Carlo*, Florence 1981

Dudok, Willem Marinus

Willem M. Dudok 1884-1974, Amsterdam 1981

"Willem Marinus Dudok: Town Hall, Hilversum." *GA* 58, Tokyo 1981

Eiffel, Gustave

Besset, M.: *Gustave Eiffel*, Paris 1957.

Renoy, G.: *La Tour Eiffel au temps de Monsieur Eiffel*, Brussels 1976

Erskine, Ralph

"Ralph Erskine: Byker Development," *GA* 55, Tokyo 1980

Fehn, Sverre

Fjeld, P.O.: *Sverre Fehn*, New York 1983

Sverre Fehn, opera completa, Milano 1997

Furness, Frank

O'Gorman, J.F.: *The Architecture of Frank Furness*, Philadelphia 1973

Gaudí, Antoni

Collins, G.R.: *Antonio Gaudí*, New York 1960

Sweeney, J.J.; Sert, J.L.: *Antoni Gaudí*, Stuttgart 1960

Martinell, C.: *Gaudí*, Barcelona 1975 (1967)

Sterner, G.: *Antoni Gaudi, Architektur ak Ereignis*, Cologne 1979

Graves, Michael

Michael Graves, London 1979

Michael Graves, Buildings and Projects 1966-1981 (ed. K.V. Wheeler, P. Arnell, T. Bickford), New York 1982

Michael Graves. Buildings and Projects 1982-89, New York 1990

A Tower for Louisville (ed. P. Arnell, T. Bickford), New York 1982

Greene, C.S, & Greene, H.M.

Greene & Greene, Architects (ed. W. & K. Current), Fort Worth 1974

Gropius, Walter

Giedion, S.: *Walter Gropius, Mensch und Werk*, Teufen 1954

Argan, G.C.: *Walter Gropius e la Bauhaus*, Turin 1951

Weber, H.: *Walter Gropius und das Faguswerk*, Munich 1962

Fitch, J.M.: *Walter Gropius*, New York 1962

Norberg-Schulz, C.: *Bauhaus*, Rome 1980

Guimard, Hector

Hector Guimard, Architektur in Paris um 1900, Munich 1975

Hector Guimard (introd. by G. Naylor), London 1978

Rheims, F.: *Hector Guimard*, New York 1988 (1985)

Häring, Hugo

Joedicke, I.: Lauterbach, H.: *Hugo Häring. Schriften, Entwarfe, Bauten,* Stuttgart 1965

Hoffmann, Josef

Baroni, D.; d'Auria, A.: *Josef Hoffmann e la Wiener Werkstätte*, Milan 1981

Sekler, E.F.: *Josef Hoffmann*, Salzburg 1982

Gresleri, G.: *Josef Hoffmann.* Bologna 1981

Horeau, Hector

Hector Horeau 1801-1872, Paris 1980

Horta, Victor

Borsi, F.; Portoghesi, P.: *Victor Horta,* Rome 1969

Howe, George

Stern, R.A.M.: *George Howe*, New Haven 1975

Isozaki, Arata

Drew, P.: *The Architecture of Arata Isozaki*, London 1982

Johnson, Philip

Philip Johnson, Architecture 1949-1965, London 1966

Johnson/Burgee: Architecture (introd. by N. Miller), New York 1979

Jacobus, J.M.: *Philip Johnson*, New York 1962

Kahn, Louis I.

Giurgola, R.; Mehta, J.: *Louis I. Kahn*, Boulder 1975*

Scully, V.: *Louis I. Kahn*, New York 1962

Lobel, J.: *Between Silence and Light*, Boulder 1979

Ronner, H.; Jhaveri, S.; Vasella, A.: *Louis I. Kahn, Complete Work 1935-74*, Basle 1977

Norberg-Schulz, C.; Digerud, J.G.: *Louis I. Kahn, idea e immagine*, Rome 1980

Wurman, R.S.: *The Notebooks of Louis I. Kahn*, Cambridge, Mass. 1973

Wurman, R.S. (ed.): *What will be has always been. The Words of Louis Kahn,* New York 1986

Kohn, Pedersen, Fox

James, W.A. (ed.): *Kohn, Pedersen, Fox,* New York, 1993

Lauwericks, J.L. Mathieu

N. Tummers: *Der Hagener Impuls*, Hagen 1972

Le Corbusier

Moos, S. von: *Le Corbusier. Elemente einer Synthese*, Frauenfeld 1968

Rowe, C.; Slutzky, R.; Hoesli, B.: *Transparenz*, Basle/Stuttgart 1968

Pauly, D.: *Ronchamp*, Paris 1980

Gresleri, G.: *L 'esprit nouveau*, Milan 1979

Venezia. F.: *La torre d'ombre*, Naples 1978

Jencks, C.: *Le Corbusier and the Tragic View of Architecture*, Harmondsworth 1973*

Choay, F.: *Le Corbusier*, New York 1960

Le Corbusier. Oeuvre Complète I/VIII. (ed. W. Boesiger), Zürich 1937ff.

Ledoux, Claude-Nicholas

Christ, Y.: *Projets et divagations de Claude-Nicholas Ledoux*, Paris 1961

Raval, M.: *Claude-Nicholas Ledoux 1756-1806*, Paris 1945

Loos, Adolf

Münz, L.; Künstler. G.: *Der Architekt Adolf Loos*, Vienna 1964

Lutyens, Edwin

Weaver, L.: *Houses and Gardens by E.L. Lutyens*, London 1914

O'Neill, D.: *Lutyens, Country Houses*, London 1980

The Work of the English Architect Sir Edwin Lutyens, London 1981

Mackintosh, Charles Rennie

Macleod, R.: *Charles Rennie Mackintosh*, Feltham 1968

Howarth. T.: *Charles Rennie Mackintosh and the Modern Movement*, London 1952

Billcliffe, R.: *Charles Rennie Mackintosh*, London 1977

Cooper, J.: *Mackintosh Architecture.* London 1978

Buchanan, W. (ed.): *Mackintosh's Masterwork. The Glasgow School of Art*, Glasgow 1989

Maillart, Robert

Bill, M.: *Robert Maillart*, Zürich 1949

May, Ernst

Boekschmitt, J.: *Ernst May, Bauten und Planungen*, Stuttgart 1963

Maybeck, Bernard

Cardwell, K.H.: *Bernard Maybeck. Artisan, Architect, Artist*, S. Barbara 1977

Mendelsohn, Erich

Erich Mendelsohn. Das Gesamtschaffen des Architekten, Berlin 1930

Eckardt, W. von: *Erich Mendelsohn*, New York 1962

Mies van der Rohe, Ludwig

Johnson, P.: *Mies van der Rohe*, New York 1947

Hilbersheimer, L.: *Mies van der Rohe*, Chicago 1956

Blaser, W.: *Mies van der Rohe. Die Kunst der Struktur*, Zürich 1965

Neumeyer, F.: *Mies van der Rohe*, Berlin 1986

Tegethoff, W.: *Die Villen und Landhausprojekte von Mies van der Rohe*, Essen 1981

Drexler, A.: *Mies van der Rohe*, New York 1962

Blake, P.: *Mies van der Rohe. Architecture and Structure*, New York 1960

Glaeser, L.: *Ludwig Mies van der Rohe.* Drawings in the Collection of the Museum of Modern Art, New York 1969

Norberg-Schulz, C.: *Casa Tugendhat*, Rome 1983

Moore, Charles W.

The Work of Charles W. Moore, Tokyo 1978

"Charles Moore and Company," *GA Houses* 7, Tokyo 1980

Neutra, Richard

McCoy, E.: *Richard Neutra*, New York 1962

Nervi, Pier Luigi

Huxtable, A.L.: *Pier Luigi Nervi*, New York 1962

Pier Luigi Nervi. Bauten und Projekte, Stuttgart 1957

Pier Luigi Nervi. New Structures, London 1963

Olbrich, Joseph Maria

Latham, I.: *Joseph Maria 0lbrich*, London 1980

Joseph Maria 0lbrich. Die Zeichnungen in der Kunstbibliothek Berlin, Berlin 1972

Oud, Jacobus Johannes Pieter

Veronesi, G.: *J.J.P. Oud*, Milan 1953

Paxton, Joseph

Chadwick, G.F.: *The Works of Sir Joseph Paxton*, London 1961

Beaver, P.: *The Crystal Palace, 1851-1936*, London 1970

Perret, Auguste

Collins, P.: *Concrete*, London 1959

Pietilä, Reima

Benincasa, C.: *Il labirinto dei Sabba*, Bari 1979

Quantrill, M.: *Reima Pietilä*, New York, 1985

Intermediate Zones in Modern Architecture, Helsinki 1985

Conah, R. (ed.): *Tango Mantyniemi*, Helsinki 1994

Poelzig, Hans

Posener, J.: *Hans Poelzig*, Berlin 1970

Portoghesi, Paolo

Norberg-Schulz, C.: *On the Search for Lost Architecture*, Rome 1975

Priori, G: *Simpatia delle cose*, Rome 1982

Paolo Portoghesi: Projects and Drawings 1949-1979, Florence 1979

Pran, Peter

Peter Pran, London 1998

Richardson, Henry Hobson

Rensselaer, M.G. van: *Henry Hobson Richardson and His Works*, New York 1888

Hitchcock, H.-R.: *The Architecture of Henry Hobson Richardson and His Times*, New York 1936

Rietveld, Gerrit

Brown, T.M.: *The Work of Gerrit Rietveld Architect*, Utrecht 1959

Rossi, Aldo

Savi, V.: *L'architettura di Aldo Rossi*, Milan 1978

Aldo Rossi. Projects and Drawings 1962-1979, Florence 1979

Saarinen, Eero

Temko, A.: *Eero Saarinen*, New York 1962

Eero Saarinen on His Work (ed. A. Saarinen), New Haven 1962

Saarinen, Eliel

Christ-Janer, A.: *Eliel Saarinen*, Chicago 1979 (1948)

Hausen, M. et.al.: *Eliel Saarinen Projects 1896-1923*, Hamburg 1990

Sant'Elia, Antonio

Caramel, L., Longatti, A.: *Antonio Sant'Elia*, Como 1962

Schmidt-Thomsen, J.P.: *Floreale und futuristische Architektur*, Berlin 1965

Scarpa, Carlo

dal Co, F.; Mazzariol, G.: *Carlo Scarpa, opera completa*, Milan 1984

Scharoun, Hans

Pfankuch, P.: *Hans Scharoun*, Berlin 1974

Blundell-Jones, P.: *Hans Scharoun. A Monograph*, London 1978

Schoder, Thilo

Riedler, U. (ed.): *Thilo Schoder*, Gera 1997

Sonck, Lars

Lars Sonck 1870-1956, Helsinki 1981

Stern, Robert A.M.

Robert Stern (introd. by V. Scully), London 1981

Robert A.M. Stern 1965-1980 (ed. P. Arnell, T. Bickford), New York

Stirling, James

James Stirling. Bauten und Projekte, 1950-1974 (introd. by J.J. Jacobus), Teuten 1975*

James Stirling, London 1982

Sullivan, Louis

Bush-Brown, A.: *Louis Sullivan*, New York 1960

Elia, M.M.: *Louis Sullivan 1856-1924.* Milan 1995

Tange, Kenzo

Boyd, R.: *Kenzo Tange*, New York 1962

Taut, Bruno

Bruno Taut 1880-1938 (introd. by K. Junghanns), Berlin 1980

Terragni, Giuseppe

Schumacher, T.L.: *Il Danteum di Terragni*, Roma 1980

Tessenow, Heinrich

Wangerin, G.; Weiss, G.: *Heinrich Tessenow*, Essen 1976

Tschumi, Bernard

Ungers, Oswald Mathias

O.M. Ungers. Works in Progress 1976-80, New York 1981

Utzon, Jørn

"Jørn Utzon. Sydney Opera House" (introd. by C. Norberg-Schulz), *GA 54*, Tokyo 1980

"Jørn Utzon. Church at Bagsvaerd" (introd. by C. Norberg-Schulz), *GA 61*, Tokyo 1981

Norberg-Schulz, C.; Faber, T.: *Utzon Mallorca*, Copenhagen 1996

van de Velde, Henry

Sembach, K.J.: *Henry van de Velde*, Stuttgart/London 1989

Voysey, Charles F.A.

Simpson, D.: *C.F.A. Voysey*, London 1979

Venturi, Robert

Venturi and Rauch. The Public Buildings, London 1976

"Venturi and Rauch. Vanna Venturi House, Brant House, Tucker House," *GA 39*, Tokyo 1976

von Moos, S.: *Venturi, Rauch & Scott Brown*, New York 1987

Wagner, Otto

Lux, J.A.: *Otto Wagner*, Munich 1914

Geretsegger. H.; Peintner, M.: *Otto Wagner*, Salzburg 1964

Wilson, Colin St. John

The Design and Construction of the British Library, London 1988

Wright, Frank Lloyd

Hitchcock. H.-R.: *In the Nature of Materials*, New York 1942

Manson, G.C.: *Frank Lloyd Wright to 1910*, New York 1958

Smith, N.K.: *Frank Lloyd Wright. A Study in Architectural Content*, Englewood Cliffs, New Jersey 1966

Hanks. D.A.: *The Decorative Designs of Frank Lloyd Wright*, London 1979

Frank Lloyd Wright Disegni 1887-1959, Florence 1976

Scully, V.: *Frank Lloyd Wright*, New York 1960

Houses by Frank Lloyd Wright I-II (ed. Y. Futagawa), Tokyo 1975-76

Frank Lloyd Wright: complete works I-XII (ed. Y. Futagawa), Tokyo 1984-88